FIRST EDITION

# Avoid Employee Lawsuits

## Commonsense Tips for Responsible Management

by attorney
Barbara Kate Repa

# KEEPING UP-TO-DATE

To keep its books up to date, Nolo issues new printings and new editions periodically. New printings reflect minor legal changes and technical corrections. New editions contain major legal changes, major text additions or major reorganizations. To find out if a later printing or edition of any Nolo book is available, call Nolo at 510-549-1976 or check our website: www.nolo.com.

To stay current, follow the "Update" service at our website: www.nolo.com. In another effort to help you use Nolo's latest materials, we offer a 35% discount off the purchase of the new edition of your Nolo book when you turn in the cover of an earlier edition. (See the "Special Upgrade Offer" in the back of the book.) This book was last revised in: **OCTOBER 1999**.

| | |
|---|---|
| FIRST EDITION | **October 1999** |
| PRODUCTION | Sarah Hinman |
| EDITOR | Ralph Warner and Shae Irving |
| PROOFREADER | Robert Wells |
| INDEX | Nancy Mulvany |
| PRINTING | Consolidated Printers, Inc. |
| COVER | Toni Ihara |

K3464
.Z9R373
1999

UC

Repa, Barbara Kate.

    Avoid employee lawsuits : commonsense tips for responsible management / by Barbara Kate Repa.

        p.  cm.

    Includes index.

    ISBN 0-87337-463-0

    1. Discrimination in employment--Law and legislation--United States--Popular works.  2. Employees--Dismissal of--Law and legislation--United  States--Popular works.  3. Executives--United States--Handbooks, manuals, etc.  I. Title.

KF3464.Z9R373  1999

344.7301'133--dc21             99-42369

                 CIP

## Dedication

To my parents, Frank and Vera, who always knew the right answers—and do still.

With special thanks to the legions of employers and employees who shared their stories and solutions.

And with gratitude to my editor, Janet Portman, who ferreted out the egregiousness—and to Biff, for helping her have the strength to do it.

# CONTENTS

## CHAPTER 4

## KEEPING RECORDS

## CHAPTER 5

## PAYING WORKERS

## CHAPTER 6

## GIVING TIME OFF

## CHAPTER 7

## COMPLYING WITH THE AMERICANS WITH DISABILITIES ACT

## CHAPTER 8

## GUARDING AGAINST DISCRIMINATION

## CHAPTER 9

## GUARDING AGAINST SEXUAL HARASSMENT

## CHAPTER 10

## GUARDING AGAINST VIOLENCE

**CHAPTER 11**

## CONDUCTING INVESTIGATIONS

**CHAPTER 12**

## FIRING WORKERS

## INDEX

# FOREWORD

This is a tense time for employers. There are a burgeoning number of laws that give workers rights and protections on the job—and a growing number of workers anxious to enforce them.

This book covers the current toughest workplace problems—a collection that is bound to change if not grow over time. It gives you clear explanations of the law and a succinct summary of your state law where needed. But the most valuable thing it gives you is something you will not find in the courtroom or the boardroom: commonsense advice on how to avoid the mistakes others have made.

Here you will learn how to avoid common legal pratfalls in hiring workers, from investigating job applicants to testing workers to keeping records that the law requires. You will learn the legal basics in paying employees and giving them time off—two topics quite dear to employees' hearts. And you will find helpful guidance on complying with the murkier new workplace legalities such as the Americans With Disabilities Act and laws against sexual harassment.

If something goes amiss, you will find here practical advice on how to investigate a workplace wrong—and even tips on getting up the paper trail and gumption to fire employees when you can do no other. ■

# Hiring Workers

**F**erreting out the best job candidates and hiring them can be a grueling, time-consuming process. And these days, it can turn into something scary, too: a sticky bunch of wickets fraught with potential pitfalls and legal liability for the unwary employer. Something as basic as your choice of words can be your undoing. Ask an applicant a friendly question about a spouse, work habits or social activities, and you could be accused of violating laws that protect privacy and ban discrimination.

One comforting truth is that most people will not sue you for not hiring them—simply because they are not in good positions to do so. Unless you have said or done something truly offensive, clunky and egregious during the hiring process, most job applicants simply will not know why you did not offer them the job. But do not allow that to make you complacent or cocky. There are still plenty of points in the hiring process—from advertising to interviewing to investigating applicants to offering a job—where you can run afoul of the subtle laws dictating hiring rights and wrongs. And the price you pay can be high—in fines and penalties exacted, in loss of good faith in the workforce and in damages to your good name in the community.

To stay out of trouble, be mindful of the two most common stumbling points while filling a staff slot. You must:

- avoid treating any applicant differently from the others based on race, color, gender, religious beliefs, national origin or age, and
- be aware of newish twists in the law that might require special treatment for disabled applicants.

Both of these cautions concern forms of discrimination. Federal and state laws prohibit you from discriminating against an employee or applicant because of race, color, gender, religious beliefs, national origin, physical disability or age if the person is at least 40 years old. Also, many states and cities have laws prohibiting employment discrimination based on marital status or sexual orientation. And finally, the Americans With

Disabilities Act (ADA) makes it illegal for you to discriminate against people who have or are perceived to have a disability.

Under the federal Civil Rights Act and many state and local anti-discrimination laws, an employer may intentionally use gender, religious beliefs or national origin as the basis for employment decisions only if the employer can show that the job has special requirements that make discrimination necessary. When an employer establishes that such a special circumstance exists, it is called a bona fide occupational qualification (BFOQ).

As you might imagine, it is not easy to make an acceptable plea that you must discriminate. In general, the courts, the Equal Employment Opportunity Commission and state equal employment opportunity agencies prohibit the use of BFOQs except where they are clearly necessary. An employer asserting a BFOQ in a workplace decision typically must prove that the BFOQ is essential for the company or organization to operate successfully.

There are three situations in which BFOQs typically have been recognized.

- **Gender.** The most common type of permissible discrimination turns on gender. The tried but still true example is the job of a wet nurse, who must be female; it is elementary to see why men can—and should—be turned down for such a position. But theaters, cosmetic companies and modeling agencies have also succeeded in arguing that workers need to be a particular gender to get their jobs done.

- **Religion.** When a job involves performing religious duties, the workers hired to do it must believe in the particular religion. For example, a religious denomination that employs counselors who answer telephone inquiries from those interested in joining would typically be allowed to hire only adherents of the religion. Being a member of the denomination would be considered a BFOQ.

- **National origin.** National origin can sometimes, but rarely, be a BFOQ. A few courts have opined that national origin may be a BFOQ in cases where a particular language, cultural background and client perception were essential—for example, an accounts manager in an American subsidiary of a Yugoslavian trading company. But as the homogenizing effect of a global economy takes a stronger hold on American businesses, it is likely that this assertion will become ever more difficult to prove.

## WHOSE WORKPLACE IS IT, ANYWAY?

While the long arm of the law does reach in and tinker with your hiring practices, it may soothe you to know that the laws that prohibit discrimination still allow you considerable discretion in deciding which souls you will welcome under your workplace roof.

You remain free, for example, to hire employees based on what you can glean about their skills, experience, performance and reliability—factors that are logically tied to a valid business purpose. It is also legally permissible—and essential for the health and happiness of the collective workforce—for you to make hiring decisions based on your assessment of a candidate's personality and character. This last comes as a shock to many, since it seems to smack of a hiring standard that might not pass muster under the scrutiny of a discrimination claim. But in truth, if the candidate sets off a signal in your head that reads Does Not Play Well With Others, you should probably pass on hiring him or her. The likelihood that a person might be a bad fit with your current workforce is a valid business reason not to bring him or her aboard and make those already on ship feel strained and uncomfortable.

You only risk violating the law when you treat a person or a group of workers differently than others for reasons that legislators and judges have decided do not serve a valid business purpose and so are considered illegal.

# A. Job Descriptions

No matter how disorganized you are and no matter how informal your workplace, it is wise to start your applicant search by writing a job description for the position you want to fill. This little exercise can feel like annoying busywork. But it can be invaluable in helping you understand what you are after in an ideal hire. And at least as important, it can go a long way toward keeping you on the legal straight and narrow if your hiring practices are ever questioned.

If you are stumped or stuck when doing this, look to other employees for help with the task. If someone on staff is currently doing the job, he or she is the logical person to draft a description of it. You are free to hone it, of course, to meet your needs.

Some additional guidance to get you started: Barebones is best. Be sure that all the functions of the job you list are true and have valid business purposes. Write down everything you envision the worker doing on the job. Then label which tasks are essential and nonessential and group them together. What remains should be a fairly solid description.

- **Essential job functions.** First list the tasks that are absolutely necessary to get the job done.
- **Nonessential job functions.** You may also wish to specify functions and duties that are desirable but not required for a particular job.

## 1. Legal Effect

You may squirm and complain that writing a job description feels like one of those touchy feely exercises with questionable value. But the act of doing it has a few practical benefits: It can help point out whether your job descriptions—perhaps even your expectations—have become dated or unrealistic.

There are legal benefits to the exercise, too. It can keep you out of a lawsuit. An applicant who is unable to do a job's enumerated essential functions—or an employee who fails to deliver on any one of them—will be hard-pressed to claim that he or she was passed over or fired unfairly.

A specific law also comes into play. The Americans With Disabilities Act (ADA) has forced employers to take a fresh look at job descriptions—and to be more scrupulous about discerning what is at the core of each job. To help eliminate unfair discrimination against people with disabilities, the ADA seeks to make sure a person is not excluded from a job simply because he or she cannot perform some marginal or nonessential duties listed in a job description.

## 2. Tips for Writing Descriptions

Well-crafted job descriptions contain a number of similar elements. And the cautions and pointers here will also spill over into your next task: writing a job advertisement. (See Section B.)

Be honest about the skills the job requires. Many employers fall into the trap of inflating the skills required to perform the job. There is not a clear legal risk in this, but it does put you in jeopardy of getting a pool of applicants that is not a good match for the available position. You can safeguard against this by making sure your description accurately reflects the essential and nonessential skills discussed above.

**EXAMPLE:** *The position of Account Representative at Fairweather Phones requires skills in making cold sales calls and entering orders in the company's computerized database. Fairweather is overstating its skill needs if the job description states that applicants need an accounting degree.*

Requiring a high school or college degree may be discriminatory in some job categories—as it disproportionately narrows your pool of applicants to those of a certain socio-economic group or race. You avoid problems by stating that an applicant must have a "degree or equivalent experience."

It is also acceptable to hedge and state your preference here.

**EXAMPLE:** *Bailey & Best, an insurance defense firm, is hiring a person to research the history and help evaluate the legality of claims it handles. While management personnel there feel that the best candidate would have a degree in Library Science, a smart soul with an inquiring mind would fit the bill, too. The job description for the Bailey & Best researcher should contain a qualifier: Degree in Library Science a plus.*

Clearly describe the experience the ideal candidate would have. Here, you are free to specify your own bottom line. Just be sure that you do not unwittingly drag age or education into the requirement—two legally sensitive areas.

If the job you wish to fill requires a licensed or certified practitioner, specify it. You do not risk illegality here as much as you risk drawing in an overqualified or underqualified pool of applicants. The particulars of the job should dictate whether you specify that licenses are required. Obviously, do not go for overkill; include the need for a license or certification—a J.D., an R.N., even a driver's license—only if it is essential for an integral part of the job.

# B. Job Advertisements

After you have written a job description for the position you want to fill, be wary about how you summarize that job in an advertisement. The best way to write an ad that does not run afoul of legal requirements is to concentrate on the skills needed and the basic responsibilities of the job.

A thoughtful choice of words is more important in ads than in any other workplace situation. The worst mistakes happen when you or someone within the company writes an ad without being aware that nuances in it can be used as evidence of discrimination by applicants of a particular gender, age or marital status.

There are a number of semantic pitfalls to avoid in job ads.

| DO NOT USE | USE |
| --- | --- |
| Salesman | Salesperson |
| College Student | Parttime Worker |
| Recent graduate | Up-to-date knowledge |
| Handyman | General Repair Person |
| Gal Friday | Office Manager |
| Married Couple | Two-Person Job |
| Waiter | Wait Staff |
| Young | Energetic |

Federal contractors are legally required to state in their Help Wanted ads that all qualified applicants will be considered for employment without regard to race, color, religion, sex or national origin. Ads often express this with the phrase An Equal Opportunity Employer—a phrase you might consider including even if you are not a federal contractor.

One final caveat. Be careful about defining the job through words that imply that the job is long-term or permanent—a promise you should not make to any employee. Best to steer away from Career Position, Job Tenure, Partnership Track, Career Path, Security, Annual Salary Increases and Merit Raises—all of which infer there is status or money that may not materialize. And resist the temptation to dangle your Comprehensive Benefits Package as an incentive; economic cutbacks can—and have—forced many employers to change the benefits offered over time. It is disingenuous and potentially dangerous, from a legal standpoint, to make promises and not deliver on them.

## THE CYNICS ARE ONTO YOU

Beware of puffing. Today's sophisticated jobseekers can see right through the smoke. There's incontrovertible proof of that in this Eyes Rolling Heavenward guide on how to interpret employment ads. Written by an anonymous author, it was recently widely circulated on employee email systems in workplaces throughout the land.

In each case, the common Adspeak language is translated by experienced jobseekers who know or suspect what the ad actually means. Silly, indeed. But if the words look overly familiar to you, take a look at revising your ad—or your workplace policies.

Competitive Salary
*We remain competitive by paying less than our competitors.*

Join Our Fast Paced Company
*We have no time to train you.*

Casual Work Atmosphere
*We don't pay enough to expect that you will dress up.*

Must Be Deadline Oriented
*You will be six months behind schedule on your first day.*

Some Overtime Required
*Some time each night, some time each weekend.*

Duties Will Vary
*Anyone in the office can boss you around.*

Must Have an Eye for Detail
*We have no quality control.*

Seeking Candidates With a Wide Variety of Experience
*You will need to replace three people who just left.*

Problem Solving Skills a Must
*You are walking into a company in perpetual chaos. Haven't heard a word from anyone out there. Your first task is to find out what is going on.*

Requires Team Leadership Skills
*You will have the responsibilities of a manager without the pay or respect.*

Good Communication Skills
*Management communicates poorly, so you have to figure out what they want and do it.*

# C. Interviewing Applicants

There are two things to keep in mind while interviewing hopeful applicants for a job position. One is to stay focused: You are in the process of winnowing out the candidates to find the best match for the job, not winning friends.

The second caveat has legal overtones: To avoid claims of discrimination and unfair treatment, you must treat all applicants consistently. Ask them the same questions—and evaluate their responses in the same manner.

---

### I DON'T LIKE YOUR AURA

Surprising as it may seem, it's perfectly legal to reject a candidate because he or she seems to have an attitude problem or a personality that would not fit in well in your workplace. You can justifiably shy away from someone who comes across in an interview as a bit dull-witted, with low job and life expectations, who would probably not add much to the life and liveliness of the current staff.

The reality is that it is easy to get rid of employees who show overtly inappropriate behavior—who are caught with their hands in the till, who are chronically absent, who consistently do not perform up to their job descriptions. But it is more difficult to weed out employees with more nebulous problems in workplace performance. As a check on this, think back to workers who gave off telltale signs during a job interview, but you hired them anyway and they turned out to be the bad blood you feared they might become. Typical examples of these queasy-making workplace misfits are employees who customarily:

- gossip
- spread rumors
- seem lazy
- arrive late
- fixate on personal business on the job, and
- are the subject of frequent complaints from customers or clients.

Pay attention to your instincts during the interview process. It is relatively easy to evaluate technical proficiency and expertise, but perhaps more important to pay attention to potential problems with infectious bad attitudes. During interviews, beware of the red flags that surround applicants who:

- have frequent job changes within a short period
- are overly eager to blame others for an unhappy work past—management problems, inept co-workers, jealous supervisors, or
- have resumes containing the obvious screamer: large, unexplained gaps in work—often, attempts to mask a firing or two.

## 1. Interview Questions

Before you begin to interview applicants for a job opening, write a set of questions you want to ask. Focus on the job duties and the applicant's skills and experience. If other people will also be conducting interviews, create a more formalized interviewing policy—and clearly identify questions and topics that are verboten under the law.

Open-ended questions are often best in eliciting the type of information you most want to learn from job applicants. Some examples:

"If asked to write a memo about the fishing operations in this region, what main points would you want to address?"

"What did you like most and least about your last job?"

"Tell me about your experience in running a warehouse."

"Describe how you would forecast demand for a hotel in this area."

"Tell me about the best job you ever had—and describe what you liked the most about it."

"If I were your boss, what would be the most important thing for me to say or do to support you?"

If you write down the questions and stick to the same format at all interviews for the position, you reduce the risk that a rejected applicant will later complain about unequal treatment. It is also smart to summarize the applicant's answers for your files. But do not get so involved in documenting the interview that you forget to listen closely to the responses. Try to pin down ambiguous or evasive responses. And be flexible—not so intent on making it through your question list that you neglect to follow up on something significant that an applicant has said.

## INTERVIEWING PROTOCOL

A good icebreaker is to give the applicant some information about the job—the duties, hours, pay range, benefits and career opportunities. Questions about the applicant's work history and experience that may be relevant to the job opening are always appropriate. But don't encourage the employee to divulge the trade secrets of a present or former employer—especially a competitor. That can lead to a lawsuit. And be cautious about an employee who volunteers such information or promises to bring secrets to the new position. Given the chance, such an employee will probably play fast and loose with your company's secrets, too.

Also, keep your antennae tuned carefully to the applicant who spouts a litany of complaints against former employers. Hire that person and your business may well become the next object of the applicant's invective. And employees with a ton of gripes also tend to have an appetite for litigation.

Give applicants plenty of time to answer questions. Make sure they understand your questions; ask them to let you know if something is unclear. And ask them if they have any questions about your company or the job for which they're applying. Finally, let them know your timeframe for getting back to them with a hiring decision so they won't bug you with premature phone calls.

Adapted from *The Employer's Legal Handbook,* by Fred S. Steingold (Nolo).

## 2. Tips for Conducting Interviews

An interview is simply not a natural conversation. As the person conducting it, your natural tendency will be to put the eager applicant at ease, to be friendly and unimposing. And you, too, might be a bit nervous about the time, money and other high stakes riding on the interview—a nervousness far too many people cover with meaningless chatter that can veer into the realm of the illegal.

These days, it is easy to trip over your tongue during the interview process and end up on the wrong side of the law. There are subtle differences—many would argue imperceptible differences—in queries that are legally permitted and those that are forbidden. The constraints are most confounding when it comes to questions that might relate to a health condition or disability the applicant might or might not have. As the law sits now, it is safest for employers to steer completely clear of questions about health or medical conditions in an interview.

If the applicant has an obvious disability—blindness or a paralyzed limb, for example—you are legally allowed to ask what type of accommodation the applicant might need to do the job. But because this area is such a tricky one, your safer route is not to mention accommodations unless the applicant brings up the topic, first. Should you want to pursue the topic of effective accommodations, it may be best to make a conditional offer to the applicant before proceeding.

And to avoid claims of privacy violations, you should also steer clear of intimate queries about family or personal predilections. Some workplace experts recommend that employees require applicants to sign written consent forms that:

- define the scope of the pre-employment investigation
- describe the type of information you seek, and
- state clearly that the applicant authorizes the employer to seek the information.

The most anal among you will opt to follow this advice about adding still another piece to your growing pile of paperwork. But keep in mind that a consent form will be worth only the paper upon which it is written if your loose lips violate the law during the actual interview.

There are a few tips to keep in mind that will help keep you on the legal up and up during the interview.

➡️ Limit your questions and discussion to the main duties of the job. Stick to accepted icebreakers such as observations about the weather or the commute. This will not put you in the running for a Fine Conversationalist Award, but it should keep you safely away from legally hazardous topics. Then cut to the chase. Describe the job and its requirements. But avoid delivering a monologue. This is your chance to gauge whether the applicant sitting before you might be a good fit for the available job.

➡️ You can usually ask the applicant to describe or demonstrate how to do a task. This bit of commonsense can be a lifesaver, as it can quickly help you separate the serious contenders for the position from the wannabes. You must be careful to apply this one across the board to all applicants, however. It is not permissible to single out applicants with perceived disabilities to demonstrate their abilities unless you have what the law terms a reasonable belief that a particular disability might hamper job performance.

**EXAMPLE:** *An applicant with one leg applies for a position as an office receptionist—a position that mainly involves greeting the public, answering phones and sorting mail. You should not ask the person to demonstrate how he or she would perform tasks associated with the receptionist job—unless you ask all applicants for such a demonstration.*

**EXAMPLE:** *An applicant with one leg applies for a position as a telephone lineperson. Because the job involves climbing poles and you might reasonably surmise that the applicant would be hampered in this, you can ask for a description or demonstration of how he or she would accomplish the task.*

Do not follow up on volunteered information. It may be tough, even counterintuitive, not to pose a question or respond when an applicant reveals something that might set off warning signals in you—a weakness for martinis, a habit of taking long stretches of time off, an inability to see or hear clearly. But you are pinned by the law here. You may have the opportunity to check out your reservations later while investigating the applicant, but the interview is not the place to do it. Better to deftly switch topics—or, if the comment you hear seems especially loaded, make clear that your decision about whether to hire or not will not be based on it.

Common slip-ups involve prying—often unwittingly—into an applicant's national origin or ethnicity. For example, if an applicant mentions she attended a big family reunion the previous weekend, beware of asking too much about it. Innocuous as this may seem, the topic could naturally elicit questions from you about cuisine, family traditions, religious customs—all of which could skirt perilously close to the danger zones of ethnicity or national origin. Better to change the subject.

And contrary to what might be your own instincts to keep the conversational ball rolling, you may not ask follow-up questions even if an applicant opens the door by revealing information about a protected area such as marital status, a disability, or age. As tempting as it may be to tap the well for some added facts, your best response is to steer the conversation away from the potential hot zone by noting simply that it is not related to the applicant's qualifications or your decisionmaking.

An increasingly touchy area involves disabilities or sickness. Remember that the Americans With Disabilities Act is so all-encompassing that it forbids discriminating against applicants who:

- are disabled
- are perceived as disabled, or
- associate with those who are disabled.

**EXAMPLE:** *During the course of an interview, an applicant mentions that he had to miss two months of work last year. As unnatural and unfeeling as it may seem, you cannot ask whether he had been sick. That might be uncomfortably close to an impermissible inquiry about a disability.*

The most important defense you can present to any potential claim of an ADA violation in hiring is not that you made or even attempted to make every change possible so that a disabled worker could do the job. The keys are your openness to considering changes—to "go the extra mile," as a judge in one recent case put it colloquially. A number of courts have also emphasized that it is important to narrow the focus on the particular applicant and the job for which he or she is applying; it is irrelevant whether there are other positions within the company to meet the applicant's capabilities.

Do not worry about remaining forever in the dark about a promising applicant's qualifications. The minute you make a conditional job offer to an applicant, you can be more overtly nosy in gathering relevant information about him or her. You have the latitude to require the applicant to pass a medical exam, for example, and can also ask specific questions about health conditions. There is one possible catch: You must require the same tests and ask the same questions of all candidates for a particular job. You cannot single out individuals about whom you harbor suspicions.

⚠ **Mum's the Word on References, Too.** Some employers try to skirt the prohibition on questions about an applicant's medical history and attendance by attempting to glean that same information from former employers. The ADA also prohibits this form of potential sneakiness.

## THE CARROTS BEFORE THE WORKHORSES

Low unemployment rates have forced employers to confront a new problem: keeping workers from jumping ship. A recent survey of companies polled about what benefits they offer to induce employees to stay on the job yielded mixed results. For senior level executives, promises of better compensation and benefits delivered the most staying power—although this group generally demonstrated the most allegiance to their employers. But to retain workers with the largest turnover—those described by the pollsters as frontline employees—you may simply need to make good hiring decisions in the first place.

The top ten methods that businesses are using to retain senior level executives—who have the lowest turnover—are:

| | |
|---|---|
| Better compensation and benefits | 67% |
| Stock options | 52% |
| More careful selection in hiring | 47% |
| Profit-sharing | 27% |
| Retention bonuses | 26% |
| Tuition reimbursement | 23% |
| Adoption of a casual dress code | 22% |
| Exit interviews | 19% |
| Flexible hours and schedules | 18% |
| Improved orientation programs | 15% |

The top ten methods that businesses are using to retain frontline employees—who have the highest turnover—are:

| | |
|---|---|
| More careful selection in hiring | 57% |
| Better compensation and benefits | 50% |
| Tuition reimbursement | 47% |
| Improved training programs | 45% |
| Better orientation programs | 39% |
| Adoption of a casual dress code | 38% |
| Flexible hours and schedules | 33% |
| Providing health insurance | 29% |
| Exit interviews | 28% |
| Profit-sharing | 17% |

Information technology employees are the most difficult to retain today, according to half of the survey respondents. The second most difficult type of employees to retain are those who work in sales, marketing and customer service positions, according to 47% of businesses.

Source: 1998 Retention and Staffing Survey by Manchester Partners International, an employment consulting firm based in Bala Cynwyd, Pa.

## 3.  Guidance on Interview Questions

Despite the proliferation of rules now evolving around permissible and impermissible interview questions, sometimes there is information you just have to know. But you must choose your words with the utmost care.

Many of the questions below are based on examples given by the Equal Employment Opportunity Commission or EEOC, the agency charged with ferreting out and clamping down on violations. The theory, at least, is that some questions are forbidden because they might cause you to exclude an applicant because of a disability or other protected characteristic such as age, national origin or religion.

| IF YOU ARE CURIOUS ABOUT | YOU CAN ASK | YOU CANNOT ASK |
| --- | --- | --- |
| Name | What is your full name? Have you ever worked for this company under a different name? | What was your maiden name? |
| Residence | Any question about applicant's residence is permitted. | No questions prohibited. |
| Age | Are you 18 or older? | Any other question about specific age. |
| Birthplace | No questions allowed. | The applicant's birthplace, or where his or her parents, spouse or other relative was born. |
| Gender | No questions allowed. | Have you ever had a sex change operation? (Yes, it seems like an unlikely question, but it has actually been asked.) |

| | | |
|---|---|---|
| **Marital or family status** | No questions allowed. | Are you married? What is your husband or wife's name? Do you have any children? |
| **Race or color** | No questions allowed. | Do you identify yourself more as black or Shiite? |
| **Religion or creed** | No questions allowed. | Are you a member of the Greek Orthodox Church on the corner? What is your religious denomination? What religious holidays do you observe? |
| **National origin** | No questions allowed. | Interesting name; is it Yugoslavian? How did you learn to read, write or speak a foreign language? |
| **Citizenship** | Are you a U.S. citizen? If not, do you have a green card or other authorization to work here? | Were you native born or naturalized? Are your parents citizens, too? When did you become a citizen? |
| **Arrest record** | No questions allowed. | Have you ever been arrested for a crime? |
| **Conviction record** | Have you ever been convicted of a crime? | Have you ever been arrested but not convicted of any particular offense? |
| **Education** | What schools have you attended? | What racial or religious affiliation were the schools you attended? |
| **Military experience** | What experience did you have in the military that might relate to this job? What branch were you affiliated with? What rank did you attain? | What type of discharge did you get? |

| | | |
|---|---|---|
| **Membership in organizations** | Did you have any experience as a volunteer or club member that may be related to this job? | Name all the groups and organizations of which you are a member. |
| **Stress** | How well do you handle stress? Do you work better under pressure? | Does stress affect your ability to be effective on the job? Have you ever been unable to handle stress on the job? |
| **Disabilities** | Do you have the ability to perform this job, with or without accommodations? This job requires you to lift 40-pound kegs and carry them down two flights of stairs. Can you do that, with or without an accommodation? Do you have 20/20 corrected vision? | Do you have a disability that would prevent you from performing this job? Are you an alcoholic? Do you have AIDS? What effect does being in a wheelchair have on your daily life? What is your corrected vision? What is your uncorrected vision? |
| **Impairments** | How did you break your arm? | How extensive was the break—and will you likely have full use of your arm once the cast comes off? |
| **Activities and job functions** | Can you life three-pound boxes and load them onto four-foot shelves as this job requires? | Can you stand? Can you walk? |
| **Attendance** | How many days were you absent from work last year? How many Mondays and Fridays were you absent from work last year other than on approved vacation? | How many days were you sick last year? How How often will you require sick leave so that you can obtain treatment for your disability? |

| History of receiving Workers' Compensation | No questions allowed. | No questions allowed. |
|---|---|---|
| **Drug use** | Are you currently using any illegal drugs? | What medications are you currently taking? Have you ever been on AZT? |
| **Alcohol use** | Do you drink alcoholic beverages? | How much alcohol do you drink weekly? Have you ever been treated for alcoholism? |
| **Certifications and licenses** | If the job requires it: Do you have certification to drive trucks interstate? | If the job does not involve driving: Do you have a valid driver's license? |

## 4. Ending the Interview

While it is wise to make some allowances for the anxiety that surely accompanies the interviewee to the event, you should also feel free to cut the session short if it becomes clear that he or she is not meant for the position. The best barometer you have is your own instinct. But be particularly attuned to behavior that suggests a candidate may be primed to deliver unpleasantness in the future—a surprising number of interviewees reveal this propensity while sitting in the Hire Me hotseat. Signs that might give you cause for pause include:

- evasive or unresponsive answers
- an eagerness to trash a present or former employer
- an inflated view of accomplishments and talents
- a total lack of sense of humor, and

- an inability to describe frequent job hops or lapses in a resume.

Be succinct and dispassionate if rejecting the applicant outright. For example, you might say simply: "It doesn't appear that you and this particular position are a good fit."

## REJECTED AND WONDERING WHY

Do not be surprised if you get a call or letter from a person you have interviewed but rejected. Many au courant jobseeking manuals and counselors advise rejected applicants to contact the very people who voted thumbs down and ask why. The theory is that the rejected applicants can use the information to learn about themselves, to help hone their interviewing skills for the next round.

On the surface, this seems like a sound way to gather information about likely human responses, just as lawyers run their cases by faux juries or CEOs seeking funds practice their pitches before a room of phony venture capitalists in advance of presenting to the real things.

But in workplace reality, the rejectees likely have little to gain from you—and you have everything to lose.

Unless you are a combination of the most adept speaker, listener and job counselor, it is usually wise not to join in these Monday Afternoon Quarterbacking conversations. Your best response will probably be to merely restate that the candidate and position did not seem to be a good fit. This will prevent the uncomfortable situation of the rejected soul lobbying you to reconsider your decision—and eliminate the possibility that you will misspeak about why you rejected him or her.

## D. Making a Job Offer

There are precious few legal rules here, other than the time-tested adage: Don't Make Promises You Can't Keep. Employees have been known to reconstruct promises made during the hiring process but broken on the job—promises about job security, working conditions or raises and promotions. These broken promises can be the stuff of which lawsuits for breach of contract are made.

More often, however, the price you pay for not delivering on promises made during the hiring process is exacted in losses in the worker's morale, allegiance and eventually productivity. Beware of gilding the offer to make the job appear more golden than it is.

- **Job security.** Few employers are foolhardy enough to promise that a job will last forever. But even an off-hand comment made during hiring such as: "We have a very solid record; we've never had to lay off anyone" can later haunt you if a layoff does become necessary. Similarly, describing a job as permanent or having management potential can become embarrassing guarantees if reality later proves the descriptions false.

- **Working conditions.** Do not dangle job attractions such as flexible hours or work-at-home arrangements if they are not a tried and true part of your company culture. An employee promised this flexibility who is later up against an unbending 9 to 5 office job is sure to feel duped and resentful.

- **Raises and promotions.** Do not promise regular bonuses or raises unless you are absolutely sure you can deliver. And remember that there may be changes in the market or your workforce that you cannot anticipate.

EXAMPLE: *Bordo, a fast growing software company, lured the best and the brightest workers not with competitive salaries or benefits, but with the promises of raises, bonuses and stock options when the company turned a high enough profit. Although Bordo endured, it did not achieve a comfortable profit margin, so the owners could not distribute the promised benefits. In time, Bordo's long suffering employees had enough and looked elsewhere for work, feeling demoralized and resentful from the cycles of broken promises.*

In all these cases, clearly written policies are more useful than grandiose promises. Your employee manual and hiring letter should specify that the employment relationship is at will—that is, an employee may quit or be fired at any time. Your manual or other writing should also make clear the circumstances under which discretionary bonuses may or may not be given. And be sure that your policies give you enough flexibility to change with the times.

## KEEP YOUR EYES ON YOUR TONGUE

Not only is it wrongheaded and meanspirited to make promises about a job that you cannot keep, but in some states, it is illegal. A California law, for example, prohibits influencing, persuading or engaging any person to move to the state or within it for a job by making false representations, written or oral.

Prohibited falsehoods include those about:

- the kind, character or existence of work
- the length of time the work will last
- compensation for the work
- the sanitary or housing conditions relating to the work, and
- the existence or nonexistence of any strike, lockout or labor dispute affecting it.

California employers who knowingly break this law may be fined, imprisoned, or both. While the measure was originally passed "to protect migrant workers from the abuses heaped upon them by unscrupulous employers," it also banishes braggery at the boardroom table. (Cal. Lab. Code §972)

# Investigating Applicants

**W**hen an employee becomes a former employee, but tensions or possible claims remain behind, many employers are left to wring their hands and lament their own shortsightedness. They decry that if only they had taken the time and effort to check out the problem worker, they never would have hired him or her in the first place. Most often, they are right.

While rules that protect individual privacy rights have made it somewhat more difficult to screen and evaluate applicants before hiring them, employers can still get help in digging out signals that an applicant may become a disappointment or a menace on the job. It is still relatively easy to find telling information about an applicant's work habits, credit history, criminal records and medical information. However, if misused or obtained improperly, this information has the potential to become grist for a legal claim against the employer who had the inquiring mind.

## A. Evaluating Resumes

An applicant who gets a foot in your door is likely to be preceded by a piece of paper—a summary of education, experience and qualifications, sometimes noxiously souped up with Goals and Objectives—known as a resume or, in more affected circles, as a curriculum vitae.

Quite often, those pages are afloat in lies. Many jobseekers inflate their resumes by exaggerating their experience or credentials. A recent study revealed that:

- 9% of job applicants falsely claimed they had a college degree, listed false employers, or identified jobs that did not exist
- 4% listed incorrect job titles
- 11% misrepresented why they left a former employer, and

- nearly 33% listed dates of employment that were off by more than three months.

Employers have always been free to fire employees who lie about a significant qualification. Now they may be able to use this misinformation to defend against lawsuits for wrongful termination or discrimination. Courts reason, in essence, that employees who lied to get a job cannot later come to court and claim the employer did them wrong. The emerging legal counterattack on firing claims even has a name: the After-Acquired Evidence Theory.

Conduct that has been held sufficiently serious to be admitted as after-acquired evidence has included:

- 150 instances of falsifying company records
- failing to list a previous employer on a resume
- failing to admit being terminated for cheating on timecards
- failing to reveal a prior conviction for a felony
- lying about education and experience on a job application
- fabricating a college degree during an interview, and
- removing and copying the company's confidential financial statements.

In a recent case, the U.S. Supreme Court held that backpay awards might still be available to employees who sue before after-acquired evidence is discovered, but they could be limited by being calculated from the date of the unlawful discharge to the date the employee's fraud was discovered (*McKennon v. Nashville Banner Publishing Co.*, 115 S. Ct. 879 (1995)). The Court's decision was based specifically on an age discrimination claim; it is unclear whether this limit on damages will also apply where the employee claims a wrong other than discrimination.

Even before the practical effect of this emerging area of law becomes more clear, it does signal that resumes are important documents that deserve close scrutiny They may even be worth a second, closer look should an employee's job performance later become shaky or inept.

# B. Contacting Former Employers

Because most job applicants exaggerate their qualifications and experience and some even lie outright about it, it is a good idea to turn to outside, objective sources for the real skinny.

Unfortunately, this is becoming more difficult. Former employers—and you may at times find yourself in this position—are often reluctant to say anything negative for fear that they may be sued for defamation. In the litigation-happy era in which we live, a growing number of employers have become so squint-lipped that they will give no more than name, former rank and dates of employment when asked to dish about workers under their former employ.

You might be able to loosen the lips of the reticent if you can produce a copy of the applicant's signed consent to a full disclosure of employment information. (See Section B.) Even then, you will have to be crafty to pry out the truth. You must learn to listen between the lines. A former employer who seems hampered or unresponsive when asked to discuss a former employee may simply be The Stuffed Shirt Type. But quite possibly, he or she is hiding something damning behind the faint praise.

To get beyond bland or generic responses, you will have to try harder—and asking open-ended questions may be your best method. You can often learn a lot by asking former employers:

- Would you hire back this person if you could?
- What are this person's greatest strengths?
- What are his or her greatest weaknesses and strengths—and how did they show up on the job?
- If you could design the perfect job for this person, what would it be?
- Was this person liked and respected by his or her co-workers?

Stay focused on what you want to know most. If the position you hope to fill requires a self starter, be specific and forthright. You might say, for example: "The position I have in mind requires someone who is able to step in and reorganize our shipping system from the top down. Do you think X is up to this task?"

Finally, if your attempts at honest conversation with an applicant's former employer bear a frustrating lack of fruit, realize that it may be unrelated to the applicant's actual ability on the job. Stop flailing at the uncommunicative soul on the other end of the phone and move on— knowing that there are many other sources to which you can turn for information. (See Sections C, D and E.)

## THAT WAS THEN, THIS IS NOW

On-the-job experience generally is much more relevant to employment than an applicant's educational credentials. Still, you may have good reasons for requiring a high school diploma or college degree for some jobs. If so, you may want to see proof that the applicant really received the diploma or degree or took the courses claimed in the job application.

If you wish to see these records, ask the applicant to sign a written release acknowledging your right to obtain them. Most schools won't turn over the records without such a release—and many won't deliver them to anyone except the former student. This can, of course, complicate your verification, since it creates the possibility of forgery or tampering.

These releases can be extremely valuable if you want to broaden your information search while you are checking the applicant's background. The applicant who consents to your investigation will be hard-pressed to later claim an invasion of privacy. Suggested wording for such a consent form follows.

**Authorization.** *I authorize XYZ Company to obtain information about me from my previous employers, schools and credit sources. I authorize my previous employers, schools that I have attended and all credit sources to disclose to XYZ Company such information about me as XYZ Company may request.*

_____ *Initials*

Adapted from *The Employer's Legal Handbook*, by Fred S. Steingold (Nolo).

# C. Checking Credit Reports

Credit bureaus—profitmaking companies that gather and sell information about a person's credit history—have become a booming business. And the growing power and popularity of the computerized credit rating has found its way into the workplace, as well. Credit bureau files used by companies that issue credit cards and make loans are now also used by many employers who want to do routine credit checks on employees and, even more often, on job applicants.

## 1. Laws on Credit Records

A federal law, the Fair Credit Reporting Act or FCRA (15 U.S.C. §1681 and following), requires credit agencies to share their data only with those who have a legitimate business need for the information. Employers generally qualify and are given broad access to credit reports, which they can use to evaluate eligibility for "employment, promotion, reassignment or retention."

Credit bureaus typically track not only individual bill-paying habits, but also maintain a list of all companies that have asked to see a credit rating when the person applies for credit, insurance, a place to live or a new job. Employers increasingly use credit bureau files to see the list—and so to find out whether an employee is job hunting with other companies. And prospective employers may use a shaky credit report to conclude that it is risky to welcome a particular new worker aboard.

However, a recent amendment to the FCRA gives workers a number of protections and built-in warnings that alert them to how and whether a current or prospective employer is using credit information about them. The law requires you to get applicants' written permission before peeping at their credit reports. And the words granting permission cannot be buried deep within a job application form or other word-laden document; you must ask them to sign separately to signal their approval.

If you have questions about the form and format of this notice, contact the Federal Trade Commission by phone: 202-382-4357; TDD: 202-326-2502; or by mail: Federal Trade Commission, 600 Pennsylvania Ave, NW, Washington, DC 20580; or through the Internet: http://www.ftc.gov.

The imposed duty to get advance written approval for credit reports sounds like strong stuff at first. But the truth is that while prospective employees are legally free to refuse, most quite rightly fear that if they do, they will leave the impression they have something to hide—killing their chances for getting or keeping a job. So most will consent to the check or withdraw as applicants.

The amendment also mandates that a prospective employer who rejects an applicant for a job based in any way on an item on a credit report must give him or her:

- a copy of the report before issuing the rejection, and
- written instructions on how to challenge the accuracy of that report.

Again, while this smells at first whiff like strong consumer protection for jobseekers and a burdensome chore for employers seeking credit information, the reality is that it is tough to track whether employers have followed the letter of the law.

What baldly remains in force is that an employer who uses credit information against an applicant is not only supposed to fess up to it and get approval first, but must also give the applicant the name, address and telephone number of the credit agency that provided the report. You must also disclose to the applicant when a report has actually been requested—and must verify the request in writing to the applicant within three days of requesting the report. Many eager employers have been done in by dates on these documents showing that they jumped the gun.

## 2. When the Law Applies

The law applies to information gleaned from reports issued by any consumer reporting agency, which includes the traditional credit bureaus such as TRW and Equifax, but also includes private investigators and people and agencies hired to uncover information for employment purposes. These investigators work in mysterious ways, but generally gather their information by interviewing friends, neighbors and associates or the person under investigation. The folks who provide the information incur no liability under the Act, as you must certify to them that you will not violate any law or regulation when using the information. If you do, in fact, misuse the information, you could potentially be dinged twice: once for misusing the information in violation of the law—and again for swearing that you wouldn't misuse it.

For inquisitive employers, the foil written into the FCRA is its broad definition of consumer reports. The law defines them to include "any written, oral or other communication of any information by a consumer reporting agency bearing on a consumer's creditworthiness, credit standing, credit capacity, character, general reputation, personal characteristics, or mode of living" when the information is or may be used as the basis for an employment decision. This mouthful means that anything written or uttered by a person or service hired to do sleuthwork on employees is protected by the FCRA—and employers who intend to use this information gathered in this way must comply with the obligations and restrictions in it. This provision has been interpreted so broadly, for example, that it even applies to a lawyer hired to defend a sexual harassment claim who interviewed employees in preparation for the case.

And the law has teeth. Employers guilty of violating its many requirements can be liable for paying damages to an applicant, along with court costs and attorney's fees. Those who obtain a report under false pretenses may be fined imprisoned or both.

## 3. Taking Action Based on a Credit Report

If you do not like what you read about an applicant in a consumer report, the FCRA also imposes rather picayune requirements on what you must do before you can act.

You must compose a detailed oral or written notice telling the applicant:

- the action you have taken—such as rejecting an application or withdrawing an offer of employment
- the name, address and telephone number of the source of the information
- that the person or agency providing the information is not responsible for making the employment decision
- that for the next 60 days, he or she is entitled to get a free copy of the report from the investigating person or agency, and
- that he or she has a right to dispute the accuracy of the information directly with the investigators.

## 4. Tips on Using Credit Reports

Despite the reality that applicants rarely call out to have credit rights enforced, you may well conclude after reading through the copious rules for compliance with the FCRA that it is more trouble than it's worth to use any information that might be controlled by it. But there are a number of steps you can take to protect yourself from accusations of wrongdoing—and to allow yourself to make the fullest and best use of the credit information you do acquire.

Review your own practices—and those of any credit agency you contact—to be sure that you both comply with the many specific requirements under the FCRA, especially those requiring notice and disclosure to applicants. Also be sure that your own employees who have access to information from credit reports on others know that the information can only be used to make legitimate employment decisions.

→ Do not deny an applicant a job solely because you find out that he or she has filed for bankruptcy; that would violate federal laws against discrimination (11 U.S.C. §525(a)).

→ Limit the kinds of positions for which you conduct credit checks; if financial stability or moxie with money is not truly important to you or the position for which the applicant is being considered, consider using other sources to track information about him or her.

→ Do not adopt a rote or rigid rule about why and whether particular information will disqualify all job candidates. Be open to considering subjective information, such as the applicant's own explanation of a negative credit notation—and the length of time since a credit transgression has occurred.

# D. Checking Criminal Records

According to recent statistics collected by the Bureau of Justice, approximately one-third of the workforce has a criminal record, with the most common criminal offense being theft.

Arrest and conviction records are public records available to anyone, including an employer, who has the wherewithal and incentive to search for them. These records are also kept by a number of agencies—among them police, prosecutors, courts, the FBI, probation departments, prisons and parole boards. These recordkeepers are theoretically barred from releasing this information to anyone other than other criminal justice agencies and a few types of specialized employers such as those who help manufacture controlled substances or run childcare or eldercare facilities. In reality, however, slips of the tongue are made and persistent employers can generally find the ways and means to get the information.

Most states now have laws that specifically bar employers and prospective employers from getting access to records of arrests that did not lead to convictions. And a number of states—including California, Michigan and Rhode Island—forbid employers from even asking job applicants about such arrests.

Still, there are many exceptions to this Don't Ask, Don't Tell rule for specific categories of workers, including most bank employees, securities industry and commodities workers, nuclear power employees and daycare and eldercare workers. Depending on state law, you may actually be duty-bound to check both the arrest and conviction records of these workers.

## YOU CAN'T ALWAYS BELIEVE YOUR EYES

Many states have laws that allow individuals to expunge, or seal, their criminal records. When a record is expunged, it is usually not available to anyone other than criminal justice agencies and the courts. If a criminal record has been expunged, a person is generally allowed to deny that he or she ever had one when a prospective employer asks about it.

There are varying policies on this. In Massachusetts, for example, an employer that asks about criminal history must include on the application a statement that an applicant with a sealed record is entitled to answer "no record" regarding the underlying offenses. But in Ohio, an employer may question an applicant regarding an expunged record if the underlying incident relates to the type of job you are seeking.

Some states extend the expungement privilege only to a first arrest that did not result in a conviction. Other states are more generous, allowing a conviction for a petty offense to be expunged if probation was successfully completed. Some states limit the procedure to juvenile records. Usually, the request to seal a record will be granted only if a person has remained clear of any contacts with the criminal justice system for a specified period of time following the arrest or conviction.

The bottom line: Only small potato crimes can be easily expunged from a record—not the ones likely to derail most applicants from jobs. Records of truly serious offenses cannot be sealed and are with a person for life.

## 1. Laws on Arrest and Conviction Records

Your access to arrest and conviction records—and the procedure you must follow to obtain this information—is controlled in most states by specific laws on the subject. A summary follows.

### STATE LAWS ON EMPLOYEE ARREST AND CONVICTION RECORDS

| | |
|---|---|
| **Alabama** | A current or prospective employee who works with children must sign a statement declaring whether or not he or she has been convicted of a sex crime. The employer may verify this statement with the National Crime Information Center. |
| | Failure to disclose a sex crime conviction is grounds for criminal prosecution. An employer may also find out from the Department of Public Safety whether a current or prospective employee has been convicted of a sex crime. Ala. Code §26-20-2 |
| **Alaska** | The state can release information concerning past convictions if fewer than ten years have passed since the person was released from prison. Sealed criminal justice records cannot be released except for criminal justice employment purposes. Alaska Stat. §12.62.160, .180 |
| **Arizona** | Employers may obtain arrest or conviction records only if there is a compelling business reason for doing so. Arizona Attorney General, Civil Rights Division, "Guide to Pre-Employment Inquiries under the Arizona Civil Rights Act." |
| | Enforcing agency: |
| | Civil Rights Division |
| | 1275 West Washington Street |
| | Phoenix, AZ 85007 |
| | 602-542-5263 |
| **Arkansas** | Private investigators and security officers must provide a verified statement disclosing any convictions of a felony, Class A misdemeanor, violent crime or crime involving moral turpitude. Ark. Code Ann. §17-40-327 |

| California | Employers may not ask prospective employees to disclose information regarding an arrest or detention which did not result in conviction. They also may not ask regarding a referral to a diversion program. Employers may not seek or use as a condition of employment any such information, but may inquire as to an arrest for which a current or prospective employee is out on bail or their own recognizance. Law enforcement and criminal justice agencies are exempt. Employees and applicants for positions at health facilities and for jobs involving access to drugs and medications may be asked questions regarding certain arrests. Does not apply to applicants for public concessions. Cal. Lab. Code §432.7<br><br>Employers may not inquire about convictions involving marijuana that were earlier than January 1, 1976. Cal Labor Code §432.8 |
|---|---|
| Colorado | Employers may not require the disclosure of sealed arrest records if the employee was acquitted, no charges were filed or the case was dismissed. Does not apply to pleas or convictions for any type of offense, driving under the influence of drugs or alcohol, sexual assault, indecent exposure, incest or child prostitution. Colo. Rev. Stat. §24-72-308 |
| Connecticut | Information about the arrest record of an applicant may not be made available to anyone other than the personnel department or the person in charge of employment. Conn. Gen. Stat. Ann. § 31-51i |
| Delaware | Records of an arrest that resulted in a dismissal or an acquittal, that have been ordered expunged by a court, do not have to be disclosed for any reason as an arrest. Does not apply to applicants to law enforcement agencies. Del. Code Ann. tit. 11 §§4371 to 4374 |
| District of Columbia | No statute |

| | |
|---|---|
| Florida | If a background screening or security check is required by law—for childcare, nursing home assistants and certain state jobs—applicants and employees must undergo statewide and local criminal records checks, and people in positions of trust must undergo checks of juvenile and federal records as well. The employer may give the information to any other employer who requests it. Fla. Stat. §§435.01 and following; 400.215; 402.302; 110.1127<br>Background checks on county and municipal employees are prohibited. Fla. Stat. §125.581 |
| Georgia | The Department of Human Resources can obtain records of a job applicant's convictions if the job duties would include the care, treatment or custody of clients or if obtaining the information is otherwise necessary for the safety of clients, other employees or the general public. The Department of Human Resources may not release this information to other people or agencies. Ga. Code Ann. §49-2-14 |
| Hawaii | The state may not disqualify someone for employment or for a license, permit or certificate solely on the basis of a conviction for a crime but may consider it if it relates to the person's possible job performance.<br>Does not apply to the issuance of a liquor license nor for employment in healthcare, youth care or detention facilities. Haw. Rev. Stat. §831-3.1(a)<br>Employers may inquire into an applicant's conviction record if it bears a rational relationship to the duties and responsibilities of the job and if the employer has made a conditional offer of employment. The state can disseminate records of convictions only, and not of arrests that did not lead to convictions, expunged convictions, convictions for which no jail sentence was possible and misdemeanor convictions that are more than 20 years old. Haw. Rev. Stat. §§378-2.5; 831-3.1(a) |
| Idaho | No statute |

| | |
|---|---|
| **Illinois** | Employers, employment agencies and labor organizations may not inquire about or use arrest information or a criminal history record that has been ordered sealed or expunged as a basis to refuse to hire or take any adverse employment action against a current or prospective employee. |
| | However, the state, school districts and certain private organizations can use information from the Department of State Police in evaluating qualifications of applicants or prospective employees. 775 Ill. Rev. Stat. 5/2-103; 20 Ill. Comp. Stat. 2630/3 |
| **Indiana** | The state can release to prospective employers information on arrests or charges. Indiana Code Ann. §5-2-5 and following |
| **Iowa** | No statute |
| **Kansas** | Employers can require applicants to sign releases allowing them to access the applicant's criminal history record for the purpose of determining the applicant's fitness for employment. Kan. Stat. Ann. §22-4710 |
| **Kentucky** | A person cannot be disqualified from public employment based on a misdemeanor for which no jail sentence can be imposed. For other types of misdemeanors and felonies, the hiring agency can consider the nature and seriousness of the crime and the relationship of the crime to the job duties. If employment is denied based on a criminal record, the applicant must be given notice, a hearing and the opportunity to reapply upon rehabilitation. This law does not apply to lawyers and police. Ky. Rev. Stat. §§335B.010 and following |
| **Louisiana** | Applicants cannot be disqualified from a license, permit or certificate, required to practice a trade or profession, on account of a prior criminal record for an offense that is not a felony. An applicant who has a prior felony conviction may be disqualified only if the felony directly relates to the position or occupation sought. La. Rev. Stat. Ann. §37:2950 |

An employer of a nonlicensed person hired to perform nursing care or health-related services must ask the state police to do a criminal record check. The applicant must be told about the check before he is offered the job. The statute includes a list of prior offenses which make the applicant ineligible for employment. All information received must be kept confidential and destroyed one year after employment ceases. La. Rev. Stat. Ann. §40:1300.51

**Maine**
State licensing agencies may consider convictions involving dishonesty for which a sentence of at least one year can be imposed and convictions for sexual misconduct for which a sentence of any length can be imposed. The conviction must directly relate to the trade or occupation for which the license is sought. If more than three years have passed since the applicant was released from prison—ten years for healthcare and social workers—the licensing agency cannot consider the conviction. Me. Rev. Stat. Ann. tit. V §5301

**Maryland**
Employers or educational institutions may not require job applicants to disclose information regarding criminal charges that have been expunged. Md. Code Ann. art. 27, §740

**Massachusetts**
An applicant for public employment may not be disqualified on account of information in sealed criminal records. Any employer who asks about criminal history must include, on the application, the advice that an applicant with a sealed record is entitled to answer "no record" regarding prior convictions, court appearances or arrests. Mass. Gen. Laws. Ann. ch. 276, §100A

**Michigan**
Employers, employment agencies and labor organizations other than law enforcement agencies, the state or a political subdivision of the state may not request, make or maintain information regarding arrest or detention that did not result in conviction. This does not apply to felony charges prior to conviction or dismissal. Mich. Comp. Laws §37.2205a

| | |
|---|---|
| **Minnesota** | A person seeking public employment, or a license or a certificate from the state necessary for an occupation or a profession, cannot be disqualified because of a prior conviction unless it directly relates to the position or occupation. Records of arrest that did not lead to conviction, expunged conviction or misdemeanor conviction not subject to a jail sentence cannot be disclosed to an employer. Does not apply to law enforcement, fire protection, lawyers, doctors, schools or childcare providers. Mich. Stat. Ann. §§364.01 and following |
| **Mississippi** | Employers of those providing childcare, transportation, treatment, counseling, custody, instruction and entertainment services to children must obtain sex offense criminal history information—including arrests and charges even if the person was not convicted or prosecuted—from the state for every employee or volunteer. People with specific prior sex offenses may not be hired. Miss. Code Ann. §§45-31-1 and following |
| **Missouri** | No statute |
| **Montana** | No statute |
| **Nebraska** | No statute |
| **Nevada** | Employers may inquire if applicants have been convicted of felony or a misdemeanor within a specified time period. Employers must inform applicants that conviction does not necessarily disqualify them. Nevada Equal Rights Commission Pre-Employment Inquiry Guide<br>Enforcing agency:<br>Equal Rights Commission<br>2450 Wrondel Way, Suite C<br>Reno, NV 89502<br>702-688-1288 |
| **New Hampshire** | No statute |

**New Jersey**  In addition to federal and state employers, any private employer or volunteer supervisor may request criminal conviction and arrest information from the state Bureau of Identification to determine a person's qualifications for work. Requests must be accompanied by a set of fingerprints or the person's Social Security number and date of birth.

Employers who are required by federal or state law to perform criminal history background checks will also be given information on arrests that ended favorably for the person arrested. Employers must keep the information confidential. New Jersey Administrative Code §§ 13:59 to 13:59-1.6 Public and private employers that operate schools, daycare facilities or youth centers must perform criminal history record checks on the federal and state level for all applicants (excluding volunteers) who will regularly come into contact with students under 18 years old. Applicants with specified convictions may not be hired unless they can present proof of rehabilitation. N.J. Stat. Ann. §18A:6-7.1

**New Mexico**  An employer must conduct a nationwide criminal records check of all employees of childcare and detention facilities. N.M. Stat. Ann. §§32-A-15-1 to 4

State employers and licensing authorities can consider applicants' felony convictions and misdemeanor convictions for crimes involving moral turpitude, but the convictions are not an automatic bar to employment. A person's license can be suspended or revoked if he or she is convicted of a felony or a misdemeanor involving moral turpitude if the crime directly relates to the employment, trade or business. N.M. Stat. Ann. §§28-2-3 and 4

**New York**  Public employers and private employers with more than ten employees may not deny employment to an applicant who has one or more past criminal convictions unless there is a direct relationship between the past offense and the employment or license sought. Employment may also be denied if, in light of the applicant's record, the job or license would involve an unreasonable risk to property or the safety and welfare of individuals or to the general public. Does not apply to crimes where forfeiture of a license is part of the penalty. N.Y. Correction Law §752 and following

| | |
|---|---|
| **North Carolina** | No statute |
| **North Dakota** | Employees of licensed early childhood facilities are subject to criminal record screening. People who have been convicted of child abuse or neglect and who have not been sufficiently rehabilitated are disqualified from employment. N.D. Cent. Code §50-11.1-04<br>Teaching certificates can be revoked if a criminal conviction has direct bearing on the person's ability to serve as a teacher. N.D. Cent. Code §15-36-15<br>Criminal background checks are required on applicants for jobs in the gaming industry. N.D. Cent. Code §53-06.1-06 |
| **Ohio** | An employer may question applicants regarding only those convictions that have not been sealed by court order, unless the question bears a direct and substantial relationship to the position sought. Ohio Rev. Code §2953.33 |
| **Oklahoma** | Employers may not question a prospective employee, in any application for employment, regarding a criminal record that has been expunged. Okla. Stat. Ann. tit. 22 §19<br>Every owner or administrator of a childcare facility or home must arrange for a criminal history investigation, conducted by the Oklahoma State Bureau of Investigation, for every applicant or, if the applicant has lived in the state less than one year, by the appropriate agency in the previous state of residence. Sex crimes requiring registration under the Sex Offenders Registration Act bar employment. Okla. Stat. Ann. tit. 10 §404.1 |
| **Oregon** | Employers may seek criminal offender information after first advising the current or prospective employees that such information is being sought. The Department of State may inform the employer of the date of arrest, offense, arresting agency, court of origin, disposition and sentence. Or. Rev. Stat. §181.557 to .560<br>Employers may not discriminate against an applicant because of a juvenile record that has been expunged by law. Or. Rev. Stat. §659.030 |

| | |
|---|---|
| **Pennsylvania** | Felony and misdemeanor convictions may be considered only to the extent that they relate to an applicant's suitability for the job. 18 Pa. Stat. Ann. §9125(b) |
| **Rhode Island** | Employers may not inquire of prospective employees whether they have ever been arrested or charged with a crime. They may ask whether they have ever been convicted. Does not apply to law enforcement. R.I. Gen. Laws §28-5-7(7)<br><br>Prospective employees who have had a conviction of a crime expunged may state that they have never been convicted of a crime. Law enforcement applicants, applicants for the bar, teachers applying for certificates and operators or employees of early childhood educational facilities are excepted. R.I. Gen. Laws §12-1.3-4 |
| **South Carolina** | No statute |
| **South Dakota** | No statute |
| **Tennessee** | No statute |
| **Texas** | State-maintained criminal record history information is available to numerous specified employers—including state agencies, fire departments, hotels, schools, public housing, boards of medical and law examiners, childcare and treatment facilities and licensing and regulatory agencies. Texas Code Ann. Government §§411.081 to .128 and Health and Safety §765.001 and following |
| **Utah** | No statute |
| **Vermont** | Criminal records are confidential and may be disclosed only to specifically designated people. Records of applicants for teaching positions with the school district or with an independent school may be disclosed with the signed release of the applicant. Juvenile court records may not be disclosed. Vt. Stat. Ann., tit. 16 §251 and following; tit. 33 §5536 |
| **Virginia** | An applicant may not be required to disclose expunged arrests or charges, and need not answer questions relating to them. Va. Code Ann. §19.2-392.4 |

| | |
|---|---|
| **Washington** | Employers may request conviction records from the state of current or prospective employees for these specified purposes only: employee bonding; pre-employment and post-employment evaluation of employees with access to money or items of value; or investigation of employee misconduct which may constitute a penal offense. Employers must notify the employee or prospective employee of the inquiry and make the record available.<br>Employers who provide services to children or vulnerable adults may obtain from the state police the conviction records for employees, applicants and volunteers.<br><br>The information disclosed is limited to convictions for crimes against children or other people, and does not include expunged records. Wa. Rev. Code §§43.43.815 and .830 to .839 |
| **West Virginia** | If an employee's or applicant's juvenile records have been expunged—at age 19 or when jurisdiction of the court over the individual has ceased, whichever is later—no employer may discriminate on the basis of those records against that individual with respect to employment or its terms or conditions. W. Va. Code §49-5-17 |
| **Wisconsin** | Employers may not discriminate on the basis of an arrest or conviction record. Wis. Stat. Ann. §111.321 However, employers may ask about pending charges. Questions may be asked about past arrests or convictions if the position requires bonding. Employment may be denied based on pending charges or past record if the applicant is not bondable or if the circumstances substantially relate to the job or activity being offered. Wis. Stat. Ann. §111.335 |
| **Wyoming** | Records of an applicant's criminal background can only be disseminated to the state board of nursing or if someone voluntarily agrees to submit to a record check. Wyo. Stat. Ann. §§7-19-106 and following |

⚠ **Why You May Have Cause for Pause**

The numbers and pronouncements about the chances of being attacked or killed while at work are scary to workers and employers alike. Experts posit that an average of 20 workers are murdered each week on the job—and many more suffer assaults that are not fatal. And the chance that someone with a violent criminal history may turn violent again when on staff has made many employers especially careful about checking into applicants' criminal pasts. (See Chapter 10, Guarding Against Violence.)

## 2. Tips on Using Criminal Records

If you intend to peep into an applicant's criminal history as part of your hiring search, these tips may help you be more circumspect.

➡ Given the increase in violence on the job, many workplace experts recommend that you conduct background checks on every job applicant. Note, however, that this may be limited by the laws in some states, as summarized in the chart above.

➡ As with other investigation techniques that may turn up potentially negative information about a job applicant, keep your ears and mind open to the possibility that a person has reformed to overcome a sketchy past. Listen to the applicant's explanation before you make a decision based on the information you have uncovered in a criminal records check.

➡ Be scrupulous about conducting criminal background checks fairly and evenhandedly. A number of employers have gotten into legal trouble because they singled out minority applicants to check, for example. If you conduct criminal background checks on some applicants for a position, check the backgrounds of all those who apply.

➡ Do not divulge the information you learn. Playing fast or loose with this particular information could come back to haunt you in the form of a lawsuit for invasion of privacy.

# E. Checking Medical Records

Medical information about employees comes into the workplace a number of ways. It is volunteered by an employee who calls in sick. It becomes general knowledge after filtering through the gossip mill. It is listed on the insurance application for a group policy, which you as an employer will likely have on file. Or it can sneak into your consciousness when interviewing a job applicant.

As a general legal rule, employers are not supposed to reveal medical information about employees unless there is a legitimate business reason to do so. Again, that nebulous standard, so often used as a fallback in workplace controversies, provides little guidance because its meaning is murky.

There are, however, a number of specific guidelines that apply to medical information gathered in the workplace. The strongest directives are imposed by the Americans With Disabilities Act or ADA, which requires that you gingerly and discreetly handle information obtained from post-job offer medical examinations and investigations. (See Chapter 4 for more on employee medical exams and records.) And before an offer is made, it is essential that you steer clear of violating discrimination laws by not basing a decision to reject an applicant solely on his or her medical condition. ∎

## CHAPTER 3

# Testing Applicants and Employees

There are now a number of types of tests to examine everything from the physical conditions to the psyches of employees and prospective employees. The temptation to collect this information can be overwhelming—compelled by every motive from filling a slot with the best worker to fear that a worker's illness might drive up your insurance costs.

Be mindful, however, that workers about to be tested might not be as excited about the prospect as you are about the possibilities of what the test results might reveal. The most disgruntled of them will do what some other disgruntled workers have done before them: They have filed lawsuits for invasion of privacy. And where judges and juries have shared their sense of outrage, they have succeeded in winning apologies—and sometimes large awards of money—from the employers who have ordered the testing.

Be aware, also, that state laws often set the bounds on how, when and whether you are allowed to perform particular tests on workers. And the standards of what is allowed may also differ depending on whether the individual you choose to test is a current or prospective employee. This chapter explains the legal bounds of testing—and gives you tips on how to keep the people being tested from crying foul.

## A. Medical Examinations

A number of insurers require employees to undergo medical evaluations before they will begin coverage. Beyond that, and often in addition to that, some employers require specific physical and mental examinations in attempts to ensure a qualified workforce. However, there are strict rules on when you can conduct those exams and who can learn the results.

Courts have also ruled that the constitutional right to privacy covers medical information and that honesty is the only policy when it comes to medical tests for prospective and existing employees. That is, you must identify what conditions you are testing for—and get individual consent to perform the tests, first.

## 1. Examining Applicants

As an employer, you may legally give prospective employees medical exams to make sure they are physically able to perform their jobs. However, timing is crucial. Under the federal Americans With Disabilities Act, or ADA (see Chapter 7), covered employers—generally, those with 15 employees or more—cannot require medical examinations before offering an individual a job. Even if you are covered by the ADA, however, you are free to make an employment offer contingent upon a person passing a medical exam.

The ADA also requires that you keep all medical history and exam results in a file separate from other personnel records. (See Chapter 4, Section C.)

During the course of a medical exam, a doctor you hire may ask anything at all about an applicant's health and medical history. However, the final medical evaluation is supposed to include only a stripped-down conclusion: able to work, able to work with restrictions, not able to work.

## 2. Examining Employees

You can require employees to take a physical or psychological examination after they are hired only if you have a reason to believe they are jeopardizing the health and safety of the workplace. For example, several courts have opined that if an employee clearly appears to be homicidal or suicidal, then an employer may have the duty to require a psychological exam, or even inform co-workers of the condition, in the name of workplace safety.

Again, while an examining doctor or psychologist has freer reign to ask questions as part of the examination of these employees than of applicants, the final evaluation they reveal to you is supposed to be succinct and free of detail: able to work, able to work with restrictions, not able to work. So there may be frustratingly little you can glean from the report in the long run, anyway. But no matter the detail or lack of it in a medical report, your charge remains the same: You must keep it in a safe place, segregated from other personnel records—and away from co-workers' curious eyes.

## GENETICS: TEST AT YOUR OWN RISK

When it first became possible to test for the genetic risks of isolated diseases, the advance was widely hailed as a modern medical near-miracle, sure to improve preventative healthcare and treatment. People with the risk of contracting inherited conditions such as breast cancer, colon cancer and Huntington's disease now commonly undergo genetic testing to gauge their chances.

Some employers—about 10% and growing, according to a recent survey by the American Management Association—now routinely test employees for genetic predispositions to diseases.

But privacy experts warn that genetic test results will be misused to target and fire employees who may run up company health insurance costs or to deny them coverage. And without specific privacy controls on the evolving medical information, they claim the hardship of diagnostics can follow workers from job to potential job, hampering their chances at finding additional work.

For a number of people, the fears are already a reality. According to a recent Georgetown University poll of 332 families with perceived genetic risks:

- 22% reported they had been refused health insurance, and
- 13% had been fired from their jobs based on their perceived genetic risks.

In response to the loud public outcry over this, about half the states now have laws that either protect against genetic discrimination or prohibit the testing in employment or insurance decisions—and dozens more bills are pending. The next frontier is likely to be federal legislation curbing the use and abuse of genetic testing in the workplace. So beware that if you have used genetic testing in the past for any reason, you may have to change your ways.

# B. Drug and Alcohol Testing

The abuse of drugs such as alcohol and cocaine has been widely publicized for many years—and many private employers now test for drug and alcohol use. The laws regulating drug abuse in the workplace and the testing of employees for such abuse, however, are relatively new and still being shaped by the courts. Currently, there is a hodgepodge of legal rules controlling drug testing—some in the Americans With Disabilities Act (see Chapter 7), some set out in specific state laws (see the chart below) and a number arrived at through court decisions.

Testing in workplaces is on the rise. Some of that is explained by the passage, in 1988, of the Drug-Free Workplace Act (102 Stat. §4181). That law dictates that workplaces receiving federal grants or contracts must be drug-free or lose the funding, although it does not call for employers to test or monitor workers.

### THE LOOK AND FEEL OF THE TESTS

Work-related drug tests take a number of forms. Analyzing urine samples is the method most commonly used, but samples of a worker's blood, hair and breath can also be tested for the presence of alcohol or other drugs in the body. Typically, state laws set out the testing methods that must be used. Many statutes provide for retesting, at the employee's expense, following a positive test.

Metabolic evidence of illegal substances remains in urine for various periods: cocaine for approximately 72 hours, marijuana for three weeks or more. Detectable residues apparently remain in hair samples for several months.

## 1. Testing Applicants

In general, employers have the right to test new job applicants for traces of drugs in their systems as long as:

- the applicant knows that such testing will be part of the screening process for new employees
- you have already offered the applicant the job
- all applicants for the same job are tested similarly, and
- the tests are administered by a state-certified laboratory.

If you intend to conduct drug testing on job candidates, it is wise to include in your job applications an agreement to submit to such testing.

## 2. Testing Employees

The testing standards with which you must comply may turn on specifics of the job or workplace. There are a number of employees who, because of their specialized positions or type of work, can be tested more freely than others for drugs and alcohol use. For example, the Department of Transportation requires drug testing for some critical positions, such as airline pilots. In addition, courts have routinely approved random drug testing for employees with national security clearances, prison officers, employees at chemical weapons and nuclear power plants and police officers. Note, however, that while many laws allow that such employees be tested, they do not require you to automatically fire the employees for positive test results.

In most private employment jobs, there are some legal constraints on testing existing employees for drug usage. You are generally prohibited from conducting blanket drug tests of all employees or random drug tests; you must usually focus the testing on a particular individual. In some cases where employers have tested for drugs without good reason, the employees affected have sued successfully for invasion of privacy and infliction of emotional harm.

However, the courts have generally ruled that companies may test employees for drugs if their actions could clearly cause human injury or property damage if their performances were impaired by drugs, and in cases where there is good reason to think that the employees are abusing drugs. For example, a bulldozer operator who swerved the machine illogically through a field crowded with workers could be the legal target of drug testing. And a legal secretary found slumped at her desk who was unable to respond cogently to questions asked of her was also considered fair game for a drug test.

## WHEN IS A SUSPICION REASONABLE?

In most situations, you may test an employee for drugs only if there is a reasonable suspicion that he or she is using them. What suspicion is reasonable and what is not is in the eye and mind of the beholder, which makes it a slippery standard indeed.

But some statutes and courts have attempted to set some guidelines that may be helpful in assessing whether your own suspicions are reasonable. A reasonable suspicion of drug use must generally be based on actual facts and logical inferences such as:

- direct observation of drug use or of physical symptoms including slurred speech, agitated or lethargic demeanor, uncoordinated movement and inappropriate response to questions
- abnormal conduct or erratic behavior while at work, or significant deterioration in work performance
- a report of drug use provided by a reliable and credible source that has been independently corroborated
- evidence that the employee has tampered with current drug test results
- information that the employee has caused or contributed to an accident at work, and
- evidence that the employee has used, possessed, sold, solicited or transferred drugs while working or at work.

## 3. State and Local Drug Testing Laws

As mentioned, a number of state courts have set out rulings defining when and why drug tests may be given. For example, a New Jersey court recently held that pre-employment testing of employees is an illegal invasion of their privacy (*O'Keefe v. Passaic Valley Water Comm'n*, 602 A. 2d 760 (1992)). In California, pre-employment testing was given a court's stamp of approval, but not blanket testing of current employees up for possible promotion (*Loder v. City of Glendale*, 14 Cal. 4th 846 (1997)).

In addition, a number of states and several municipalities have laws that regulate work-related testing for substance abuse. Those that do also specify the scientific procedures to which testing labs must adhere. Some states also require you to distribute to employees written policies on drug testing and rehabilitation.

Laws in a growing number of states—including California, Florida, Georgia and Vermont—include a kinder, gentler twist for the workers, protecting employees who seek treatment for a substance abuse problem from being discriminated against or fired.

Ironically, employers who operate in states that have laws regulating the timing and procedures of drug and alcohol testing may actually have more constraints than those in states that are mum on the topic. Employers living in such lawless states, for example, are generally free to test workers without giving them advance notice.

## STATE DRUG AND ALCOHOL TESTING LAWS

Alabama

To qualify for a reduction in workers' compensation rates, an employer must require testing of all new hires and may perform tests on some applicants. Employers may test if there is a reasonable suspicion of illegal drug or alcohol use, may use regularly scheduled and random tests and must test if the employee is involved in an injury-causing accident at the workplace resulting in the loss of work time. However, if the drug test is based on reasonable suspicion, the employer must document in writing the circumstances forming the basis for the suspicion and provide the employee with a copy of this document upon request. An employee who tests positive has five days to explain the results to the employer. Employers must give employees and applicants written notice of their substance abuse policy, including the consequences for refusal to submit to a test, the resources available to employees with substance abuse problems and an employee's right to explain a positive test result. Employers must have an employee assistance program or provide a resource file on employee assistance programs. Ala. Code §§25-5-330–340

Alaska

School bus drivers must be tested for improper use of drugs or alcohol; random tests are allowed for them. Discipline or discharge is allowed for positive results. Alaska Stat. §14.09.025

Arizona

Employees are subject to random and scheduled tests for any job-related purpose. Employers must give all employees a copy of the written policy before conducting tests. The policy must give employees the right to obtain written test results and to explain positive results. Notice of test must state the consequences of a positive test or refusal to submit to testing. Employees must be given the opportunity to inform employers of prescription drugs or other medical information that might affect test. Does not apply to federal or state employees except for Department of Public Safety employees. Ariz. Rev. Stat. Ann. §23-493 and following

School district transportation employees are subject to testing if their supervisor has probable cause to believe that their job performance is impaired or they have an on-the-job accident. Ariz. Rev. Stat. Ann. §15-573

| | |
|---|---|
| **Arkansas** | No statute |
| **California** | Employers with 25 or more employees must reasonably accommodate any employee who enters an alcohol or drug rehabilitation program, unless the employee's current alcohol or drug use makes him or her unable to perform work duties or do a job safely—unless this would impose an undue hardship on the employer. An employer must make reasonable efforts to safeguard the privacy of an employee who is enrolled in a treatment program. Cal. Lab. Code §§1025 and 1026 |
| **Colorado** | No statute |
| **Connecticut** | Job applicants may be required to submit to testing if informed in writing beforehand. |

Employers may require a drug or alcohol test when there is a reasonable suspicion that an employee is under the influence and his or her job performance is or could be impaired. Employers may test randomly when authorized by federal law, when the employee works in a dangerous or safety-sensitive occupation or when the test is part of an employee assistance program in which participation is voluntary.

Testing required for intrastate truck drivers after a reportable accident, with reasonable cause or on a random basis. Testing required for applicants for school bus driver positions. Conn. Gen. Stat. §§31-51t through 51aa, 14-261b

| | |
|---|---|
| **Delaware** | Testing required to certify school bus drivers; if there is a positive result, employee can request that the employer conduct further analysis. Del. Code Ann. tit. 21, §2708 |

| | |
|---|---|
| **District of Columbia** | Random testing is required of employees who work in a Department of Corrections institution or have responsibility for the custody or care of inmates. Other Department of Corrections employees can be tested only upon reasonable suspicion or if they have been involved in a job accident involving a vehicle or resulting in personal injury or property damage, after being given 30 days notice and the opportunity to seek treatment. An employee who tests positive can request confirmation of the results by another lab. D.C. Code Ann. §24-448.1 |
| **Florida** | Employers may test for drugs and alcohol upon reasonable suspicion that an employee is under the influence, as a pre-employment screening with advance notice, during routine fitness-for-duty examinations and as a follow-up to participation in a drug treatment program. Fla. Stat. Ann. §440.101 |
| | Employers who do not have a written drug testing policy in place that has been disseminated to employees must give 60 days advance notice of testing. Employees who voluntarily seek treatment for substance abuse cannot be fired, disciplined or discriminated against, unless they have tested positive or have been in treatment in the past. Fla. Stat. Ann. §440.102 |
| | State agencies may test job applicants and employees as part of routine fitness-for-duty examinations, based upon a reasonable suspicion of substance abuse or as a follow-up to a drug treatment program. A state employee who completes a rehabilitation program must be reinstated to the same or an equivalent position. Fla. Stat. Ann. §112.0455 |
| | All employees have the right to explain positive results within five days. A positive result must be verified by a confirming test before the employer can take adverse action against the employee. All test results must be kept confidential and cannot be used in criminal proceedings against the employee. Fla. Stat. Ann. §§440.102; 112.0455 |

| | |
|---|---|
| **Georgia** | State employees who are involved in dangerous work may be subject to random drug testing. Ga. Code Ann. §§45-20-90 and 91 |
| | A public employee who, prior to any arrest, tells an employer about illegal use of a controlled substance may keep his or her job if he or she enters a licensed treatment program and does not refuse to be tested. Ga. Code Ann. §§45-23-3 to 23-7 |
| | An applicant for a state government job must submit to a drug test if the head of the agency has determined that the duties involved in that position warrant drug testing. Positive results must be verified by a confirming test—and the applicant has the right to provide proof that use of the drug is legitimate. Ga. Code Ann. §45-20-110 and following |
| | Under the Drug Free Workplace Act, the state may not enter into any contract with a private contractor unless the contractor certifies that the workplace or site is drug-free. An employer must post this policy and report any employee convictions for illegal drug use to the state agency that is part of the contract. The statute does not establish drug testing by the contractor. Ga. Code Ann. §50-24-1 and following |
| **Hawaii** | All employers may test employees or job applicants for substance abuse as long as the following conditions are met: the employers pay all costs; the tests are performed by a licensed laboratory; the individuals tested are given a list of the substances they are being tested for and disclosure forms for the medicines and legal drugs they are taking; and the results are kept confidential. Haw. Rev. Stat. §329B-1 and following |
| **Idaho** | No statute |
| **Illinois** | Drug testing of applicants and employees is permitted. Ill. Rev. Stat. 5/2-104(C)(4) |
| **Indiana** | An employer may implement reasonable policies, including drug testing, designed to ensure that an employee is no longer using illegal drugs. Ind. Code §22-9-5-6 |

| | |
|---|---|
| **Iowa** | Employers cannot request random drug testing of employees or require employees or job applicants to submit to drug testing as a condition of employment, pre-employment, promotion or change in employment status, except as part of a pre-employment or regularly scheduled physical examination under certain restrictions. An employer may require a specific employee to submit to a drug or alcohol test if there is a reasonable suspicion that the employee's faculties are impaired on the job or if the employee is in a position where such impairment presents a danger to the safety of others or if the impairment is a violation of a known rule of the employer. Random testing is prohibited.<br><br>A positive test result must be verified by a confirming test. An employee who tests positive has the right to explain the results, and the results must be kept confidential.<br><br>An employee cannot be fired after one positive test if he or she undergoes a substance abuse evaluation and, if recommended, substance abuse treatment. This law does not apply to peace or correctional officers. Iowa Code §730.5 |
| **Kansas** | Applicants for jobs in law enforcement agencies that involve carrying a firearm, corrections agencies, gubernatorial staff or appointed heads of state agencies can be required to take a drug test, after they are offered the job, as long as there is prior notice. Employees may be tested but only if there is reasonable suspicion of drug abuse. The results of drug tests are confidential. Kan. Gen. Stat. Ann. §75-4362 |
| **Kentucky** | An employer may reject an applicant based on his or her drug or alcohol addiction. Ky. Rev. Stat. §207.140 |

| | |
|---|---|
| **Louisiana** | Employers may require all job applicants and employees to submit to drug testing as long as certain procedural guidelines are followed and the specimens are collected with due regard for the individual's privacy. Employees have the right to review test results and to have a confirming test. Applicants must pay for any confirming test.<br><br>Public employers can test applicants and employees if there is an accident or reasonable suspicion of substance abuse. Public employees in safety-sensitive positions are subject to random testing. La. Rev. Stat. Ann. §§49:1001 and following |
| **Maine** | Public and private employers may require an employee to submit to a drug test when there is probable cause to believe the employee is impaired. Random testing is permitted when substance abuse might endanger co-workers or the public, during a rehabilitation program, when returning to work after a positive test or when it is permitted by a union contract. Job applicants may be tested only if offered employment or placed on an eligibility roster.<br><br>Employees and applicants cannot be denied employment, fired or reassigned without a confirmed positive test result, but may be suspended without pay pending test results. Employers must have employee assistance programs and a written policy approved by the state Department of Labor. Test results are confidential and cannot be used in criminal proceedings. Me. Rev. Stat. Ann. tit. 26, §§681-690 |
| **Maryland** | Employers may require testing for alcohol or drug abuse of employees, contractors or other people for job-related reasons as long as certain procedural guidelines are followed. Employees must be informed of the right to have a sample tested at an independent laboratory at the employer's expense. Md. Code Ann. Health Law §17-214.1 |
| **Massachusetts** | No statute |
| **Michigan** | No statute |

| | |
|---|---|
| **Minnesota** | Employers may require employees to submit to drug or alcohol testing if there is a written and posted testing policy and the test is performed by an independent, licensed laboratory. Random tests may be given only to employees in safety-sensitive positions. Employers may require a drug test as part of an annual routine physical examination after giving employees two weeks notice. Job applicants may be tested if they have been offered jobs and if testing is required of all applicants. Specific individuals may be tested when there is a reasonable suspicion that the employee is under the influence of drugs or alcohol, has violated rules against the use, possession or distribution of drugs or alcohol on the job or has caused injury or accidents at work. An employee who tests positive has the right to explain the results and to obtain a confirming test at his or her personal expense. Test results are confidential and cannot be used in a criminal proceeding. Minn. Stat. Ann. §§181.950 to 181.957 <br><br> An employer may refuse to hire and may discipline or discharge an employee who refuses or fails to comply with the conditions established by a chemical dependency treatment or aftercare program. Minn. Stat. Ann. §181.938(3)(4) |
| **Mississippi** | Public and private employers may require employees to submit to drug or alcohol testing after the policy has been posted for at least 30 days and certain prescribed procedures are followed. Testing is authorized when there is a reasonable suspicion that an employee is abusing drugs or alcohol. Random testing is also authorized. Employers may also test as part of routine fitness-for-duty examinations or as part of the follow-up to a rehabilitation program. <br><br> Employees who test positive have the right to contest or explain the results. Job applicants may be tested if they are warned when they apply for the job. Test results are confidential. Miss. Code Ann. §§71-7 and following |
| **Missouri** | No statute |

| | |
|---|---|
| Montana | No person may be required to submit to a blood or urine test unless the job involves hazardous work or security, public safety or fiduciary responsibilities. Employees subject to testing may be tested if the employer has reason to believe the employee's faculties are impaired by drug or alcohol use or that the employee contributed to a work-related accident involving injury or property damage. The employee has the right to a confirming test and to explain or rebut a positive test result. Mont. Code Ann. §39-2-304 |
| Nebraska | Employers with more than six employees may require employees to submit to drug or alcohol testing if certain screening procedures are met, including a confirming test of a positive result. Refusal to undergo a test can be grounds for discipline or discharge. Neb. Rev. Stat. §48-1901 and following |
| Nevada | Applicants for state jobs and state employees may be tested if the job involves public safety. Nev. Rev. Stat. § 284-406 and following |
| New Hampshire | No statute |
| New Jersey | The Board of Education can require drug testing of applicants who have received a conditional offer of employment. The Department of Education is responsible for developing guidelines for conducting the testing. N.J. Stat. Ann. §18A:16-2 |
| New Mexico | No statute |
| New York | No statute |
| North Carolina | Public and private employers may test applicants and employees for the presence of controlled substances as long as they follow specified procedures, including preserving the test samples so that those examined may perform their own tests. N.C. Gen. Stat. §§95-230 to 235 |
| North Dakota | No statute |
| Ohio | No statute |

| | |
|---|---|
| **Oklahoma** | Public and private employers are allowed to test applicants and employees as long as they adhere to procedures outlined in the Act and issue a written workplace policy. An applicant may be tested as long as all applicants are tested; and an employee may be tested if the employer has a reasonable suspicion that the employee has violated the written policy and after a work-related accident involving property damage or injury. Random testing is allowed for certain employees only, including peace officers and those whose jobs directly affect the safety of others. Routine testing can be done if part of fitness-for-duty exam and if all employees in the same classification are subject to routine testing. The employee must be given the opportunity to explain test results. No adverse action can be taken without a confirming test. The employer must provide an employee assistance program for drug or alcohol abuse. Test results are confidential and cannot be used in a criminal proceeding. Standards for Workplace Drug and Alcohol Testing Act, Okla. Stat. Ann. tit. 40, §§551-565 |
| **Oregon** | Employers may not require any employee or job applicant to submit to any breathalyzer alcohol test unless there is a reasonable suspicion that the employee or applicant is under the influence of alcohol. Or. Rev. Stat. §659.227 When employees are tested for drugs, the laboratory must be licensed by the state and must follow certain procedural safeguards. Or. Rev. Stat. §438.435 |
| **Pennsylvania** | No statute |
| **Rhode Island** | Public and private employers may require an employee to submit to drug or alcohol testing when there is reason to believe that the use of controlled substances is impairing the employee's ability to do the job, the test sample is provided in private, the testing is part of a rehabilitation program, positive results are confirmed by the most accurate method available, the employee is given reasonable notice that the test will be given and the employee is given a chance to explain the results. Employers may not terminate employees because they test positive but may refer them to a substance abuse professional for assistance. Employers must keep test results confidential. R.I. Gen. Laws §28-6.5-1 |

| | |
|---|---|
| **South Carolina** | An employer may establish a drug prevention program which includes testing of employees. The employer must distribute its substance abuse policy statement to employees before conducting any tests and must keep results confidential. Test results may not be used in a criminal proceeding. S.C. Code Ann. §41-1-15 |
| **South Dakota** | No statute |
| **Tennessee** | All private and certain public employers have the option of participating in the Drug-Free Workplace Program. Employers who choose to participate must post their drug-free workplace policy at least 60 days before conducting any drug or alcohol tests. Employers must test applicants who have received a conditional offer of employment for drugs and may test for alcohol. Employers may test employees for drugs and may test employees in safety-sensitive positions or upon reasonable suspicion for drugs or alcohol. Employers may test employees for drugs or alcohol as part of a routine fitness-for-duty examination and after an accident resulting in injury. Employees have the right to explain or contest the results. Employers can fire or refuse to hire someone who has a confirmed positive test. The results are confidential and cannot be used in a criminal proceeding. Tenn. Code Ann. §§50-9-101 and following Employees in security positions within the Department of Corrections may be required to submit to drug tests, but only if the supervisor has a reasonable suspicion, based on specific objective facts, that the employees' faculties are impaired and that this presents a clear and present danger to the safety of the employees, other employees or the security of the institution. If an employee tests positive, a confirming test must be done and the employee must be provided with a copy of the results. The employer must provide counseling and rehabilitation to employees who test positive. Tenn. Code Ann. §41-1-122 |
| **Texas** | An employer with 15 or more employees who has a workers' compensation insurance policy must adopt a drug abuse policy and provide a written copy to employees. |

| | |
|---|---|
| **Utah** | Private employers and public utility or transit district employers who test for drugs must have a written policy regarding the methods used, and management must submit to regular testing as well as employees. A confirmed positive test result may be used as grounds for suspension, discipline or discharge. Test results are confidential and cannot be used in any criminal proceeding. Employees who test positive are not to be considered handicapped within the state's anti-discrimination law. Utah Code Ann. §§34-38-1 to -15 |
| **Vermont** | Public and private employers may require an employee to be tested for drugs or alcohol if there is a probable cause to believe the employee is using or is under the influence on the job, if the employer provides a rehabilitation program and if the employee who tests positive is given a chance to participate in a rehabilitation program rather than being fired. Applicants may be tested if advance notice is given and an offer of a job has been made. Employees who have already been through rehabilitation and who again test positive may be fired. Job applicants may be tested when they have been offered the job conditioned upon passing the test, if they are given advance notice of the test and the test is given as part of a comprehensive physical examination. Applicants and employees must be given the opportunity to retest samples that have tested positive. Vt. Stat. Ann. tit. 21, §511 and following |
| **Virginia** | No statute |
| **Washington** | Private employers who want a discount on their workers' compensation premiums may test applicants if advance notice has been given and a job has been offered. Employees may be tested upon reasonable suspicion of drug abuse, following a workplace accident, or at random. Employer must post testing policy and must offer an employee assistance program to employees who test positive before terminating them. Employers can terminate employees who have a second confirmed positive test or refuse to participate in the employee assistance program. Employees have the right to explain or contest the results. Random testing is allowed. Results are confidential and cannot be used in a criminal proceeding. Wash. Rev. Code §§49.82.010 and following |

| West Virginia | No statute |
| Wisconsin | No statute |
| Wyoming | No statute |

## 4. Tips for Drug and Alcohol Policies

Many workplaces have policies against using alcohol or nonprescription drugs during the workday—a wise move, given that a policy that plainly and simply sets out prohibited behavior is hard to argue with later and nearly impossible to beat in court. It is often the best intentions that go the furthest awry. If you do adopt a policy prohibiting the use of drugs and alcohol on the job, ensure it has the hallmarks of a sound policy.

Make sure your policy is clear. The biggest problems concern when and whether an employee may be fired for drug and alcohol use on the job. A strict policy that decrees that an employee may be fired for a single transgression is legally permissible. The important thing is that the tippling transgressor knew of the policy and possible consequences beforehand.

Also, be sure your policy is clearly written—and devoid of vague and subjective phrases such as "under the influence." Better to bring home to employees that if drugs or alcohol hamper their judgment or threaten safety on the job, it is better for them not to be there.

➡ Be consistent. If one employee is disciplined or fired for violating a drug or alcohol policy, be sure that others experience the same truth and consequences. Do not leave yourself open to claims that you have singled out any individual for favoritism or discrimination.

➡ Be sure before acting. It is common for employees caught with incriminating blood or urine samples to attempt to cast dispersions on the form and format of the testing. Be sure your testing methods are unassailable—taken under reputable, objective supervision—and that they comply with any state standards that may be required. (See the chart above.)

And note that employers are free to add safeguards to protect against specimen tampering—requiring those taking the test to remove their own clothing and don hospital gowns, or providing a test monitor who checks the temperature of the urine and adds dye to toilet water, as examples. However, a modicum of discretion is required; while most courts have found it reasonable to have a monitor listen as a urine test is administered, a number have found it an unreasonable invasion of privacy to watch.

In addition, many laws require employers to maintain workplace counseling and outreach programs before they can test employees.

### NEW MEANING TO 'PASS THE CUP'

According to one recent study of major U.S. firms, workplace testing for drugs is at an all-time high—up 277% since 1977. Much of the increase in testing can be traced to new regulations mandating testing for certain types of workers. But employers—who reportedly spend an average of $35 per test—are also simply more anxious to weed out problem workers by testing applicants and employees whenever possible.

**Who Is Testing**

| | |
|---|---|
| Firms that test for drugs | 81% |
| Those that test current employees | 70% |
| Those that test all new hires | 68% |
| Those that test selected new hires | 9% |

**How They Test**

| | |
|---|---|
| Urine sampling | 92% |
| Blood sampling | 15% |
| Hair sampling | 2% |
| Performance testing | 2% |

**The Envelope, Please**

| | |
|---|---|
| Employees who tested positive | 2% |
| Those immediately dismissed | 22% |
| Those referred to treatment | 83% |
| Those disciplined or reassigned | 24% |
| New hires who tested positive | 4% |
| Those who were not hired | 94% |

Source: Survey of 961 member companies of the American Management Association

# C. Psychological Testing

These days, there are a number of tests that purport to take the guess-work out of finding competent employees with that something extra: Integrity.

Indeed, a number of people who market themselves as Workplace Consultants claim they have developed series of written questions—integrity tests—that can predict whether a person would lie, steal or be unreliable if hired for a particular job. And a number of other alleged experts claim to have perfected personality tests that allow employers to tell in advance whether an individual is suited by temperament and talent to a particular position.

In fact, legions of test publishers have recently cropped up everywhere from telephone listings to the Internet—most of which claim they can forecast everything from a potential employee's likelihood of being honest and hardworking to his or her absence and injury rate on the job. Most promise an analysis fast—often within 48 hours of receiving responses to test questions. Many employers are understandably drawn to these tests because they seem to short-circuit the process of interviewing—during which conversation too often degenerates into chatty small talk that takes time and cuts into productivity. Before joining their ranks, however, you should at least be aware of potential drawbacks.

Many employers—about 40% of them, according to the American Management Association—use these questionnaires in the process of screening applicants for job openings. But even that temptation has been curbed of late by a number of cases that send a clear warning: Psychological tests cannot be used as an excuse to discriminate against prospective employees—and they must be limited to job-related questions. Recently, these tests have been challenged as being discriminatory and as violating employees' rights of privacy.

A few states have enacted laws against some specific forms of psychological testing. In Nebraska, for example, an employer may not require an employee or a prospective employee to submit to a truth and deception exam unless the position involves law enforcement (Neb. Rev. Stat. §§81-1931 and 1932). And in New York, employers may not require that job applicants or employees take psychological stress evaluator tests (N.Y. Lab. Law §§733 to 739).

## TARGET LEARNS WHAT NOT TO ASK

The first major case to challenge psychological testing of job applicants recently yielded an unsettling settlement: a $2 million payment and a five-year ban on testing.

The settlement came in July 1993, in a class action brought by several people who had applied to the Target Stores chain for work as security guards. As part of the application process, they had been asked to respond to over 700 true/false statements including:

- I am very strongly attracted by members of my own sex.
- I have never indulged in unusual sex practices.
- I believe my sins are unpardonable.
- I believe in the second coming of Christ.
- I have had no difficulty starting or holding my urine.

About 30% of the 2,500 test takers did not get jobs with Target—either because of the answers they gave or because the results were deemed inconclusive.

But the test made even successful applicants queasy. Robert Marzetta worked at Target for a year before becoming one of the main plaintiffs in the case. He said that while he felt the test questions were "out of line" and made him "uncomfortable," he didn't object at exam time because he needed the job.

Sue Urry joined in the case because, she said, as a Mormon, she found the religious questions particularly offensive.

Another plaintiff, Sibi Soroka, also got a guard job. Soroka found the test questions so unsettling that he copied all 700 of them before turning in his answers—then went to the American Civil Liberties Union and a number of attorneys seeking help. He was on the job only about a month because, he said, "it's kind of difficult to work for a person you're suing."

Target argued that the test, the Rodgers Condensed CPI-MMPI, helped weed out the emotionally unstable from the pool of those who would be subjected to the stressful task of apprehending shoplifting suspects.

The applicants challenged the test as violating their privacy rights and the state Labor Code, which bans questions about sexual orientation.

They will now share in the $2 million in wealth Target has lost.

## D. Lie Detector Tests

For decades, lie detectors, or polygraphs, that purport to measure the truthfulness of a person's statements by tracking bodily functions such as blood pressure and perspiration were routinely used on employees and job applicants.

Employers could—and often did—ask employees and prospective employees questions about extremely private matters such as sexual preferences, toilet habits and family finances, while a polygraph machine passed judgment on the truthfulness of the answers. A testee who pushed the machine's needle too far by reacting to an offensive question could be labeled a liar and denied a job.

The federal Employee Polygraph Protection Act (29 U.S.C. §2001), passed in 1988, severely curbed the use of lie detectors in connection with employment. That law covers all private employers in interstate commerce, which includes just about every private company that uses the U.S. mail or the telephone system to send messages to someone in another state.

Under the Act, it is illegal for all private companies to:

- require, request, suggest or cause any employee or job applicant to submit to a lie detector test
- use, accept, refer to or inquire about the results of any lie detector test conducted on an employee or job applicant, or
- dismiss, discipline, discriminate against or even threaten to take action against any employee or job applicant who refuses to take a lie detector test.

The law also prohibits you from discriminating against or firing those who use its protections.

If the Labor Department finds that you have violated the Act, it can fine you up to $10,000 and order you to hire or reinstate an illegally tested worker to a job, promote him or her, compensate for back wages or take other logical action to correct the violation.

## 1. When Lie Detector Tests Can Be Used

The Employee Polygraph Protection Act allows employers to use polygraph tests in connection with jobs in security and handling drugs, or in investigating a specific theft or other suspected crime. However, you must first give a written notice, at least 48 hours before the test, notifying the employee that he or she is a suspect. And you must have a provable, reasonable suspicion that the individual was involved in the theft or other conduct triggering the investigation.

The Act does not apply to employees of federal, state or local government, nor to certain jobs that handle sensitive work relating to national defense.

## 2. Legal Limitations

In addition to the strict strictures on when and to whom the tests may be given, there are a number of restrictions on their format. Before you can administer lie detector tests, you must read a statement to the employees you intend to test and ask them to sign it. The statement must include:

- a list of topics they cannot be asked about, including questions on religious beliefs, sexual preference, racial matters, lawful activities of labor organizations and political affiliation
- the information that they have the right to refuse to take the test
- the fact that they cannot be required to take the test as a condition of employment
- an explanation of how the test results can be used, and
- an explanation of their legal rights if the test is not given in keeping with the law.

While the test is being administered, they have the right:

- to stop it at any time, and

- to be asked questions in a way that is not "degrading or need-lessly intrusive."

When the test is said and done, you can disclose the results only to the employee who was tested, a court or government agency or an arbitrator or mediator if there is a court order. The law specifically prohibits prospective employers from getting access to old test results.

The Employee Polygraph Protection Act is enforced by the U.S. Department of Labor. If you have questions about whether the Act applies to your workplace, call the office of the U.S. Labor Department's Wage and Hour Division nearest you. It is listed in the federal government section of the telephone directory under Labor Department.

## 3.  State Laws on Lie Detector Tests

Some states have laws prohibiting or restricting employers from using lie detectors in connection with employment, but most have been made obsolete by the federal anti-polygraph statute.

Penalties in a few states are more strict than those provided under federal law. In New York, for example, an employer who uses polygraph tests illegally may be convicted of a misdemeanor and sentenced to up to one year in jail (N.Y. Lab. Law 189 §§733 to 739).

In addition, state coverage may be broader; while the federal law does not apply to state and local government employers, many of the state statutes do.

Some states have also expanded anti-polygraph laws to cover other types of tests that probe bodily functions in connection with employment. For example, it is illegal for employers in Oregon to require employees to submit to genetic screening or brainwave testing (Or. Rev. Stat. §659.227).

## STATE LIE DETECTOR TESTING LAWS

| | |
|---|---|
| Alabama | State employees cannot be required to take a lie detector test as a condition of employment. Ala. Code §36-1-18 |
| Alaska | Employers cannot require an applicant or employee to submit to a polygraph or lie detection test as a condition of employment. Current or prospective police officers are excepted. Alaska Stat. §23.10.037 |
| Arizona | No statute |
| Arkansas | No statute |
| California | Private employers cannot require employees or applicants to submit to lie detector tests as a condition of employment. Does not apply to public employers. Does not prohibit voluntary testing as long as employees' rights are explained in writing. Cal. Lab. Code §432.2 |
| Colorado | No statute |
| Connecticut | Employers may not request or require employees or applicants to take polygraph exams as a condition of employment or dismiss or discipline them for refusing to take the tests. Not applicable to Department of Corrections employees nor to police departments except for civilian employees. Conn. Gen. Stat. Ann. §31-51g, 1998 Conn. Public Act 126, §2 |
| Delaware | Employers may not require employees or applicants to submit to lie detector tests and may not fire or discriminate against them for refusing to submit to such tests. Does not apply to law enforcement applicant background checks. Del. Code Ann. tit. 19, §704e |
| District of Columbia | Employers may not request or require an employee or applicant to submit to a polygraph or any lie detector test as a condition of employment. Does not apply to employees of the federal government, foreign governments or law enforcement agencies. However, law enforcement employees shall not be denied employment based solely on the results of polygraphs; there must be independent corroboration of the results. D.C. Code Ann. §§36-801 to 803 |

| | |
|---|---|
| Florida | No statute |
| Georgia | No statute |
| Hawaii | Employers cannot require an employee or applicant to submit to a lie detector test as a condition of employment. Employers may not terminate or otherwise discriminate against an employee or applicant for refusing to submit to an exam. Does not prohibit voluntary testing as long as the right of refusal is explained in writing. Does not apply to law enforcement agencies. Haw. Rev. Stat. §378.26 and following |
| Idaho | Private employers cannot require employees to take lie detector tests as a condition of employment. Does not apply to the federal or state government. Idaho Code §44-903, 904 |
| Illinois | No statute |
| Indiana | No statute |
| Iowa | Employers may not request, require or administer a lie detection test as a condition of new or continued employment. Does not apply to law enforcement or corrections agencies. Iowa Code §730.4 |
| Kansas | No statute |
| Kentucky | No statute |
| Louisiana | No statute |
| Maine | Employers cannot request, require, administer or suggest that an employee or applicant submit to a lie detection test as a condition of employment. However, an employee can voluntarily request a test, and an employer can refer to the results as long as the results are not used against the person for any reason. Does not apply to law enforcement agencies. Me. Rev. Stat. Ann. tit. 32, §7166 |
| Maryland | Employers cannot require that employees or applicants submit to a lie detector test as a condition of employment. This law does not apply to federal government, Division of Corrections, law enforcement nor correctional officers. Md. Code Ann. Labor and Employment §3-702 |

| | |
|---|---|
| **Massachusetts** | Employers cannot require or request employees or applicants, including police officers, to submit to lie detector tests as a condition of employment. Employers cannot fire or discriminate against them for refusing to take such tests. Mass. Gen. Laws Ann. ch. 149 §19B |
| **Michigan** | Employers cannot require employees or applicants to submit to polygraph examinations as a condition of employment. An employee or applicant may voluntarily request a polygraph examination and, if this is the case, the employer may administer it but the employer must first give the employee a copy of the statute. Mich. Comp. Laws §§37.201 and following |
| **Minnesota** | Employers may not request or require a polygraph or any test purporting to test an employee's or applicant's honesty as a condition of employment. Minn. Stat. Ann. §181.75 |
| **Mississippi** | Applicants for patrol officer training may be required to submit to a lie detector test. Miss. Code Ann. §45-3-470 |
| **Missouri** | No statute |
| **Montana** | Employers may not require employees to submit to polygraphs or any mechanical lie detection tests. Mont. Code §39-2-304 |
| **Nebraska** | No employee or applicant may be required to take a lie detector test, but voluntary tests are allowed as long as they meet specified requirements. Violation of this statute is a Class III misdemeanor. Statute does not apply to law enforcement agencies. Neb. Rev. Stat. 81 §§1932 and 1933 |
| **Nevada** | Private employers may not request or require employees or prospective employees to take lie detector tests, nor may they refer to, accept or use the results of a test. Employers cannot fire, discipline, discriminate or threaten based on results. The prohibition does not apply to an ongoing investigation of a loss to the employer's business, as long as the employer has a reasonable suspicion that the employee is involved and the job has a significant impact on the health or safety of the state. Other exceptions are also included. Nev. Rev. Stat. §§613.480 and following |

| | |
|---|---|
| New Hampshire | No statute |
| New Jersey | Employers cannot request or require an employee or prospective employee to submit to a lie detector test. The law does not apply to manufacturers of controlled dangerous substances. N.J. Stat. Ann. §2C:40A-1 |
| New Mexico | A peace officer's employer may order the employee to take a lie detector test as long as all other reasonable investigative means have been tried and the employee is told why he or she is being ordered to take the test. N.M. Stat. Ann. §29-14-5 |
| New York | An employer may not require an employee or applicant to take a lie detector test, and it is unlawful to administer the test or to use the results of the test. Violations are misdemeanors. N.Y. Lab. Code §§733 and following |
| North Carolina | No statute |
| North Dakota | No statute |
| Ohio | No statute |
| Oklahoma | No statute |
| Oregon | Employers cannot require lie detector tests, although law does not prohibit voluntary administration during a civil or criminal proceeding. Psychological stress tests, genetic screening and brainwave tests are also not allowed. Or. Rev. Stat. §§659.225 and 659.227 |
| Pennsylvania | Employers cannot require employees or applicants to take lie detector tests as a condition of employment. Does not apply to law enforcement or to dispensers of narcotic or dangerous drugs. Pa. Cons. Stat. Ann. tit. 18, §7321<br>It is a second degree misdemeanor to use a psychological stress evaluator, audio-stress monitor or similar device to test the truth of statements without the consent of the subject. Pa. Cons. Stat. Ann. tit. 18, §7507 |

| | |
|---|---|
| **Rhode Island** | Employers cannot request, require or subject any employee to a lie detector test. Written examinations are allowed as long as results are not the primary basis of an employment decision. Does not apply to law enforcement agencies. R.I. Gen. Laws §§28-6.1-1 to 28-6.1-4 |
| **South Carolina** | No statute |
| **South Dakota** | No statute |
| **Tennessee** | Employers may require an employee or applicant to submit to a polygraph test, but no personnel action may be based solely on the results. Tenn. Code Ann. §62-27-128 |
| **Texas** | The Department of Public Safety may not discharge or in any way discriminate against a commissioned officer on account of his refusal to take a lie detector test. Texas Code Ann. Government §411.007(e)<br>Peace officers and firefighters may be required to take lie detector tests under certain circumstances. Texas Code Ann., Local Gov. §§143.313, 614.063 |
| **Utah** | Employers cannot fire employees for refusing to take lie detection tests. Employers may not administer such tests without the subject knowing it. Utah Code Ann. §53-5-312 |
| **Vermont** | Employers cannot request, require or administer polygraph examinations to employees or applicants, nor fire or discriminate against them for refusing to submit to such a test.<br>Does not apply to law enforcement agencies, departments of public safety and sellers of precious metals, gems or jewelry; nor does it apply to an employer whose business includes manufacturing or selling regulated drugs—with respect to only those employees who come into contact with the drugs.<br>Penalties are fines of $500 to $1,000, six months in jail or both, and the penalties cannot be suspended by the court. Vt. Stat. Ann., tit. 21, §494a-e |

| Virginia | An employer may require a polygraph examination for any reason, except to disclose an employee's sexual activities that did not result in a criminal conviction. The employee must be given the results of the test upon request. |
| --- | --- |
| | Law enforcement agencies and regional jails cannot require employees to submit to a lie detector test except during an internal administrative investigation into allegations of misconduct or criminal activity and cannot discharge or demote employees solely on the basis of the test results. Va. Code Ann. §§40.1-51.4:3 and 4:4 |
| Washington | Employers cannot request or require an employee or applicant to submit to a lie detector test as a condition of employment or continued employment. Employers cannot fire, discipline or discriminate in any way for refusal to take such an exam. Does not apply to law enforcement applicants or applicants or employees in positions involving manufacturing, distributing or dispensing any controlled substance, or to people in sensitive positions involving national security. Wash. Rev. Code Ann. §§49.44.120 to 49.44.135 |
| West Virginia | Employers may not request or require an employee or applicant to submit to a lie detector test as a condition of employment, nor can they use the results of a test administered by someone else. Employers cannot fire or discriminate against an employee or applicant for refusing to submit to such a test. W. Va. Code §§21-5-5a to 21-5-5d |
| Wisconsin | Employers cannot request or require an employee or applicant to submit to a lie detection test as a condition of employment, nor may they use the results of a test administered by someone else. Employers cannot fire or discriminate against an employee or applicant for refusing to submit to such a test, or for filing a complaint, testifying about or exercising their rights under this law. |

|  | Does not apply to an employee who is suspected of involvement in theft, embezzlement or damage to employer's property, security-type personnel or manufacturers and sellers of controlled substances. Wis. Stat. Ann. §111.37 |
| **Wyoming** | No statute |

# E.  AIDS Testing

The disease of Acquired Immune Deficiency Syndrome (AIDS) was first identified in 1981. Fairly early on, researchers isolated its viral cause, Human Immunodeficiency Virus (HIV), which suppresses the immune systems of those who carry it, making them easy targets for various other infections and diseases. But beyond that, no great strides have been made in finding a cure. Many of those who have the HIV infection live nearly symptom-free. But ultimately, the disease is still fatal—and spreading.

The impact on American workplaces has been and will continue to be enormous. Not only have hundreds of thousands of workers died, most of them suffered also from the reactions of others—irrational fear and ostracism—that play in tandem with the AIDS epidemic. Many workplaces responded to the hysteria with more hysteria, developing intrusive policies of isolating workers suspected to have the disease. Another offshoot of this hysteria is the practice of testing employees for the HIV virus. While a number of courts have struck down state and local efforts to screen employees for HIV, the practice continues in many workplaces.

## 1. Legal Controls on Testing

Originally, HIV blood tests were fashioned to screen blood, not people. But when prospective employees and employees are subjected to testing, the reality is that people are being screened—and sometimes labeled as unfit workers.

A federal law, the Americans With Disabilities Act (see Chapter 7), prohibits you from testing job applicants to screen out workers who have HIV or AIDS. Once you offer an applicant a job, however, the legal constraints on testing become a bit murkier. To avoid singling out any individual or group, which would be illegal discrimination, you would have to test all employees. Even then, to justify giving employees an HIV test, you would have to show that the test is necessary to determine fitness to hold a job. This would be nearly an impossible task, as many people infected with HIV show no symptoms of ill health.

States are just beginning to enact laws regulating employers' uses of HIV tests. Alabama, California, Florida, Hawaii, Iowa, Maine, Massachusetts, Minnesota, Montana, New Jersey, New Mexico, Vermont, Washington and Wisconsin all have laws setting some bounds on employers.

Test results may not be used to determine suitability for insurance coverage or employment according to the laws in a number of states, including Florida (Fla. Stat. §381.6065). And Massachusetts bans employers from requiring employees to take a test as a condition of employment (Mass. Gen. Laws ch. 111, §70f).

In addition, a number of cities have enacted ordinances that put additional limits on how and when employers may test for HIV and AIDS. A strict law in San Francisco, for example, states that employers cannot test for AIDS unless they can show that the absence of AIDS is an essential employment qualification (San Francisco Police Code §§3801-16).

Laws on AIDS testing are changing very rapidly. Doublecheck your local, state and federal law for recent changes. A local clinic, support group or AIDS hotline may be able to provide you with the most current local information. A number of organizations also offer information on the HIV virus, AIDS and resources on AIDS in the workplace.

## 2. Tips on Dealing With Workers With HIV or AIDS

If someone in your workplace has HIV infection or AIDS, you may feel anxious. That's a normal reaction. People with HIV infection or AIDS also feel anxious about their health and about how supervisors and co-workers will treat them.

Be supportive of workers with HIV infection or AIDS. If you have a close relationship, you can let the person know you are concerned and offer support. Most people with HIV infection or AIDS are able to function normally and independently. They want to live and work without being singled out or harassed. They need your understanding and sensitivity. There are specific steps you can take to ensure this.

Let the person with HIV infection or AIDS decide which people he or she wants to tell about the condition. Do not spread rumors or gossip about someone with HIV infection or AIDS.

Be aware that people infected with the virus have damaged immune systems. Be careful not to expose them to colds or coughs.

Even though no one on your staff is infected with HIV or has AIDS, it is likely that someone has a spouse, family member, life partner or close friend with the virus. Be supportive of them. ■

**CHAPTER 4**

# Keeping Records

**N**othing can clutter up an office space more quickly than aging paperwork. But some of the clutter may be just what you need to refute a claim of unfair treatment—and several laws actually require you to hang onto such potential evidence for a specified time. This chapter discusses the paperwork you must keep when making new hires and the personnel records you are likely to keep on all employees. It also explains the special treatment required for medical records. Fortunately, there are limits as to how long you must store this accumulation of paper.

## A. Proof of Work Authorization

Immigration laws prohibit you from hiring those who do not have authorization to work in the United States. And they also set out specific procedures you must follow to verify an applicant's status before hiring him or her.

The government tracks your compliance with these requirements by making sure you keep a paper trail on every individual you hire. If the thought of having the IRS on your trail is scary, be mindful of its similarly acronymed cousin in government service, the INS—the Immigration and Naturalization Service—also known for its doggedness in sniffing out and clamping down on those who run afoul of the laws it polices. It behooves you to fulfill the hiring obligations the INS imposes on you—and to make sure employees do their parts, too.

New employees must complete Section 1 of INS Form I-9, which asks for cursory identifying information such as name, address, birthdate and Social Security number. But the most important part of the form asks the employee to attest that he or she can lawfully work here by virtue of being:

- a citizen or national of the United States
- a lawful permanent resident alien, or
- an alien with work authorization.

Employees must complete this section of Form I-9 by the end of their first day on the job. They then have three business days to present you with documents that prove:

- that they are who they say they are, and
- that they are legally authorized to work in the United States.

**No One Is Exempt.** You must complete and file Form I-9 paperwork for every new employee you hire. And to prevent claims of discrimination, you must ask each one to provide the required documentation, regardless of whether he or she was born in the United States and has lived here for a lifetime.

## 1. When One Document Is Sufficient

The INS recently changed rules for documents it deems sufficient to prove both identity and eligibility to be employed in the United States. The following will now be accepted:

- a United States passport—either expired or unexpired
- an unexpired foreign passport with an I-551 stamp
- an alien registration receipt card or permanent resident card
- an unexpired employment authorization card

- an unexpired employment authorization document issued by the INS which contains a photograph, or
- an unexpired foreign passport with Form I-94 containing an endorsement of nonimmigrant status.

## 2. When Two Documents Are Required

An employee who does not have any of that evidence must produce two documents: one establishing that he or she is authorized to work in the United States, and another verifying identity.

As documents proving employment authorization, the INS will accept:

- a Social Security card
- a U.S. birth or birth abroad certificate
- a Native American tribal document
- a U.S. citizen ID card
- a resident citizen ID card, or
- unexpired employment authorization documents issued by the INS.

As documents proving identity, the INS will accept:

- a current U.S. or Canadian driver's license
- a federal, state or local identification card with a photograph on it
- a school ID card with a photograph
- a voter's registration card
- a U.S. military card or draft record
- a military dependent's ID card
- a U.S. Coast Guard Merchant Mariner card, or
- a Native American tribal document.

For workers 16 and under, the INS considers a school report card or a hospital record such as a birth certificate acceptable as proof of identity.

## 3. Time Limits

These time limits requiring employees to complete the form during the first day on the job and provide the required documents within three days are strict. However, those who require extra time to pull together the documents proving identity and authorization—for example, to obtain a certified copy of a birth certificate from another state—may be allowed an additional 18 business days to produce the required documents. To get an extension of time, however, they must show you proof that they have applied for the documents by producing, for example, a receipt for the fee charged for a certified birth certificate.

## 4. Employer Duties

For your part, you must complete Section 2 of the form, indicating that you have reviewed the documents the employee has presented as proof of identity and employment eligibility. Do your utmost to be sure that these documents are current and authentic. In this regard, the INS has appointed you as the initial immigration police; you are charged with accepting only documents that appear to be genuine.

For additional information on completing Form I-9, see the INS website at http://www.ins.usdoj.gov. Or obtain their free publication, *Handbook for Employers;* you can obtain a copy from the nearest regional office of the INS—or order it from the agency's website.

Employees who attempt to dupe you with doctored documents may face the big troubles of being fired and getting into immigration trouble, but you also face the risks of being fined or jailed for violating this law.

**⚠ The One Time It's Better Not to Keep Copies.** Return to employees any documents that they give you in the process of completing their I-9 Forms—and do not keep any copies of them on hand. This warning has a bit of a cloak and dagger ring to it, but it can be a valuable safeguard for you if the INS decides to investigate whether you have complied with I-9 requirements.

If you have no copies of the documents on hand to review, the INS will be hard-pressed to question your good faith in accepting the proof provided as genuine.

Note that if you do make copies of the documents, however, you must keep them on file with the completed Form I-9.

## WHAT IF TIME REALLY IS MONEY?

Bureaucratic clockwatchers recently put the following estimates on the time it takes to comply with Form I-9 recordkeeping requirements:

| | |
|---|---|
| Learning about the form | 5 minutes |
| Completing the form | 5 minutes |
| Assembling and filing the form | 5 minutes |

Those who watch both clocks and calculators have computed that about 78,000,000 new employees and 20,000,000 employers complete Form I-9 each year. The total time spent annually on completing Form I-9: well over 13 million hours.

# B. Personnel Records

You are required by law to keep some tabs on employees—including information on their wages and hours, workplace injuries and illnesses and tax withholding, as well as records of accrued vacation and other benefits. That information is usually gathered together in one place: a personnel file.

But personnel files can sometimes become the catch-alls for other kinds of information—references from previous employers, comments from customers or clients, employee reprimands, job performance evaluations, memos of management's observations about an employee's behavior or productivity. When employment disputes develop, or an employee is demoted, transferred or fired, the innards of his or her personnel file often provide essential information—often unknown to the employee—about the whys and wherefores.

A federal law, the Privacy Act (5 U.S.C. §552a), limits the type of information that federal agencies, the military and other government employers may keep on their workers.

However, private employers have a nearly unfettered hand when it comes to the kind of information they can collect. The laws in only a few states restrict the information in personnel files. Michigan, for example, bars employers from keeping records describing an employee's political associations (Mich. Stat. Ann. §17.62 (8)). And employers in Minnesota may not retaliate with any information intentionally left out of a personnel file (Minn. Stat. Ann. §§181.960 to .965).

While the content of personnel files may be a hot subject for legislation, there are reams of laws on who gets access to the files. Many states now have some type of law regulating personnel files for private employers. (See the chart in Section B3 below.) These laws control:

- whether and how employees and former employees can get access to their personnel files

- whether employees are entitled to copies of the information in them, and
- how employees can contest and correct erroneous information in their files.

## 1. Content of Files

Workplace experts frequently advise troubled employees that the best way for them to find out what a company knows about them, or what it is saying about them to outside people who inquire, is to obtain a copy of the contents of their personnel file from a current or former employer. This should be a heads up to you that these files are becoming fertile grounds for disgruntled employees who comb through them looking for evidence of potential wrongdoing or unjust treatment. Do use personnel files as a way to collect and organize information about employees. But it is wise to be discreet. Restrict file entries to information that is related to work. Do not include gossip or unsubstantiated criticism in personnel files.

**The Importance of Keeping Secrets.** Employers are supposed to collect only information that is job-related. And only those people with a proven need to know are supposed to have access to any individual employee's personnel file. For example, you cannot tell workers the results of a drug screening test that a co-worker was required to take. Keep personnel files locked up and in a safe place. And make sure that only those within the company who truly have a need to know the information have access to it.

## 2.  Access by Employees

Whether and when you must show employees what lurks within their personnel files depends on the particulars of your state law.

In some states, the only way they can see those files is by suing you. And even then, you might be able to successfully defend that portions of the files are not relevant to the case and should be kept out of sight.

But in many states, employees have the right to see the contents of their personnel files without filing a lawsuit. For example, Oregon law gives employees the right to a copy of any document an employer uses in making a workplace decision—including promotions, raises or firings.

And a number of states limit what documents employees have the legal right to see. In California, Nevada and Wisconsin, for example, employees need not be shown references from past employers. And those three states in addition to Michigan, New Hampshire and Washington limit employees' access to their files if employers are investigating them for a possible crime or other misconduct. The rationale behind this is to protect incriminating evidence from being destroyed.

## 3.  State Laws

State laws on employee access to personnel records generally cover technical matters, such as when a request for a viewing must be made and how long you have to respond to it. In general, employees must make a written request to an employer or former employer if they want to see a personnel file.

## STATE LAWS ON EMPLOYEE ACCESS TO PERSONNEL RECORDS

| | |
|---|---|
| Alabama | No statute |
| Alaska | Employees have the right to see their personnel files and make a copy of them. Alaska Stat. §23.10.430 |
| Arizona | No statute |
| Arkansas | Public employees have right of access to their personnel and evaluation records. Ark. Code Ann. § 25-19-105(c)(2) |
| California | Private employees have the right to have a copy of any document that they have signed relating to employment. Cal. Lab. Code §432<br><br>Private employers must maintain a copy of the employee's personnel file where the employee reports to work, or must make the file available at that location within a reasonable time after the employee asks to see it.<br><br>Does not apply to letters of reference or records relating to the investigation of a possible offense. Cal. Lab. Code §1198.5 |
| Colorado | No statute |
| Connecticut | Employees have the right to see their personnel files and to insert rebuttals of information with which they disagree. Conn. Gen. Stat. Ann. §31-128b and e |
| Delaware | Employees have the right to see their personnel files and to insert rebuttals of information with which they disagree. Del. Code Ann. tit. 19 §§730 through 735 |
| District of Columbia | Employees have the right to review their personnel records, to insert rebuttal information and to request the removal of information that is irrelevant or more than three years old. D.C. Code Ann. §16-632.5 |
| Florida | No statute |
| Georgia | No statute |
| Hawaii | No statute |

| | |
|---|---|
| **Idaho** | School district employees have the right to review and obtain copies of their personnel files—except for letters of recommendation—and to attach rebuttals to any material in the file. Idaho Code §33-518 |
| **Illinois** | Employers with five or more employees must allow them to see their personnel files—except for letters of reference, testing documents and investigatory records concerning possible criminal conduct of the employee which could harm the employer—and to insert rebuttals of any information with which they disagree. Personnel Record Review Act, 820 Ill. Rev. Stat. 40/2-10 |
| **Indiana** | No statute |
| **Iowa** | Employees have the right to see and copy personnel files, including performance evaluations and disciplinary records, but not references. Iowa Code §91B.1 |
| **Kansas** | No statute |
| **Kentucky** | No statute |
| **Louisiana** | Current or former employees, or their designated representatives, have a right of access to employers' records of employee exposure to toxic substances, medical records and analyses using employee records. La. Rev. Stat. Ann. §23.1016 |
| **Maine** | Employees have the right to see and make copies of their personnel files, including workplace evaluations. Me. Rev. Stat. Ann. tit. 26 §631 |
| **Maryland** | No statute |
| **Massachusetts** | Employees have the right to see their personnel files and to insert rebuttals of any information with which they disagree. Employees may take court action to expunge from personnel records any information that the employer knows, or should have known, was incorrect. Does not apply to employees of private institutions of higher learning who are tenured, on tenure track or have positions or responsibilities similar to those who are tenured or in tenure track positions. Mass. Gen. Laws Ann. ch. 149 §52C |

| | |
|---|---|
| **Michigan** | Employees have the right to see and make a copy of their personnel files—except for employee references—and to insert rebuttals of any information with which they disagree. |
| | Access is not available to employees whom the employer is investigating for criminal activity that may cause loss to the employer's business. When the investigation ends or after two years, whichever comes first, the employee must be told of the outcome and, if no disciplinary action is taken, the investigation file must be destroyed.  Right to Know Act, Mich. Comp. Laws §§423.501 to 505 |
| **Minnesota** | Employees have the right to see their personnel files and to insert rebuttals of any information with which they disagree. |
| | Does not apply to public employers. A former employee may inspect once within the year following termination. An employer may not use in any retaliatory way any information intentionally left out of the personnel record. Minn. Stat. Ann. §§181.960 to 965 |
| **Mississippi** | No statute |
| **Missouri** | No statute |
| **Montana** | No statute |
| **Nebraska** | Employees of counties with more than 300,000 inhabitants have access to their personnel records. Neb. Rev. Stat. §23-2507 |
| **Nevada** | Employees who have been employed at least 60 days have the right to see and copy any records that the employer used to confirm the employee's qualifications, or as the basis for any disciplinary action. If those records contain incorrect information, the employee may notify the employer of the errors in writing. The employer is required to correct the challenged information if the employer decides it is false. |
| | However, the employee may not inspect confidential reports from past employers or reports from an investigative agency regarding the employee's violation of any law. Nev. Rev. Stat. §613.075 |

| | |
|---|---|
| **New Hampshire** | Employees have the right to see and copy their personnel files and to insert rebuttals of any information with which they disagree.<br>Employers may not disclose information that relates to a government security investigation or information regarding an investigation of the employee if that disclosure would prejudice law enforcement. N.H. Rev. Stat. §275:56 |
| **New Jersey** | No statute |
| **New Mexico** | No statute |
| **New York** | No statute |
| **North Carolina** | Employees have access to records of their exposure to toxic substances. N.C. Gen. Stat. §95-143.<br>State employees and their authorized representatives have access to personnel records except for letter of reference. N.C. Gen. Stat. §126-24 |
| **North Dakota** | State employees, but not those of political subdivisions, must be given the opportunity to read information regarding their performance or character before it is placed in their files. The employee must be given an opportunity to reproduce the material, and no anonymous entries are permitted. Employer may maintain separate performance notes to use in evaluating the employee or in disciplinary actions. N.D. Cent. Code Ann. §54-06-21 |
| **Ohio** | Employees have the right to copies of medical reports furnished to employers. Ohio Rev. Code §4113.23<br>Public employees have the right to review records of their exposure to toxic substances. Ohio Rev. Code §4167.11 |
| **Oklahoma** | An employee is entitled to a copy of a report of a required medical examination. Okla. Stat. Ann., tit. 40, §191 |
| **Oregon** | Employees have the right to see and copy any documents used by the employer in making work-related decisions, such as promotions, wage increases or termination. Or. Rev. Stat. §652.750 |

| | |
|---|---|
| **Pennsylvania** | Employees and their designated agents have the right to see their personnel files. The files may not be copied or removed. Pa. Cons. Stat. Ann. tit. 43, §§1321 through 1323 |
| **Rhode Island** | Employees have the right to see their personnel files up to three times per year. The file may not be copied or removed, but the employee may request that specific documents be copied. Employers do not have to allow employees to review letters of reference, criminal investigation records, managerial records or confidential reports from prior employers. R.I. Gen. Laws §§28-6.4-1 and 28-6.4-2 |
| **South Carolina** | Employees have the right to review records of their exposure to toxic substances. S.C. Code Ann. §14-15-100 |
| **South Dakota** | Public employees have the right to review their personnel records. S.D. Codified Laws §3-6A-31 |
| **Tennessee** | State employees have the right to review their personnel records and to make copies at their own expense. Tenn. Code Ann. §8-50-108 |
| **Texas** | If a negative document is placed in the personnel file of a firefighter or police officer, the employer must notify him or her, give him or her a copy upon request and allow him or her to file a written response. Texas Code Ann. Local Gov. §143.089 |
| **Utah** | Public employees have the right to examine and make copies of their personnel files. Utah Code Ann. §§67-18-1 and following |
| **Vermont** | No statute |
| **Virginia** | No statute |
| **Washington** | Employees have the right to see their personnel files, and to insert rebuttals of any information with which they disagree. A former employee retains the right of rebuttal or correction for two years. Does not apply if employee is subject to criminal investigation or if the records have been compiled in preparation of an impending lawsuit. Wash. Rev. Code §§49.12.240 to 260 |
| **West Virginia** | No statute |

| Wisconsin | Employees have the right to see and copy their personnel files up to twice a year, and to insert rebuttals of any information with which they disagree. The rebuttal must be attached to the record and transmitted with it to any third party.<br><br>Does not apply if employee is subject to a criminal investigation, to references or recommendations or to records subject to a pending claim in a judicial proceeding. Personnel records include medical records, but if the employer thinks that disclosure of these would be detrimental to the employee, the employer may instead disclose them to a physician designated by the employee. Wis. Stat. §103.13 |
|---|---|
| Wyoming | No statute |

# C. Medical Records

The Americans With Disabilities Act, or ADA, imposes very strict limitations on how you must handle information you obtained about employees through medical examinations and inquiries. You must keep the information in medical files that are separate from non-medical records such as personnel files, and you must store the medical files in a separate locked cabinet. To further guarantee the confidentiality of medical files, it is a good idea to designate a specific person to have access to those files.

The ADA allows very limited disclosure of medical information. Under the ADA, you may:

- inform supervisors about necessary restrictions on an employee's duties and about necessary accommodations

- inform first aid and safety workers about a disability that may require emergency treatment and about specific procedures that are needed if the workplace must be evacuated, and

- provide medical information required by government officials and by insurance companies that require a medical exam for health or life insurance.

Because medical information can be used and misused for various personal and business purposes, you may find yourself up against unusual requests from outsiders—from private investigators to former spouses. Keep your lips firmly zipped. Treat all medical information about all employees as confidential.

# D. How Long You Must Keep Records

Employers with the itch to pitch out old files often question how long they must retain the musty things. Here is help.

### One Year

Keep all personnel and employment records for at least one year.

If a worker is fired, keep all his or her personnel records for at least a year after the firing.

### Two Years

Keep all records related to pay such as wage rates, job evaluations, merit raises or bonuses for at least two years.

### Three Years

Keep all payroll records for at least three years. This is mandated by both the Age Discrimination in Employment Act or ADEA and the Fair Labor Standards Act, or FLSA.

Keep all Form I-9s for three years after hiring an employee or a year after he or she leaves the company—whichever is longer.

### Other Time Periods

Keep all employee benefit plans—such as health insurance, pensions, 401(k)s—as long as the plans are in effect and for at least one year after any plan is terminated.

If an employee or former employee files a claim of discrimination or other wrongdoing, be sure to keep all records relating to the employee and to the claim until it is finally resolved. ■

**CHAPTER 5**

# Paying Workers

**T**he topic discussed in this chapter—paying employees—at first glance does not seem particularly compelling or sexy. But when you consider that today's hottest commodity in the workplace is money, it soon becomes clear why you need to pay careful attention to this concern.

Some money concerns are matters of commonsense and fairness. Workers are more apt to stay on the job longer and stay on it more happily if they have the anticipation and reality of pay raises to boost their morales. But there are additional money concerns, such as how and when employees must be paid, that you need to heed. These are dictated to employers by laws that spell out to the penny what will pass legal muster.

## A. The Federal Fair Labor Standards Act

The most important and most far-reaching law concerning how you pay workers is the federal Fair Labor Standards Act or FLSA (29 U.S.C. §§201 and following). The FLSA:

- defines the 40-hour workweek
- covers the federal minimum wage
- sets requirements for overtime, and
- places restrictions on child labor.

Basically, the FLSA establishes minimums for fair pay and hours— and it is the single law most often violated by employers. An employer must also comply with other local, state or federal workplace laws that set higher standards. So in addition to determining whether you are paying workers properly under the FLSA, you may need to check whether the other laws discussed in this chapter also apply to your workplace.

**MONEY TALKS—LOUDLY**

In a recent survey of about 2,500 employees, 60% responded that salary was their top concern—ranking it way above the more ethereal concerns of job security and opportunities to learn.

Source: Challenger, Gray & Chritman, Employment Consulting Firm

## 1. Who Is Covered

The FLSA applies only to employers whose annual sales total $500,000 or more, or who are engaged in interstate commerce.

You might think that this would restrict the FLSA to covering only employees in large companies, but in reality the law covers nearly all workplaces. This is because the courts have interpreted the term interstate commerce very broadly. For example, courts have ruled that companies that regularly use the U.S. mail to send or receive letters to and from other states are engaged in interstate commerce. Even the fact that employees use company telephones to place or accept interstate business calls has placed an employer under the FLSA.

## 2. Who Is Exempt

A few employers, including small farms—those that use relatively little outside paid labor—are explicitly exempt from the FLSA. In addition, some employees are exempt from the FLSA even though their employers are covered. As explained below, a few common categories of employees are exempt from certain FLSA requirements, such as pay for overtime and minimum wages.

## a. Executive, administrative and professional workers

Executive, administrative and professional workers are exempt from the FLSA. This is the most confusing and most often mistakenly applied broad category of exempt worker.

The requirements for executive workers are most rigorous. To qualify as an exempt executive, a worker must:

- be paid with a salary, so that compensation is not subject to reductions for quality and quantity of work
- use discretion in performing job duties
- regularly direct the work of two or more people
- have the authority to hire and fire other employees, or to order such hiring and firing
- be primarily responsible for managing others, and
- devote no more than 20% of worktime to other tasks that are not managerial. For certain retail and service companies, 40% of nonmanagerial time is allowed.

**It's the Work, Not the Pay, That Matters.** An employee is not automatically exempt from the FLSA solely because you pay him or her a salary. The work performed must correspond to the kind of work a salaried employee normally does. Be mindful of the common mistake employers make in docking or pumping up a salaried employee's pay. If you pay a worker as a salaried employee, but cut his or her pay for work or award a bonus for working more hours, the worker might legally be deemed to be an hourly rather than a salaried employee.

The definitions of administrative and professional employees are similar, but contain minor differences. For example, employees categorized as professionals must perform work that is primarily intellectual.

The definitions also change with the employee's salary level. For example, if the weekly salary of the executive, administrative or professional employee exceeds a certain minimum, fewer factors are required to qualify for the exemption.

At the first few glances, how you classify employees does not seem to be a particularly evocative issue. But keep in mind that nothing speaks more loudly to many disgruntled employees than the thought of being shortchanged. And those who have been classified incorrectly as exempt might find they are legally entitled to the pay for overtime and compensatory time that they were denied.

To be truly exempt, employees must meet specific tests set out for the government agency famous for setting out tests: the Internal Revenue Service. Even if you initially set things up to qualify the workers for exempt status, you may inadvertently jeopardize that status by certain policies. For example, to be exempt, employees must be paid a set weekly amount that is not reduced by the quality or quantity of their work. Similarly, you may transform an exempt employee to a nonexempt one if you require the worker to reimburse the company for cash or inventory shortages.

### EXEMPTION GUIDELINES

The chart below summarizes exemption guidelines for the unwieldy category of executive, administrative and professional employees. Be aware, however, that not all of the legal nuances appear in the chart. Unless an employee fits squarely into the simplified guidelines, your best bet is to dig further. Contact your state labor department for more specific guidance.

Note that there's a long test and a short test for each category. A worker who meets all of the requirements of the short test is exempt and need not meet the long test.

The long test requirement that executives and administrators spend at least 80% of the workday in certain activities is reduced to 60% for employees who work in retail and service establishments. Further, the percentage test does not apply at all to an executive who is in charge of an independent business establishment or branch or who owns at least a 20% interest in the business.

**Exemption Guidelines**

| Executive Exemption | Administrative Exemption | Professional Exemption |
|---|---|---|
| **Short Test** | | |
| Primarily manages a business or department | Meets the first test described below under Long Test | Duties as described below under Long Test |
| Routinely supervises two or more employees | Work includes discretion and independent judgment | Duties need only include work requiring discretion and independent judgment |
| Earns salary of at least $250 per week | Earns salary of at least $250 per week | Earns salary of at least $250 per week |
| **Long Test** | | |
| Primarily manages a business | Primary duties include work acquired by a prolonged course of specialized intellectual study requiring advanced knowledge | Mainly performs office or non-manual work directly related to management policies |
| | -or- | -or- |
| | | Original and creative work stemming primarily from invention, imagination or talent |
| Routinely supervises two or more employees | Routinely exercises discretion and independent judgment | Work requires consistent exercise of discretion and judgment |
| Can hire, fire or and promote workers Routinely exercises discretion | Routinely assists a proprietor or executive Performs technical work under general supervision | Work is intellectual varied, not routine |
| | -or- | |
| | Executes special assignments under general supervision | |
| Spends at least 80% of workday in above activities | Spends at least 80% of workday in above activities | Spends at least 80% of workday in above activities |

| Earns salary of at least $155 per week | Earns salary of at least $155 per week | Earns salary of at least $170 per week; does not apply to doctors and lawyers |

Adapted from *The Employer's Legal Handbook,* by Fred Steingold (Nolo).

 The fine points of these exemptions are explained in a free booklet titled "Regulations Part 541: Defining the Terms— Executive, Administrative, Professional and Outside Sales." It is available from the nearest office of the Wage and Hour Division of the U.S. Department of Labor—or call 202-219-8743.

### b. Outside salespeople

An outside salesperson is exempt from FLSA coverage if he or she:

- regularly works away from the employer's place of business while making sales or taking orders, and
- spends no more than 20% of worktime doing work other than selling.

Typically, an exempt salesperson will be paid primarily through commissions and will require little or no direct supervision in doing the job.

### c. Computer specialists

This exemption applies to computer system analysts and programmers who receive a salary of at least $170 a week or who, if paid by the hour, receive at least 6.5 times the minimum wage. That works out to $27.63 an hour.

Employees will likely be exempt from the wage and hour laws as computer specialists if their primary duties consist of determining functional specifications for hardware and software, designing computer systems to meet user specs or creating or modifying computer programs.

## d. Miscellaneous workers

Several other types of workers are exempt from the minimum wage and overtime pay provisions of the FLSA. The most common include:

- employees of seasonal amusement or recreational businesses
- employees of local newspapers having a circulation of less than 4,000
- newspaper delivery workers
- switchboard operators employed by phone companies that have no more than 750 stations
- workers on small farms, and
- personal companions and casual babysitters. Officially, domestic workers—housekeepers, childcare workers, chauffeurs, gardeners—are covered by the FLSA if they are paid at least $1,000 in wages from a single employer in a year, or if they work eight hours or more in a week for one or several employers.

## e. Apprentices

An apprentice is a worker who is at least 16 years old and who has signed an agreement to learn a skilled trade. Apprentices are exempt from the requirements of the FLSA. But beware that your state may have a law limiting the number of hours someone is allowed to work as an apprentice. If you employ apprentice workers, check with your state labor department for more information.

FLSA exemptions for employers change often. Doublecheck any exemption by calling the local U.S. Labor Department, Wage and Hour Division office, listed in the federal government section of your telephone directory. Keep in mind, however, that the FLSA is so broadly written and so full of amendments and cross-references that it applies to most employers.

Most of the exemptions to FLSA coverage are listed in federal statute 29 U.S.C. §213. The most direct way to become familiar with these exemptions is to read about them in an annotated edition of the code, which is what your local law library is most likely to have.

---

**GETTING AROUND A TIGHT BELT**

If budget constraints make it truly impossible for you to offer increased—or even competitive—salaries to employees, there may be other benefits you can offer that will seem more valuable than gold. Some of these benefits are what prompts a worker to accept or stay at a job over one dangled before them with much better pay. They can be important in luring the best and the brightest new employees—and invaluable in holding onto those who have demonstrated loyalty by staying on the job for a long time. These morale boosters include:
- lengthier vacations
- flexible work hours
- training to increase job skills
- seminars of general interest to workers ranging from the practical, such as Financial Planning—to the creative, such as Life Drawing
- a willingness to accommodate a reasonable wish, such as allowing an employee to occasionally bring a pet to work, and
- making the workplace a pleasant and friendly place to be, with comfortable furnishing, music, art and—that universal seducer—good food.

---

## 3. Employer Duties

The FLSA imposes on employers a number of duties, primarily aimed at ensuring that workers get paid fairly for the time they work.

## a. Paying minimum wage

You must pay all covered employees not less than the minimum wage—currently set at $5.15 an hour.

Some states have established a minimum wage that is higher than the federal one—and you must comply with the higher rate if your state allows for one. Employers not covered by the FLSA, such as small farm owners, are required to pay all workers the state minimum wage rate. (See the chart below in this section.)

The FLSA does not require any specific system of paying the minimum wage, so you may base pay on time at work, piece rates or according to some other measurement. In all cases, however, an employee's pay divided by the hours worked during the pay period must equal or exceed the minimum wage.

Many employers become confused by the nuances and exceptions in the wage and hour law or bend the rules to suit their own pocketbooks. You would do well to doublecheck your math and abandon any inclinations to skirt the law. A few simple rules may help.

- *Hourly.* Hourly employees must be paid minimum wage for all hours worked. You cannot take an average—or pay less than minimum wage for some hours worked and more for others.
- *Fixed rate or salary.* You can check the minimum amount you must pay employees who receive fixed rate wages by dividing the amount they are paid in a pay period by the number of hours worked. The resulting average must be at least minimum wage.
- *Commissions and piece rates.* The total you pay divided by the number of hours worked must average at least the minimum hourly wage rate.

⚠ **Rules on Tips and Commissions.** If you have any employees who routinely receive at least $30 per month in tips as part of their jobs, you are not required to pay more than $2.13 an hour—and credit the tips received against the minimum wage requirement. However, your offset may not exceed the tips the employee actually receives. Also, the employee must be allowed to keep all of the tips he or she receives.

When people are paid commissions for sales, those commissions may take the place of wages. However, if the commissions do not equal the minimum wage, the FLSA requires that you make up the difference.

As mentioned, all but a few states have laws specifying wage and hour standards. They are summarized in the chart below.

## STATE MINIMUM WAGE LAWS

| | |
|---|---|
| **Alabama** | No statute |
| **Alaska** | 50 cents above federal minimum wage. Alaska Stat. §23.10.065 |
| **Arizona** | No statute |
| **Arkansas** | $5.15. Fulltime students working 20 hours per week or less are entitled to only 85% of the minimum wage. Ark. Code Ann. §11-4-210 |
| **California** | $5.75. 85% of minimum wage for learners during their first 160 hours of employment if they have no prior related experience and for minors if less than 25% of the employees are minors. California Code of Regulations, tit. 8, ch. 5, Group 1, §11000 |
| **Colorado** | $5.15. By order of the Department of Labor and Employment, 1515 Arapahoe Street, Tower 2, Suite 400, Denver, CO 80202-2117; 303-620-4700. Authorizing statute: Colo. Rev. Stat. §8-6-109 |

| | |
|---|---|
| | Minimum wage for minors may be 15% below the regular minimum wage unless the minor is married and living away from parents or guardians, or supports himself or herself or can show that his or her well-being is substantially dependent on being employed. Colo. Rev. Stat. §8-6-108.5 |
| **Connecticut** | $5.65, or at least 1/2% above the federal minimum wage, whichever is higher. Starting on January 1, 2000, the minimum wage is $6.15 or at least 1/2% above the federal minimum wage, whichever is higher. For employees under the age of 18, learners and beginners, the minimum wage for the first 200 hours of work is 85% of the regular minimum wage. Conn. Gen. Stat. §31-58j, Conn. Public Act 98-44 |
| **Delaware** | The federal minimum wage. Del. Code Ann. tit. 19, §902a |
| **District of Columbia** | $6.15, or the federal minimum wage plus $1.00. D.C. Code Ann. §§36-220.1 and 36-220.2 |
| **Florida** | No statute |
| **Georgia** | $3.25. Ga. Code Ann. §34-4-3a |
| **Hawaii** | $5.25. Employees who receive tips can be paid 20 cents/hour less. Haw. Rev. Stat. §387-2 |
| **Idaho** | $5.15. For tipped employees, 65% of minimum wage. For employees under 20 years old, $4.25 for first consecutive 90 days. Idaho Code §44-1502 |
| **Illinois** | $5.15. For employees under the age of 18, minimum wage is 50 cents less. 820 Ill. Comp. Stat. 105/4 |
| **Indiana** | $5.15 for employers who employ at least two employees. For employees under the age of 20, minimum wage for first 90 consecutive days is $4.25. Ind. Code Ann. §22-2-2-4 |
| **Iowa** | $4.65 or federal minimum, whichever is greater. Iowa Code Ann. §91D.1 |
| **Kansas** | $2.65. Kan. Stat. Ann. §44-1203 |

| | |
|---|---|
| **Kentucky** | Federal minimum wage. For employees who earn more than $30 per month in tips, minimum wage is 50% of regular minimum wage so long as salary plus tips is at least equal to the minimum wage. Ky. Rev. Stat. Ann §337.275 |
| **Louisiana** | No statute |
| **Maine** | Same as federal minimum wage. |
| | Employers can deduct up to 50% off the minimum wage for employees who receive tips. Me. Rev. Stat. Ann. tit. 26, §664 |
| **Maryland** | At least the federal minimum wage. Employers can deduct $2.77 from minimum wage for employees who receive tips. Md. Code Ann., Labor and Employment, §§3-413, 419 |
| **Massachusetts** | $5.25. Set by the Labor and Industries Department, 100 Cambridge Street, Room 1100, Boston, MA 02202; 617-727-3465. Authorizing statute: Mass. Gen. Laws Ann. ch. 151, §1 |
| **Michigan** | $5.15. Mich. Comp. Laws §408.384 |
| **Minnesota** | $5.15 for employers grossing more than $500,000 per year. For others, $4.90. Minn. Stat. Ann. §177.24 |
| **Mississippi** | No statute |
| **Missouri** | The federal minimum wage. Mo. Ann. Stat. §290.502 |
| **Montana** | Federal minimum wage for businesses with gross annual sales of $110,000 or more. For others, $4.00. Mont. Code Ann. §§39-3-404; 39-3-409; Dept. of Labor & Industry Rules §24.16.15104 |
| **Nebraska** | $5.15. The minimum wage for student learners is 75% of the regular minimum wage. Neb. Rev. Stat. §48-1203 |
| **Nevada** | $5.15. Minimum wage for minors is 85% of regular minimum wage. Nev. Rev. Stat. §608.250 |

| | |
|---|---|
| **New Hampshire** | $5.15. For tipped employees (except for domestic or farm labor, summer camp employees, newsboys, golf caddies and nonprofessional ski patrol), minimum wage is $2.38, or 45% of regular minimum wage, whichever is higher. For employees under the age of 16 or with less than six months' experience, minimum wage is 75% of regular minimum wage. N.H. Rev. Stat. Ann. §279:21 |
| **New Jersey** | $5.05. Law does not apply to car salespeople, parttime home childcare workers or workers under the age of 18 who do not have a special vocational school graduate permit. N.J. Stat. Ann. §34:11-56a4 |
| **New Mexico** | $4.25. N.M. Stat. Ann. §50-4-22 |
| **New York** | $4.25. $1.34 can be deducted from wages of hotel service employees who receive tips. $1.05 can be deducted from wages of tipped chambermaids. N.Y. Labor Law §652 |
| **North Carolina** | Federal minimum wage. Fulltime students, learners, apprentices and messengers entitled to 90% of regular minimum wage. N.C. Gen. Stat. §95-25.3 |
| **North Dakota** | $5.15. For employees who receive tips, the minimum wage is $3.45. Commissioner of Labor sets the standards of minimum wages, hours of employment and conditions of employment. Labor Department, 600 East Boulevard, Bismarck, ND 58505; 701-328-2660. Authorizing statute: N.D. Century Code §34-06-03 |
| **Ohio** | $4.25; 85% of regular minimum wage for students in cooperative vocational education programs approved by the board of education. Ohio Rev. Code Ann. §4111.02 |
| **Oklahoma** | Not less than current federal minimum wage. Okla. Stat. Ann. tit. 40, §197.2 |
| **Oregon** | $6.50. Or. Rev. Stat. §653.025 |

| Pennsylvania | The federal minimum wage. Employees under the age of 18, seasonal employees, employees under the age of 21 at summer day camps, golf caddies, switchboard operators at small phone companies, farm laborers, domestic servants in private homes and news delivery workers are not covered under the minimum wage law. Pa. Cons. Stat. Ann, tit. 43, §§333.104, 105 |
|---|---|
| Rhode Island | $5.15. R.I. Gen. Laws §28-12-3 |
| South Carolina | No statute |
| South Dakota | $5.15. Statute does not apply to employees under the age of 18, babysitters or outside salespeople. S.D. Codified Laws Ann. §60-11-3 |
| Tennessee | No statute |
| Texas | $3.35, except that an employer may pay only 60% of the minimum wage if the employee's earning or productive capacity is impaired by age, physical or mental deficiency or injury; or if the person is over 65 years old. Lower wages may not be paid to agricultural piece rate workers. |
| | Statute does not apply to employees under the age of 18 who are not graduates of high school or a vocational training program, employees under the age of 20 who are students in high school or in a vocational training program, employees under the age of 21 who are disabled and who are clients of vocational rehabilitation and are in a school-work program, amusement parks or recreational establishments that operate less than seven months out of the year, dairy and livestock production workers, inmates, patients and clients of state mental health facilities. Tex. Labor Code Ann. §§62.051, .055., .057, .155, .156, .158, .160 |
| Utah | $5.15 for employees 18 and older; does not apply to waitressing, personal attendants, domestic employees, seasonal employees of nonprofit camping, religious or recreational programs, prisoners, livestock or harvest laborers, agricultural employees who worked less than 13 weeks during the prior year, registered apprentices or students employed by the school they are attending, employees of seasonal amusement parks. |

|  | Set by the Industrial Commission of Utah, but may not be more than the federal minimum wage. Industrial Commission of Utah, 160 East 300, 3rd Floor, P.O. Box 146600, Salt Lake City, UT 84114-6600; 801-530-6921. Authorizing statute: Utah Code Ann. §34-40-103 |
| Vermont | $5.25 or the federal minimum wage, if it is higher. Not applicable to state employees, retail or service establishments, amusement or recreational facilities, hotels, restaurants. certain hospitals, public health centers or nursing homes. Vt. Stat. Ann. tit. 21, §384a |
| Virginia | Not less than the federal minimum wage. Va. Code Ann. §40.1-28.10 |
| Washington | $4.90. Wash. Rev. Code Ann. §49.46.020 |
| West Virginia | $5.15. Training wage of $4.25 for employees under age 20 for first 90 days. W.Va. Code §21-5C-2a |
| Wisconsin | $5.15. Minimum wage for employees under 20 years old during their first 90 days of employment is $4.25. Minimum wage for adult agricultural workers is $4.05, for minor agricultural workers the wage is $3.70. Minimum wage for employees who receive tips is $2.33.<br>Set by wage order of the Dept. of Industry, Labor and Human Relations Regulations, P.O. Box 7946, Madison, WI 53707; 608-266-6860. Authorizing statute: Wis. Stat. Ann. §104.02 |
| Wyoming | $1.60. Wyo. Stat. §27-4-202 |

## b. Paying for overtime

The FLSA does not limit the number of hours an employee may work in a week—except through some of the child labor rules. But it does require that any covered worker who works more than 40 hours in one week must be paid at least one-and-one-half times his or her regular rate of pay for every hour worked in excess of 40.

There is no legal requirement that workers must receive overtime pay simply because they worked more than eight hours in one day. Nor is there anything that requires a worker to be paid on the spot for overtime. Under the FLSA, you are allowed to calculate and pay overtime by the week—which can be any 168-hour period made up of seven consecutive 24-hour periods.

However, the FLSA requires consistency. You cannot manipulate the start of the workweek to avoid paying overtime.

Also, because of the nature of the work involved, commonsense—and the law—both dictate that some jobs are exempt from the overtime pay requirements of the FLSA.

The most common of these jobs include:

- commissioned employees of retail or service establishments
- some auto, truck, trailer, farm implement, boat or aircraft workers
- railroad and air carrier employees, taxi drivers, certain employees of motor carriers, seamen on American vessels, and local delivery employees
- announcers, news editors and chief engineers of small nonmetropolitan broadcasting stations
- domestic service workers who live in their employer's residence
- employees of motion picture theaters, and
- farmworkers.

And finally, some employees may be partially exempt from the FLSA's overtime pay requirements. The most common of this hybrid type is an employee who works in a hospital or residential care establishment who agrees to work a 14-day work period. However, these employees must be paid overtime pay for all hours worked over eight in a day or 80 in the 14-day work period, whichever is the greater number of overtime hours.

## REVAMPING THE OVERTIME SYSTEM

Under current laws, the strict but confusing rules on overtime entitle about 75 million workers to overtime pay for hours they work over 40 in a week.

The notion of paying a premium for overtime work hours harkens back to the 1930s, when employers were encouraged to hire more workers rather than pay high rates to a select few.

But these days, a growing number of people claim that overtime pay is an anachronism.

Many employers, oblivious to or unmindful of overtime pay strictures, routinely deny workers the extra pay they have coming. Few of them get caught. The Labor Department currently collects only about $100 million a year in back overtime—a small drop in its oversize bucket.

But those that do get caught by the Department of Labor pay dearly. Employees lose their exempt status, which means they must be paid overtime—and they must be paid any overtime pay due them during the last two years.

Some employers unwittingly become liable for large overtime claims by putting conditions on exempt, salaried employees. Some courts have held, for example, that executive employees who are suspended without pay or docked for taking partial days off have been treated as nonexempt workers and so become entitled to overtime pay and other benefits guaranteed by the FLSA.

Many employees, citing increased difficulties over balancing time between work and personal lives, say they would prefer more flexibility over more take-home pay. Restructuring proposals which also have the support of many small business organizations include the plan to abandon the 40-hour workweek. If, for example, entitlement to overtime were based on a two-week, 80-hour work schedule, an employee would be free to work 75 hours in one week and a mere five the next without being entitled to overtime pay.

### c. Paying for compensatory time

Most employers are familiar with compensatory or comp time—the practice of offering employees time off from work in place of cash payments for overtime. What comes as a shock to many is that the practice is illegal in most situations. Under the FLSA, only state or government agencies may legally allow their employees time off in place of wages (29 U.S.C. §207(o)).

Even then, comp time may be awarded only:

- according to the terms of a collective bargaining unit agreement, or

- if the employer and employee agree to the arrangement before work begins.

When compensatory time is allowed, it must be awarded at the rate of one-and-a-half times the overtime hours worked—and comp time must be taken during the same pay period that the overtime hours were worked.

Many employers and employees routinely violate the rules governing the use of compensatory time in place of cash overtime wages. However, such violations are risky. As an employer, you risk feeling the pain in your pocketbook: You could end up owing large amounts of overtime pay to employees as the result of a labor department investigation and prosecution of compensatory time violations.

**Beware of State Law Twists.** Some states do allow private employers to give employees comp time instead of cash. But there are complex, often conflicting laws controlling how and when it may be given. A common control, for example, is that employees must voluntarily request in writing that comp time be given instead of overtime pay—before the extra hours are worked. Check with your state's labor department for special laws on comp time in your area.

## WHEN IS ON THE JOB ON THE JOB?

In calculating hours worked, most concerns and claims focus on how to deal with specific questionable situations, such as travel time, time spent at seminars, waiting periods, on-call periods and sleeping on the job.

**Travel time.** The time spent commuting between home and the normal place of work is not considered to be on-the-job time for which you must pay. But it may be payable time if the commute is actually part of the job or if you require employees to go to and from the normal worksite at odd hours in emergency situations.

**Lectures, meetings and training seminars.** Generally, if you require a nonexempt employee to attend a lecture, meeting or training seminar, you must pay him or her for that time—including travel time if the meeting is away from the worksite.

The specific exception to this rule is that you need not pay if:
- the event is outside of regular working hours
- attendance is voluntary
- the instruction session isn't directly related to the employee's particular job, and
- the employee does not perform any productive work during the instruction session.

**Waiting periods.** Time periods when employees are not actually working, but are required to stay on the work premises or at some other designated spot while waiting for a work assignment, are covered as part of payable time. For example, a driver for a private ambulance service who is required to sit in the ambulance garage waiting for calls must be paid for the waiting time.

**On-call periods.** A growing number of employers are paying on-call premiums—or sleeper pay—to workers who agree to be available to be reached outside regular worktime and respond by phone or computer within a certain period. Some plans pay an hourly rate for the time spent on call; some pay a flat rate. If you require employees to be on call but do not require them to stay on the company's premises, then the following two rules generally apply.

- On-call time that they are allowed to control and use for their own enjoyment or benefit is not counted as payable time.

- On-call time over which they have little or no control and which they cannot use for their own enjoyment or benefit is payable time.

Unless there's an employment contract that states otherwise, employers are generally allowed to pay a different hourly rate for on-call time than they do for regular worktime, and many do. You need only make sure that the employees are paid at least the minimum amount required under wage and hour regulations.

**Sleep time.** If you require an employee to be on duty at your place of employment for less than 24 hours at a time, any time they are allowed to sleep during a shift of duty is counted as payable time. If you require them to be at work for more than 24 hours at a time, you may exclude up to eight hours per day from the payable time as sleep and meal periods.

## 4. Penalties for Retaliation

A whopping majority of the states have laws that specifically protect from retaliation employees who file complaints or testify in investigations controlled by the wage and hour statutes. Most of these laws simply provide that employees cannot be fired for filing wage and hour complaints. Several protect those who testify at a wage and hour dispute on their own behalf or on behalf of another employee.

A number of laws pack a wallop for employers who violate their strictures. In Alaska, for example, violators can be fined up to $2,000 and jailed for up to 20 days—and each day of a violation counts as a separate offense.

## STATE LAWS PROHIBITING RETALIATION

| | |
|---|---|
| Alabama | No statute |
| Alaska | An employer may not discriminate against or discharge an employee who has complained, instituted a proceeding or testified in a proceeding regarding the minimum wage act. Violations are a fine of $100 to $2,000, ten to 20 days in jail or both. Each day a violation occurs constitutes a separate offense. Alaska Stat. §§23.10.135 and 140 |
| Arizona | Employees cannot be fired or discriminated against for serving on or testifying before a wage board. Ariz. Rev. Stat. Ann. §23-329<br>An employer may not discriminate against anyone who has opposed, made a charge, testified or participated in a hearing of an alleged violation of the Arizona Civil Rights Act. Ariz. Rev. Stat. Ann. §§41-1401 and following, Ariz. Rev. Stat. Ann. §41-1464 |
| Arkansas | It is a misdemeanor to retaliate against an employee who complains, testifies or participates in proceedings instituted by the Department of Labor with respect to equal wages for males and females. Ark. Code Ann. 11-4-608 |
| California | Employees cannot be fired for asserting rights under the jurisdiction of the Labor Commissioner. Cal. Lab. Code §98.6<br>Employees cannot be fired for refusing to work hours in excess of those permitted by the Industrial Welfare Commission. Cal. Lab. Code §1198.3 |
| Colorado | Employers cannot fire or otherwise discriminate against employees for participating in any wage and hour proceeding. Colo. Rev. Stat. §8-6-115<br>It is a misdemeanor to threaten, blacklist or in any way discriminate against an employee who has complained about a violation of the state wage law or who has instituted a proceeding concerning the state wage law. Colo. Rev. Stat. §8-4-124 |

| | |
|---|---|
| **Connecticut** | Employees may not be disciplined in any manner for reporting violations of minimum wage laws. Conn. Public Act 97-263, §18 |
| **Delaware** | Employees may not be fired for participating in a proceeding under wage payment and collection law. Del. Code Ann. tit. 19 §1112 |
| **District of Columbia** | Employees may not be fired for filing a complaint or participating in a proceeding to enforce the minimum wage law. D.C. Code Ann. §36-220.9 |
| **Florida** | No statute |
| **Georgia** | No statute |
| **Hawaii** | Employees may sue employers if they are fired for reporting a violation of law to a public agency. Haw. Rev. Stat. §378.62 |
| **Idaho** | Employees cannot be fired or discriminated against for participating in proceedings under the minimum wage law. Idaho Code §44-1509 |
| **Illinois** | An employer may not discharge or discriminate against any employee who testifies, cooperates or brings a complaint to a wage board; or who serves as a member of a wage board. 820 Ill. Comp. Stat. 125/15<br>A whistleblower under the Prevailing Wage Act may not be discriminated against or discharged. 820 Ill. Comp. Stat. 130/11b |
| **Indiana** | Employees may not be fired for participating in an action to recover wages  under the state wage and hour law. Ind. Code Ann. §22-2-2-11 |
| **Iowa** | Employees cannot be fired for participation in wage and hour proceedings. Iowa Code §91A.10(5) |
| **Kansas** | An employer who discharges or discriminates against an employee who has filed a complaint, participated in proceedings or initiated proceedings with respect to the wage board shall be fined $250 to $1,000. Kan. Stat. Ann. §44-1210 |
| **Kentucky** | Employees cannot be fired for exercising rights under wage and hour law. Ky. Rev. Stat. §337.550 |

| | |
|---|---|
| **Louisiana** | Employees may not be fired or in any way discriminated against for testifying regarding enforcement of any labor laws. Criminal penalties are a fine of $100 to $250, 30 to 90 days in jail or both. La. Rev. Stat. Ann. §23:964 |
| **Maine** | An employer who discharges or otherwise discriminates against an employee who makes a complaint concerning minimum wages is subject to a $50 to $200 fine. Me. Rev. Stat. tit. 26 §671 |
| **Maryland** | An employer may not discharge an employee because that employee made a complaint to the commissioner of labor or an authorized representative that the employee has not been paid in accord with the minimum wage law. Md. Labor and Emp. Code §3-428 <br><br> An employer may not discharge or otherwise discriminate against an employee who makes a complaint to the commissioner of labor or any person regarding equal pay for equal work or any subject that relates to equal pay for equal work. Md. Labor and Emp. Code §3-308 |
| **Massachusetts** | No employee may be penalized by an employer for seeking rights under the wage and hours law. Mass. Gen. Laws Ann. ch. 149 §148A |
| **Michigan** | Employees may not be fired for protesting violations or participating in proceedings regarding the state minimum wage law. Mich Stat. Ann. §17.255(15) |
| **Minnesota** | Employees cannot be fired for giving testimony with regard to minimum wage violations. Minn. Stat. Ann. §177.32 <br><br> The same protections apply to testimony concerning violations of the Minnesota Labor Relations Act. Minn. Stat. Ann. §179.12 |
| **Mississippi** | No statute |
| **Missouri** | An employer may not discharge or in any way discriminate against an employee who has complained, testified or caused a proceeding to be instituted regarding the minimum wage law. Mo. Ann. Stat. §290.525(7) |
| **Montana** | No statute |

| | |
|---|---|
| **Nebraska** | Employees who attempt to enforce the state's equal pay law for women's and men's wages are protected from retaliation. Neb. Rev. Stat. §48-1221(4) |
| **Nevada** | An employee who is paid less than the minimum wage can sue for the difference within two years. Neither a contract for employment that specifies a lower wage, nor the employee's acceptance of the lower wage, shall bar the employee's lawsuit. An employer who violates the minimum wage law is guilty of a misdemeanor. If a district attorney fails to commence an investigation within 20 days of receiving a complaint, and the complaint is taken over by the attorney general and proves meritorious, the district attorney is guilty of a misdemeanor and shall be removed from office. Nev. Rev. Stat. §608.260 and §608.290 |
| **New Hampshire** | No statute |
| **New Jersey** | An employer who fires or in any way discriminates against an employee who complains, institutes a proceeding or testifies regarding wage law violations will be guilty of a disorderly person offense and fined $100 to $1,000, and ordered to reinstate the employee or to correct any discriminatory action. Further penalties may be imposed. N.J. Stat. Ann. 34:11-56a24 |
| **New Mexico** | No statute |
| **New York** | Employers cannot fire or in any way discriminate against employees because of labor complaints to the employer or Labor Commissioner. N.Y. Lab. Law §215 Employers cannot fire or in any way discriminate against employees because of wage complaints. N.Y. Lab. Law §662 |
| **North Carolina** | Employers cannot fire or take any retaliatory action against employees who, in good faith, file or threaten to file a wage claim. N.C. Gen. Stat. §§95-240 and 95-241(a)(1)(b) |
| **North Dakota** | An employer may not discharge or in any way discriminate against an employee who has testified or is about to testify in any proceeding relative to hours and wages. N.D. Century Code §34-06-18 |

| | |
|---|---|
| **Ohio** | An employer may not discharge or discriminate against an employee for filing a complaint, lodging a claim or testifying in any proceeding regarding the wage laws. Ohio Rev. Code §4111.13(B) |
| **Oklahoma** | It is a misdemeanor for any employer to discharge or penalize an employee who files a complaint, institutes an investigation or testifies in any proceeding relative to the minimum wage law. Okla. Stat. Ann. tit. 40 §199 |
| **Oregon** | Employers cannot fire employees because of filing a wage claim. Penalties include actual damages not less than $200, but not reinstatement. Or. Rev. Stat. §652.355 |
| **Pennsylvania** | An employer who discharges or in any way discriminates against an employee who testifies in any proceeding under the wage laws is liable for a fine of $500 to $1,000 or, if the employer fails to pay the fine, of imprisonment of ten to 90 days. 43 Pa. Stat. Ann. §333.112 |
| **Rhode Island** | An employer may not discharge or discriminate against an employee because he or someone acting on his behalf reports or is about to report to the Department of Labor a violation of the wage laws. R.I. Gen. Laws §§28-14-16 and 18 |
| **South Carolina** | No statute |
| **South Dakota** | Employers may not fire or otherwise discriminate against employees for wage complaints. S.D. Codified Laws Ann. §60-11-17.1 |
| **Tennessee** | Employees who invoke the state's equal pay laws for women and men are protected from retaliation. Tenn. Code Ann. §50-2-202(c) |
| **Texas** | No statute |
| **Utah** | Employers may not discharge or threaten to discharge an employee who files a complaint or testifies in proceedings to enforce the state wage laws. Utah Code Ann. §34-28-19 |

| Vermont | An employer may not discharge or in any way discriminate against an employee who has served or is about to serve on a wage board or has testified or is about to testify before a board or because the employer thinks an employee is about to serve or testify. Vt. Stat. Ann. tit. 21 §394 |
|---|---|
| Virginia | No statute |
| Washington | An employer who discharges or discriminates against an employee who files a complaint, institutes a proceeding or has testified or is about to testify before a wage board is guilty of a gross misdemeanor. Wash. Rev. Code Ann §49.46.100(2) |
| West Virginia | Employers who fire or otherwise discriminate against employees for wage complaints are guilty of a misdemeanor and subject to a fine of not more than $100. W. Va. Code §21-5C-7 |
| Wisconsin | Employers cannot fire employees for testifying at wage complaint proceedings. Wis. Stat. Ann. §104.10 |
| Wyoming | No statute |

# B. Payroll Withholding and Deductions

The laws that created the income tax and Social Security programs typically authorize payroll withholding to finance those programs. But a growing number of additional deductions are now also authorized.

## 1. What You Can Deduct or Withhold

In addition to Social Security and local, state and federal taxes, you may also make several other deductions from minimum wages: costs of meals, housing and transportation, loans, debts owed the employer, child support and alimony, payroll savings plans and insurance premiums. As in most other workplace laws, there are exceptions to these rules. And there are often limitations on how much you may withhold or deduct from a paycheck.

### a. Meals, housing and transportation

You may legally deduct from an employee's paycheck the "reasonable cost or fair value" of meals, housing, fuel and transportation to and from work.

But to deduct any of these amounts from a paycheck, you must show that you customarily paid these expenses and that:

- they were for the employee's benefit
- the employee was told in advance about the deductions, and
- the employee voluntarily accepted the meals and other accommodations against minimum wage.

### b. Loans

If you have loaned an employee money, you can withhold money from his or her pay to satisfy that loan. However, it is illegal to make any such deduction if it would reduce the pay to below the minimum wage.

### c. Wage garnishments

A judge may send you a legal order requiring that you withhold money from an employee's paycheck to satisfy a debt the employee owes to someone else. This process is called wage attachment or garnishment.

The order itself should state the timelines and procedures you must follow in enforcing it. You will be fined if you fail to comply.

There are also limits on how much particular creditors can take each pay period. A federal law, the Consumer Credit Protection Act (15 U.S.C. §1673), prohibits judgment creditors from taking more than 25% of an employee's net earnings through a wage garnishment to satisfy a debt. A few states offer employees greater protection, however. In Delaware, for example, judgment creditors cannot take more than 15% of an individual's wages.

The Consumer Credit Protection Act also prohibits you from firing an employee because his or her wages are garnished to satisfy a single debt. If two judgment creditors garnish wages or one judgment creditor garnishes wages to pay two different judgments, however, you are free to fire that employee. Also, many state statutes prohibit employers from retaliating against an employee for being subject to a wage garnishment. They differ in how many garnishments an employee is allowed per year and still have his or her job protected.

Another type of anti-retribution for wage garnishment statute is one that applies when income is withheld to satisfy child support obligations. You may not fire employees merely because they are subject to this type of order, regardless of the quantity of garnishments.

Of course, none of these statutes prohibit firing for just cause. They only prohibit firing an employee solely because of the wage garnishment.

A number of states—including Nebraska, New York, Utah, Washington, West Virginia and Wisconsin—extend some protections to job applicants as well.

## STATE LAWS ON WAGE GARNISHMENTS

| | |
|---|---|
| Alabama | Employees may not be fired for having wages garnished for child support obligations. Ala. Code §30-3-70 |
| Alaska | Employees may not be fired for having wages assigned for child support obligations. Alaska Stat. §25.27.062 |
| Arizona | Employees may not be fired or disciplined because of wage assignment to provide child support obligations. Ariz. Rev. Stat. §23-722.02 |
| Arkansas | Employees may not be fired or disciplined for having a wage assignment for child support obligations. Ark. Stat. Ann. §9-14-226 |
| California | Employees may not be fired for having one wage garnishment. Cal. Lab. Code §2929b |
| Colorado | Employees may not be fired for having wages garnished. Colo. Rev. Stat. §13-54.5-110 |
| Connecticut | Employees may not be fired for having wages garnished unless they have more than seven in one calendar year. Conn. Gen. Stat. Ann. §52-361a(j) |
| Delaware | Employees may not be fired for having wages garnished. Del. Code Ann. tit. 10 §3509 |
| District of Columbia | Employees may not be fired for having wages garnished. D.C. Code Ann. §16-584 |
| Florida | Any disciplinary action by an employer against an employee because of a garnishment order constitutes contempt of court. Fla. Stat. §61.12(2) |
| Georgia | Employees may not be fired for having one wage garnishment. Ga. Code Ann. §18-4-7 |
| Hawaii | Employees may not be fired for having a wage assignment for child support obligations. Haw. Rev. Stat. §378-2(2)(5)<br>Employees may not be fired for having wages garnished. Haw. Rev. Stat. §378-32(1) |

| | |
|---|---|
| Idaho | An employer may not discharge an employee on the basis of a garnishment order to pay a judgment arising from a regulated consumer credit transaction. Idaho Code §28-45-105 |
| Illinois | An employee may not be discharged because of a single garnishment. The law does not protect against firing for multiple garnishments. 735 Ill. Comp. Stat. 5/12-818 |
| Indiana | Employees may not be fired for having one or more wage garnishments. Ind. Code Ann. §24-4.5-5-106 |
| Iowa | An employer who dismisses an employee due to an assignment order for child support commits a simple misdemeanor. Iowa Code §252D.17 |
| Kansas | Employees may not be fired for having wages garnished. Kan. Stat. Ann. §60-2311 |
| Kentucky | Employees may not be fired for having one wage garnishment. Ky. Rev. Stat. §427.140 |
| Louisiana | Employees may not be fired for having one wage garnishment. An employee may be discharged for having three or more garnishments in a two-year period. La. Rev. Stat. Ann. §23:731 |
| Maine | Employees may not be fired for having wages garnished. Me. Rev. Stat. Ann. tit. 14, §3127-B(6) |
| Maryland | Employees may not be fired for having one wage garnishment in a year. Md. Com. Law Code Ann. §15-606 |
| Massachusetts | No statute |
| Michigan | Employees may not be fired for having one or more garnishments. Mich Comp. Laws §§600.4015 and following |
| Minnesota | Employees may not be fired for having wages garnished. Minn. Stat. Ann. §571.927 |
| Mississippi | Employees may not be fired for having wages garnished for child or spousal support obligations. Miss. Code Ann. §93-11-111 |

| | |
|---|---|
| **Missouri** | Employees may not be fired or discriminated against for having one wage garnishment. Mo. Ann. Stat. §525.030 Employees may not be fired for having wages assigned for child support obligations. Mo. Ann. Stat. §452.350 |
| **Montana** | Employees may not be fired or discriminated against for having wages assigned for child support obligations. Mont. Code Ann. §40-5-422 An employer may not fire an employee because of a garnishment of wages. Mont. Code §39-2-302 |
| **Nebraska** | Employees may not be fired for having one wage garnishment. Neb. Rev. Stat. §25-1558 Employees may not be discriminated against in hiring or be fired, demoted or disciplined for having wages assigned for child support obligations. Neb. Rev. Stat. §43-1725 |
| **Nevada** | Employees may not be fired for having wages garnished. Nev. Rev. Stat. §31.298 |
| **New Hampshire** | Employees may not be fired for having wages garnished for child support obligations. N.H. Rev. Stat. Ann. §458-B:6 |
| **New Jersey** | Employees may not be fired for having one or more wage garnishments. N.J. Stat. Ann. §2A:170-90.4 |
| **New Mexico** | Employees may not be fired for having wages garnished for child support obligations. N.M. Stat. Ann. §40-4A-11 |
| **New York** | Prospective employees cannot be denied employment because of past wage garnishments or the pendency of a court action for a wage garnishment. Current employees may not be fired or disciplined because of a past or current garnishment, nor because of a pending court action to garnish wages. N.Y. Civ. Prac. L. & R. §5252 |
| **North Carolina** | Employees may not be fired for having wages garnished for child support obligations. N.C. Gen. Stat. §110.136.8 Employees may not be fired for having wages garnished to pay debts for services rendered at a public hospital. N.C. Gen. Stat. §131E-50 |

| | |
|---|---|
| **North Dakota** | Employees may not be fired for having wages garnished, and may sue for twice the amount of wages withheld, plus reinstatement. N.D. Cent. Code §32-09.1-18<br>Employers who fire or in any way penalize an employee whose wages have been ordered withheld for child support may be sued for reinstatement, lost wages and attorneys' fees. N.D. Cent. Code §§14.09-09.3 |
| **Ohio** | An employer who discharges an employee because of a child support deduction order is subject to a fine of $50 to $250 and ten to 30 days in jail. Ohio Rev. Code §§2301.39 and .99<br>No employer may discharge an employee on the basis of one garnishment in any 12-month period. Ohio Rev. Code §2716.05 |
| **Oklahoma** | An employer may not discharge or discipline an employee because of a wage assignment. An employer who does becomes liable for all lost wages and benefits, plus reinstatement. Okla. Stat. Ann. tit. 56 §240.2.E.8<br>Employees may not be fired for having wages garnished, unless more than two in a year. Okla. Stat. Ann. tit. 14A, §5-106 |
| **Oregon** | Employees may not be fired for having wages garnished. Or. Rev. Stat. §23.185 |
| **Pennsylvania** | Employees may not be fired or disciplined for having wages garnished for child support obligations. Pa. Cons. Stat. Ann. tit. 23, §4348 |
| **Rhode Island** | An employer who discharges or discriminates against an employee on account of a garnishment for child support shall be liable for all damages, a $100 fine and an order of reinstatement. R.I. Gen. Laws §15-5-26 |
| **South Carolina** | Employees may not be fired for having wages garnished for consumer debt. S.C. Code Ann. §37-5-106<br>Employees may not be fired for having wages garnished for child support. S.C. Code Ann. §§20-7-1315(F)(9) and (I)(1)<br>An employer who discharges an employee for wage garnishment or refuses to withhold wages per the order is subject to a fine of up to $500. |

| | |
|---|---|
| **South Dakota** | Employers who discharge or discriminate against an employee because of a garnishment order for child support are guilty of a petty offense. S.D. Codified Laws Ann. §25-7A-46 |
| **Tennessee** | No statute |
| **Texas** | Employees may not be fired or disciplined for having wages garnished for child support obligations, nor may an employer refuse to employ because of an order to withhold wages. Tex. Fam. Code Ann. §158.209 |
| **Utah** | Employees may not be fired for having one wage garnishment. Utah Code Ann. §70C-7-104<br>An employer who discharges, refuses to employ or takes disciplinary action against an employee because of an order to withhold wages for child support is liable for the amount not withheld up to the date of discharge or $1,000, whichever is greater. Utah Code Ann. §62A-11-316 |
| **Vermont** | Garnishment is known in Vermont as the trustee process. No employer may discharge an employee because of trustee process. Any firing within 60 days of trustee process is presumed to be in retaliation, which the employer may disprove with evidence that it was done for cause. An employee fired in retaliation for trustee process is entitled to reinstatement, back wages, damages and court costs. Vt. Stat. Ann. tit. 12 §3172<br>Employees may not be fired for having wages assigned for child support. Vt. Stat. Ann. tit. 15 §790 |
| **Virginia** | Employees may not be fired for having wages garnished for one debt. Va. Code §34-29f<br>No employer shall discharge or take any retaliatory action against an employee or refuse to employ an applicant because his or her earnings have been subjected to a withholding order for child support. Va. Code Ann. §20-79.3.A(9)<br>No employer may discharge an employee because of a voluntary assignment of earnings to settle a support debt or lien or because an order to withhold has been served against the employer. Va. Code Ann. §63.1-271 |

| Washington | Employees may not be fired for having wages garnished, unless the employee has three or more within a year. Wash. Rev. Code Ann. §6.27.170 <br> No employer may discharge or discriminate against an employee, or refuse to hire an applicant, because of an assignment of earnings for child support. Violations of the statute subject the employer to double the amount of lost wages, damages, costs and attorney fees and a civil penalty of not more than $2,500 per violation, plus court orders to rehire, reinstate or hire. Wash. Rev. Code Ann. §§26.18.110 and 74.20A.230 |
|---|---|
| West Virginia | Employees may not be fired or receive any reprisals for having wages garnished for a consumer credit sale or loan. W. Va. Code §46A-2-131 <br> Employees may not be fired or discriminated against, nor applicants not hired, for having wages garnished for spousal or child support obligation. W. Va. Code §48A-5-3(r) |
| Wisconsin | Employees may not be fired for having wages garnished. Wis. Stat. Ann. §812.43 <br> Employees may not be fired or disciplined, nor may job applicants be refused, for having wages garnished for child support. Wis. Stat. Ann. §767.265(6)(c) |
| Wyoming | Employees may not be fired, disciplined or penalized for having wages garnished. Wyo. Stat. §1-15-509 <br> Employees may not be fired for having wages garnished for child support obligations. Wyo. Stat. §20-6-218 |

## d. Student loans

The federal Emergency Unemployment Compensation Act of 1991 authorizes the U.S. Department of Education or any agency trying to collect a student loan on behalf of the Department of Education to garnish up to 10% of a former student's net pay if he or she is in default on a student loan.

### e. Child support and alimony

The federal Family Support Act of 1988 (102 U.S. Stat. §2343) requires that all new or modified child support orders include an automatic wage withholding order. If you have an employee subject to such an order, you must send a portion of his or her pay to the parent who has custody.

In most states, where there is not an automatic wage attachment—usually, where the support order has been in effect for a while—you must withhold wages if an employee is one month delinquent in paying support. But you cannot discipline, fire or refuse to hire an employee because his or her pay is subject to a child support wage withholding order. You are subject to a fine if you do discriminate in this way.

### f. Back taxes

If an employee owes back taxes and does not pay, the IRS, known for its tenacity, can grab most—but not all—of his or her wages. The amount that an employee can keep is determined by the number of dependents and the standard tax deduction to which he or she is entitled.

Most state and some municipal taxing authorities also have the power to seize a portion of your employee's wages—and some act even more quickly than the IRS does when the employee owes back taxes. State laws vary, however, as to the maximum amount of wages that the state can take.

## 2. What You Cannot Deduct or Withhold

Only a few things are sacrosanct and may not usually be deducted from an employee's paycheck:

- the value of time taken for meal periods (see Chapter 6)
- the cost of broken merchandise
- tools and materials used on the job
- required uniforms, and
- cash register shortages and losses due to theft. ■

# Giving Time Off

No law requires you to pay employees for time off, such as vacation, holidays or sick days. Although most employers give fulltime workers some paid time off each year, laws such as the Federal Labor Standards Act currently cover payment only for time on the job. (See Chapter 5.)

However, there are a number of legal mandates, most often buried in state labor and employment codes, that contain detailed requirements for how and when you must give workers time off to attend to personal needs or business. This chapter contains a passel of charts that summarize individual state requirements for situations when you must allow employees time off—including meal and rest breaks, jury duty, voting, military leave and more.

## A. Meal and Rest Breaks

Federal law does not require that you give time off or pay for breaks to eat meals. However, many states have laws specifically requiring that employees be allowed a half hour or so in meal and rest breaks during each workday. (See the chart below.)

You usually need not count meal breaks of 30 minutes or more as part of payable work hours—as long as you completely relieve workers of work duties during that time. Technically, however, if you either require that employees work while eating—or allow them to do so—you must pay for time spent during meals. Also, you must pay for break periods that are less than 20 minutes.

## STATE MEAL AND REST BREAK LAWS

**Alabama**

No one 15 or younger shall be required to work five continuous hours without a meal or rest break of at least 30 minutes. Ala. Code §25-8-38(c)

**Alaska**

Employees under the age of 18 who work at least a six-hour shift have the right to take an unpaid 30-minute break after their first five hours of work. Does not apply to employees in fishing or farming or who work for a family member. Alaska Stat. §23.10.350

**Arizona**

No statute

**Arkansas**

No statute

**California**

Meal—30 minutes within five hours of starting work if workday is six hours or more. If less, waivable.
Rest—ten minutes per four-hour period. Compensated. Does not apply to motion picture, agricultural and household occupations. Cal. Code of Regs., tit. 8, ch. 5, Group 2

**Colorado**

Meal—30 minutes unpaid within five hours of starting work.
Rest—ten minutes per four hours paid.
Applies only to employees in retail, service, commercial support service, food and beverage and health industries. Wage Order No. 22

**Connecticut**

Meal—30 minutes per 7 1/2 hour workday; given after second hour and before last two hours. Conn. Gen. Stat. §31-51ii

**Delaware**

Meal—30 minutes for 7 1/2 hour workday; given after second hour and before last two hours. Does not apply to public school teachers. Del. Code Ann. tit. 19, §707

**District of Columnia**

No statute

| | |
|---|---|
| Florida | Employees age 17 and under are entitled to a 30-minute break for every four hours of work. Does not apply to minors with high school diplomas, who are employed as domestic servants or by their parents, who are pages in the state legislature, who have a certificate of exemption from compulsory education or who receive a hardship or family emergency waiver from the school superintendent. Fla. Stat. Ann. §450.081 |
| Georgia | No statute |
| Hawaii | Meal—45 minutes for government employees only. Haw. Rev. Stat. §80—1 |
| Idaho | No statute |
| Illinois | Meal—20 minutes for a 7 1/2 hour workday beginning no later than five hours into the work period. 820 Ill. Comp. Stat. 140/3 |
| Indiana | No statute |
| Iowa | Employees under the age of 16 who work five or more hours are entitled to an intermission of 30 minutes. Iowa Code §92.7 |
| Kansas | No statute |
| Kentucky | Meal—"Reasonable" break between three and five hours into the work period. Rest—ten minutes per four hours. Statute does not apply to railroad employees. Ky. Rev. Stat. Ann. §§337.355 and 337.365 |
| Louisiana | Divers and tunnel and caisson workers who use compressed air must be given the following rest intervals between shifts, in the open air: 0–26 pounds, one hour; 26–33 pounds, two hours; 33–38 pounds, three hours; 38–43 pounds, four hours; 43–48 pounds, five hours; 48–50 pounds, six hours. La. Rev. Stat. Ann. §23:486 |
| Maine | Meal—30 minutes per six hours of work for meals or rest. Does not apply if there are fewer than three employees on duty. Me. Rev. Stat. Ann. tit. 26, §§601 and 602 |

| Maryland | Employees under the age of 18 get a 30-minute break every five hours. Md. Code Ann. Lab. and Emp. §3-210(a) |
|---|---|
| Massachusetts | Meal—30 minutes per six-hour work period. Mass. Gen. Laws Ann. ch. 149, §100 |
| Michigan | Minors who are employed more than five continuous hours must be given 30 minutes for a meal or rest break. Mich. Comp. Laws §409.112 |
| Minnesota | Meal—Employer must allow "adequate time" to eat a meal during an eight-hour work period. Minn. Stat. Ann. §177.254<br>Rest—Employer must allow a "reasonable" amount of time in a four-hour period to use the restroom. Minn. Stat. Ann. §177.253 |
| Mississippi | No statute |
| Missouri | No statute |
| Montana | No statute |
| Nebraska | All employees in assembly plants, workshops or mechanical establishments are required to have at least 30-minute lunch breaks between noon and 1 p.m. without having to remain on the premises unless it operates 24 hours per day. Neb. Rev. Stat. §48-212 |
| Nevada | Meal—30 minutes per eight hours of work.<br>Rest—ten minutes per four hours of work.<br>Nev. Rev. Stat. Ann. §608.019 |
| New Hampshire | Meal—30 minutes per five hours of work, except if it is feasible for the employee to eat while working and the employer allows him or her to do so. N.H. Rev. Stat. Ann. §275:30-a |
| New Jersey | Employees under the age of 18 are entitled to take a 30-minute break for every five hours of work. N.J. Stat. Ann. §34-2-21.4 |
| New Mexico | Women's working hours are restricted to eight hours per day and 48 hours per week, except for domestic workers and workers in interstate commerce. Those employees must be given a 30-minute rest period, which is not counted as part of the working day. N.M. Stat. Ann. §§50-5-1 to 4 |

| | |
|---|---|
| **New York** | Meal—Mercantile or similar establishments: 30 minutes; Factory: 60 minutes. If shift begins before 11 a.m. and extends past 7 p.m., an additional 20 minutes is given to factory and mercantile workers between 5 p.m. and 7 p.m. |
| | If shift is more than six hours long and begins between 1 p.m. and 6 a.m., mercantile employees must receive 45 minutes and factory employees 60 minutes at a point midway through the shift. N.Y. Labor Law §162 |
| **North Carolina** | Minors are entitled to take a 30-minute break for every five hours of work. N.C. Gen. Stat. §95-25.5 |
| **North Dakota** | Meal—30 minutes if shift is over five hours. By wage order. Commissioner of Labor sets the standards. N.D. Century Code §34-06-03 |
| **Ohio** | No statute |
| **Oklahoma** | Employees under the age of 16 may take a one-hour break for every eight hours of work and cannot work more than five consecutive hours without at least a 30-minute break. Okla. Stat. Ann., tit. 40, §75 |
| **Oregon** | Meal—30 minutes for each work period of between six and eight hours within the 2nd and 5th hour worked. Or, if work period is more than seven hours, a break must be given between the third and sixth hour worked. Rest—ten minutes for every four hours worked. Or. Admin. Rules §839-020–050 |
| **Pennsylvania** | Seasonal farmworkers and employees under the age of 18 are entitled to take a 30-minute break per five hours of work. Pa. Cons. Stat. Ann., tit. 43, §46 |
| **Rhode Island** | Meal—20 minutes per six hours of work. R.I. Gen. Laws §28-3-14 |
| **South Carolina** | No statute |
| **South Dakota** | No statute |

| | |
|---|---|
| **Tennessee** | Meal—30 unpaid minutes for six-hour work period, except in workplaces that by their nature provide for ample opportunity to rest or take an appropriate break. Tenn. Code Ann. §50-2-103 |
| **Texas** | No statute |
| **Utah** | No statute |
| **Vermont** | Employees must be afforded a reasonable opportunity to eat and use toilet facilities during work periods. Vt. Stan. Ann. tit. 21, §304 |
| **Virginia** | No statute |
| **Washington** | Meal—30 minutes per five-hour work period. Rest—ten minutes per four-hour work period unless the nature of the work allows the employee to take intermittent rest breaks equivalent to ten minutes per four hours. Wash. Admin. Code 296-126-092 |
| **West Virginia** | Meal—20 minutes per six-hour work period. W.Va. Code §21-3-10a |
| **Wisconsin** | Meal—30 minutes close to usual meal time or near middle of shift. Shifts of more than six hours without a meal break should be avoided. Break mandatory for minors. Wis. Admin. Code, Ind. 74.02 |
| **Wyoming** | No statute |

# B. Jury Duty

Legislators treat jury duty as a serious civic charge. Many state laws contain an anti-discrimination twist—baldly stating that employees called to serve on juries may not be fired or otherwise treated negatively for doing so. And a few laws broadly restrict employers from attempting to intimidate employees not to serve on juries.

But these days, with employees laboring under the fear of losing their jobs and employers anxious watching their bottom lines, the issue of taking time off for jury duty looms ever larger. The two major concerns are:

- whether employers must pay employees who are called as jurors, and

- what the penalties are for employers who violate statutes that protect employees on jury duty.

Unless your employee handbook or other published policies state otherwise, employees are not generally entitled to be paid for time off work spent responding to a summons or serving on a jury. However, a number of states have exceptions to this rule. State laws that set out some qualified rights to payment include: Alabama, Alaska, Colorado, Connecticut, Hawaii, Kentucky (for teachers and state employees), Louisiana, Massachusetts, Nebraska, New Jersey, New York, Ohio (state employees), Tennessee and West Virginia.

Most of the statutes do not specify what penalties can be imposed if you do not live up to your legal rights and responsibilities when it comes to employee-jurors. But some laws specifically allow discharged employees to file lawsuits for back wages. And some states—Indiana, Kentucky, Michigan, Nevada, North Dakota, Oklahoma, Tennessee, Virginia and Washington—make a violation a misdemeanor, so that employees who claim they have been discriminated against or fired in violation of a jury duty law need only complain to the district attorney or other local prosecuting authority, who will decide whether to prosecute the case.

South Carolina has a harsh consequence: Employers who fire an employee because of jury duty are liable for up to one year of the discharged employee's salary, or the difference between the original and the lessened salary if the employee is demoted. But New York's law is the toughest on employers who break jury duty laws; it leaves the employer open to criminal contempt charges.

The chart below summarizes state laws on jury duty.

## STATE LAWS ON JURY DUTY

**Alabama**        Employees may not be fired for taking time off to serve on a jury. A fulltime employee is entitled to usual pay less any compensation received from the court for service. Ala. Code §12-16-8

**Alaska**         Public employees may not be fired or penalized for taking time off to serve on a jury and are entitled to paid leave for their absence from employment. Alaska Stat. §39.20.270
Private employers cannot penalize employees for serving on a jury but are not required to pay the employees during their leave. Alaska Stat. §9.20.037

**Arizona**        Employees may not be fired for serving on a jury. Employers are not required to pay employees when absent from employment for jury service. Ariz. Rev. Stat. Ann. §21-236

**Arkansas**       City, county and school employees may not be fired for taking time off to serve on a jury. Ark. Stat. Ann. §21-12-304
Employees may not be fired for taking time off to serve on a jury—and cannot be required to use sick leave or vacation to cover time off spent serving on a jury. Ark. Stat. Ann. §16-31-106

**California**     Employees may not be fired or discriminated against for taking time off to serve on a jury, but employees must give employers a reasonable amount of advance notice. Cal. Labor Code §230

**Colorado**       Employees may not be fired for taking time off to serve on a jury. Regular employees, including parttime, temporary and casual workers, are entitled to regular wages up to $50 per day for the first three days of jury service. Colo. Rev. Stat. §§13-71-126 and 13-71-134

**Connecticut**    Employees may not be fired for taking time off to serve on a jury. Conn. Gen. Stat. Ann. §54-247a
Fulltime employees are entitled to be paid their regular wages by their employer for the first five days of jury service. Conn. Gen. Stat. Ann. §51-247

| Delaware | An employer cannot fire, threaten or coerce an employee who responds to a summons or serves as a juror. Del. Code Ann. tit. 10, §4515 |
|---|---|
| District of Colombia | An employer cannot fire, threaten or coerce an employee who responds to a summons or serves as a juror. D.C. Code Ann. §11-1913 |
| Florida | Employees may not be fired for taking time off to serve on a jury. Fla. Stat. §40.271<br>Regular employees, including parttime, temporary and casual workers, who continue to receive their regular wages are not entitled to be compensated by the court for the first three days of jury duty. Employers are not required to pay jurors during absence. Fla. Stat. §40.24 |
| Georgia | An employer may not discharge, discipline or otherwise penalize an employee who responds to a judicial summons, including a jury subpoena. Ga. Code Ann. §34-1-3 |
| Hawaii | Employees may not be fired for taking time off to serve on a jury. Haw. Rev. Stat. §612-25<br>Public employees may not be fired for taking time off to serve on a jury and are entitled to paid leave during their absence from employment. Haw. Rev. Stat. §79-14 |
| Idaho | Employees may not be fired for taking time off to serve on a jury. Idaho Code §2-218 |
| Illinois | Employees may not be fired for taking time off to serve on a jury. Nightshift employees cannot be required to work while they do jury duty during the day. 705 Ill. Comp. Stat. 310/10.1 |
| Indiana | It is a misdemeanor to dismiss an employee or to deprive an employee of benefits, or to threaten to do either, because an employee has responded to a jury summons or served on a jury. An employee who is fired for responding to a jury summons may sue for lost wages and a reinstatement order, plus attorney's fees. Ind. Code §35-44-3-10 |

| | |
|---|---|
| Iowa | Employees may not be fired for taking time off to serve on a jury. Iowa Code §607A.45 |
| Kansas | Employers may not discharge or threaten to discharge employees who serve as jurors. Kan. Stat. §43-173 |
| Kentucky | Employees may not be fired for taking time off to serve on a jury. Ky. Rev. Stat. §29A.160 Teachers and state employees must be granted leave with pay while serving on a jury—minus any compensation for serving on a jury. Ky. Rev. Stat. §161.153 |
| Louisiana | Employees may not be fired for taking time off to serve on a jury. Regular employees get one day of paid leave for either responding to a summons or serving on a jury. La. Rev. Stat. Ann. §23:965 |
| Maine | Employees may not be fired for taking time off to serve on a jury. Me. Rev. Stat. Ann. tit. 14, §1218 |
| Maryland | Employees may not be fired for taking time off to serve on a jury. Md. Cts. and Jud. Proc. Code Ann. §8-105 |
| Massachusetts | Employees may not be fired for taking time off to serve on a jury. Regular employees, including parttime, temporary and casual workers, are entitled to regular wages for the first three days of jury service. However, a court may excuse an employer from his obligation to pay the employee if it finds that "extreme financial hardship" would result. In that case, the court must compensate the employee for up to $50 per day for the first three days of service. Mass. Gen. Laws Ann. ch. 234A, §§48 and 49 |
| Michigan | Employees may not be fired or disciplined for taking time off for jury service. An employer who forces an employee to work hours which, when added to jury duty time, exceed the number of hours that the employee usually works, is guilty of a misdemeanor and may be punished for contempt of court. Mich. Comp. Laws 600.1348 |
| Minnesota | Employees may not be fired for taking time off to serve on a jury. Minn. Stat. Ann. §593.50 |

| | |
|---|---|
| **Mississippi** | Employers may not intimidate employees to keep them from jury service. Miss. Code Ann. §13-5-23 |
| **Missouri** | An employer cannot fire, discipline or take any adverse action against an employee on account of receiving or responding to a jury summons. Mo. Ann. Stat. §494.460 |
| **Montana** | No statute |
| **Nebraska** | Employees may not be fired or otherwise penalized for taking time off to serve on a jury and are entitled to regular pay during absence from employment less any compensation received from court. Neb. Rev. Stat. §25-1640 |
| **Nevada** | An employer who fires or threatens to fire an employee because the employee received or responded to a jury summons is guilty of a misdemeanor. In addition, the employee may sue for lost wages, reinstatement, damages equal to the lost wages and punitive damages up to $50,000. Employee must give the employer at least one day's notice of intended absence.  Nev. Rev. Stat. §6.190 |
| **New Hampshire** | Employer may not retaliate against an employee who performs jury service. N.H. Rev. Stat. Ann. §500-A:14 |
| **New Jersey** | State, county, local and mass transit employees may not be fired for taking time off to serve on a jury. Any fulltime employee is entitled to regular pay less any pay received for being a juror. N.J. Stat. Ann. §2B:20-16 |
| **New Mexico** | Employees may not be fired for taking time off to serve on a jury. N.M. Stat. Ann. §§38-5-18 and 38-5-19 |
| **New York** | An employee who receives a summons and gives notice to an employer may not be discharged or penalized. Employers with more than ten employees must pay the first $40 of the employee's daily wages for up to three days of jury service. Employer may be subject to criminal contempt of court for violations. N.Y. Judiciary Law §519 |

| | |
|---|---|
| **North Carolina** | An employer may not discharge or demote an employee who was called to perform jury duty. N.C. Gen. Stat. §9-32 |
| **North Dakota** | An employer who fires or in any way penalizes an employee because the employee receives a jury subpoena or serves on a jury is guilty of a misdemeanor. Employees may sue for reinstatement and back wages. N.D. Cent. Code §27-09.1-17 |
| **Ohio** | Employees may not be fired for taking time off to serve on a jury. Ohio Rev. Code Ann. §2313.18 State employees are entitled to paid leave when summoned for jury duty. Ohio Rev. Code Ann. §124.135 |
| **Oklahoma** | Employees may not be fired for taking time off to serve on a jury. Okla. Stat. Ann. tit. 38, §35 It is a misdemeanor to discharge an employee for sitting on a jury. The employer is liable for up to $5,000 in lost earnings, mental anguish and the costs of securing suitable employment. Okla. Stat. Ann. tit. 38, §34 |
| **Oregon** | Employees may not be fired for taking time off to serve on a jury. Or. Rev. Stat. §10.090 |
| **Pennsylvania** | Employees may not be fired for taking time off to serve on a jury. The statute does not protect employees of retail or service businesses with fewer than 15 employees or employees of manufacturing businesses with fewer than 40 employees. 42 Pa. Stat. Ann. §4563 |
| **Rhode Island** | Employees may not be fired or otherwise disadvantaged for taking time off to serve on a jury. R.I. Gen. Laws §9-9-28 |
| **South Carolina** | Employers who dismiss or demote an employee for service on a jury are liable for up to one year of the discharged employee's salary or the difference between the original and the lessened salary of the demoted employee. S.C. Code Ann. §41-1-70 |
| **South Dakota** | Employees may not be fired for taking time off to serve on a jury. S.D. Codified Laws Ann. §§16-13-41.1 and 16-13-41.2 |

| | |
|---|---|
| **Tennessee** | An employer with five or more employees may not discharge an employee for serving on a jury or responding to a summons, provided that the employee shows the summons to the employer the day after receiving it. Employees are entitled to regular pay less any jury pay received. Statute protects only permanent employees and parttime employees who have worked more than six months. An employer who discharges an employee in violation of the law is guilty of a misdemeanor. Tenn. Code Ann. §§22-4-108 and 39-16-514 |
| **Texas** | Employees may not be fired for taking time off to serve on a jury. Texas Code Ann. Civil Prac. & Remedies Code §122.001 |
| **Utah** | Employees may not be fired for taking time off to serve on a jury. Utah Code Ann. §78-46-21 |
| **Vermont** | Employees may not be fired for taking time off to serve on a jury. Vt. Stat. Ann. tit. 21, §499 |
| **Virginia** | Any person summoned to jury service shall not be discharged or discriminated against or be forced to use sick leave or vacation time. Violations are Class 4 misdemeanors. Va. Code §18.2-465.1 |
| **Washington** | Employers who do not give an employee a leave to serve as a juror are guilty of a misdemeanor and may be sued by the employee for reinstatement. Wash. Rev. Code Ann. §2.36.165 |
| **West Virginia** | Employees may not be fired for taking time off to serve on a jury and are entitled to regular wages for time absent. W. Va. Code §§52-3-1 |
| **Wisconsin** | Employees may not be fired or otherwise penalized for taking time off to serve on a jury and are entitled to paid leave while serving on a jury. Wis. Stat. Ann. §756.255 |
| **Wyoming** | Employees may not be fired, threatened or coerced for taking time off to serve on a jury. Wyo. Stat. §1-11-401 |

# C. Voting

Some state laws set out a specific amount of time that employees must be allowed off from work to cast their ballots. In some states, the time off must be paid; not in others. And most state laws prohibit employers from disciplining or firing employees who take time off work to vote.

Finally, some states impose hardball restrictions on employees who want to claim protection under the voter laws. In Maryland and Oklahoma, for example, employees may be required to show proof that they actually cast a ballot before they can claim the time off. In California, Iowa and Wisconsin, employees must give their employers previous notice that they intend to take time off work to vote.

### STATE LAWS ON VOTING

| | |
|---|---|
| Alabama | No statute |
| Alaska | Employees may not be fired for taking two hours off without loss of pay unless the employee has two nonwork hours to vote. Alaska Stat. §15.56.100 |
| Arizona | Employees may not be fired for taking three hours off without loss of pay unless the employee has three nonwork hours to vote. Ariz. Rev. Stat. Ann. §16-402 |
| Arkansas | Employers must change work schedules to allow employees to vote. No specific amount of time off is required. Ark. Stat. Ann. §7-1-102 |
| California | Employees may take enough time off work to vote if they do not have enough time to vote outside of working hours. Up to two hours may be taken without loss of pay. Employees must give two workdays' prior notice. Cal. Elec. Code §14000 |
| Colorado | Employees cannot be fired for taking two hours off without loss of pay unless the employee has three nonwork hours to vote. Colo. Rev. Stat. §1-7-102 |
| Connecticut | No statute |

| | |
|---|---|
| Delaware | No statute |
| District of Columbia | No statute |
| Florida | It is a misdemeanor to discharge or threaten to discharge an employee for voting or not voting. Fla. Stat. §104.081 |
| Georgia | Employees cannot be fired or disciplined for taking two hours off of unpaid time unless the employee has two nonwork hours to vote. The employee must give the employer reasonable notice. Ga. Code Ann. §21-2-404 |
| Hawaii | Employees cannot be fired for taking two hours off without loss of pay unless they have two nonwork hours to vote. Hawaii Rev. Stat. §11-95 |
| Idaho | No statute |
| Illinois | Employees cannot be fired for taking two unpaid hours off to vote. 10 Ill. Comp. Stat. 5/7-42 |
| Indiana | No statute |
| Iowa | Employees may take as much time off as will, when added to nonworking time, give the employee three consecutive hours during which the polls are open. The time taken from work is paid, but the employee must apply for the leave in writing and the employer designates the period of time to be taken off. Iowa Code §49.109 |
| Kansas | It is a misdemeanor for an employer to refuse to give an employee two hours leave with pay in order to vote. However, if the polls are open before or after work, the employee is entitled to take only as much time off as will constitute a two-hour block. Kan. Stat. Ann. §25-418 |
| Kentucky | Employees cannot be fired for taking off four unpaid hours to vote. An employee who takes time off to vote but fails to vote, under circumstances which did not prevent him from voting, may be subject to disciplinary action. Ky. Rev. Stat. §118.035 |
| Louisiana | No statute |

| | |
|---|---|
| Maine | No statute |
| Maryland | Employees cannot be fired for taking two hours off without loss of pay unless they have two nonwork hours in which to vote. Employee must furnish proof that they have voted. Md. Ann. Code art. 33, §24-26 |
| Massachusetts | Manufacturing, mercantile and mechanical employees must be given time off for the first two hours the polls are open without loss of pay. Mass. Gen. Laws Ann. ch. 149, §178 |
| Michigan | No statute |
| Minnesota | Employees cannot be fired for taking time off to vote and must be given an unspecified amount of morning time without loss of pay for this purpose. Minn. Stat. Ann. §204C.04 |
| Mississippi | No statute |
| Missouri | Employees cannot be fired for taking three hours off to vote without loss of pay. Statute does not apply if the employee has three successive nonworking hours while the polls are open. Mo. Ann. Stat. §115.639 |
| Montana | No statute |
| Nebraska | No statute |
| Nevada | Employees cannot be fired for taking up to three hours off, depending upon where they live in relation to the polling place, without loss of pay unless they have enough time during nonwork hours to vote. Nev. Rev. Stat. §293.463 |
| New Hampshire | No statute |
| New Jersey | No statute |
| New Mexico | Employees cannot be fired for taking two hours off without loss of pay unless they have two hours before or three hours after work to vote. N.M. Stat. Ann. §1-12-42 |

| | |
|---|---|
| **New York** | Employees cannot be fired for taking up to two hours off without loss of pay unless they have four hours of nonwork time to vote. Employers must post these provisions in a conspicuous place in the workplace not less than ten days before the election. N.Y. Elect. Law §3-110 |
| **North Carolina** | No statute |
| **North Dakota** | Employers are encouraged to grant employees time off to vote. No specific requirements are mandated. N.D. Cent. Code §16.1-01-02.1 |
| **Ohio** | Employees cannot be fired for taking a reasonable amount of time off to vote without loss of pay. Ohio Rev. Code Ann. §3599.06 |
| **Oklahoma** | Employees cannot be fired for taking two hours off to vote without loss of pay, unless the employee has three nonwork hours in which to vote. If the worksite and the polling place are at a distance, employers must grant "sufficient time" in which to vote. Employees must present proof of having voted. Does not apply to school board or bond elections. Okla. Stat. Ann. tit. 26, §7-101 |
| **Oregon** | No statute |
| **Pennsylvania** | No statute |
| **Rhode Island** | No statute |
| **South Carolina** | No statute |
| **South Dakota** | Employees may not be fired for taking two hours off without loss of pay unless they have two nonwork hours to vote. S.D. Codified Laws Ann. §12-3-5 |
| **Tennessee** | An employee may be absent for a reasonable period, up to two hours, to vote, unless there are three hours during which the polls are open and the employee is not at work. Tenn. Code Ann. §2-1-106 |
| **Texas** | It is a misdemeanor for employers to refuse to allow employees to be absent from work to vote, or to threaten employees for attending the polls. Employees are not entitled to time off if they have two nonwork hours in which to vote. Tex. Elect. Code §276.004 |

| | |
|---|---|
| **Utah** | Unless an employee has three or more hours of nonwork time in which to vote, he or she cannot be fired for taking paid time off. Employees must request time off before election day. Utah Code Ann. §20A-3-103 |
| **Vermont** | No statute |
| **Virginia** | No statute |
| **Washington** | Employers must arrange employees' work schedules so that they will have a reasonable amount of nonwork time, up to two hours, in which to vote. If a work schedule cannot be arranged to give an employee two free hours (not counting meal and rest breaks), the employer must grant up to two paid hours leave. Paid leave applies only if, during the time between when the employee is informed of his or her work schedule and election day, there is insufficient time to apply for an absentee ballot. Wash. Rev. Code Ann. §49.28.120 |
| **West Virginia** | Employees cannot be fired for taking three hours off without loss of pay unless they have three nonwork hours to vote. W. Va. Code §3-1-42 |
| **Wisconsin** | An employee is entitled to up to three hours unpaid leave to vote, but must notify the employer first. The employer may designate which hours are to be taken off. Wis. Stat. Ann. §6.76 |
| **Wyoming** | Employees cannot be fired for taking one hour, other than meal time, without loss of pay to vote, providing the employee actually votes. Wyo. Stat. §22-2-111 |

# D. Military Leave

Most states have laws requiring employers to give time off for National Guard or state militia members or reservists to serve. A number of laws set a minimum amount of paid or unpaid time off that you must give. And most laws include a provision preventing discrimination against employees who take military leave.

When an employee takes military leave, you must usually reemploy him or her without loss of benefits, status or reduction in pay. These reemployment guarantees usually contain a number of additional conditions. Typical rights and restrictions are that:

- the employee must not have been dishonorably discharged
- the employee must present proof that he or she has satisfactorily completed service
- the employee must request reinstatement within a specified time
- if the employee is not able to do the job he or she left, you must offer an appropriate substitute position, and
- you need not reinstate the serviceperson if changes in the workforce have made that unreasonable.

## STATE LAWS ON MILITARY LEAVE

| | |
|---|---|
| **Alabama** | Active members of the Alabama National Guard or any reserve of the armed forces are entitled to up to 21 days paid leave of absence. Ala. Code §31-2-13(a). But *White v. Associated Industries of Alabama, Inc.*, 373 So.2d 616 (Ala. 1979), held this statute unconstitutional as applied to private employers. |
| **Alaska** | Public employees are entitled to 16 1/2 days of paid leave if they are members of the reserves and are called to training, duty or a search and rescue mission. Alaska Stat. §39.20.340<br>Private employers must grant unpaid leaves of absence to state militia members called to active service. Alaska Stat. §26.05.075 |
| **Arizona** | Employers may not discriminate against employees because of membership in the National Guard or other state or federal military forces or for absence from work for military duty. Employers must allow National Guard members an unpaid leave of absence for active duty or training. State employees can take up to 30 days paid leave in a two-year period for National Guard training. Ariz. Rev. Stat. Ann. §§26-167 and 26-168 |

| Arkansas | Fulltime state employees may not be fired or discriminated against for membership in the military reserves. Ark. Stat. Ann. §21-3-306 |
|---|---|
| | Public employees who are National Guard members or reservists must receive 15 days of paid leave for training or other official duties per year. If called to active duty in an emergency situation, they must receive 30 days of paid leave. |
| | Unused portions of the paid leave may be carried over to the next year, but the total days available per year shall not exceed 30 days. Ark. Stat. Ann. §21-4-212 |
| | National Guard or militia members who are called to active duty by the governor are entitled to the same reemployment rights, benefits and protections as those afforded employees who are called to active duty in the U.S. forces. Ark. Stat. Ann. §12-62-413 |
| California | Employers may not discriminate against employees on account of membership in state or federal military forces. Employees who are members of the National Guard or reserves are entitled to 17 days leave for active military duty for training. Public employees who are members of the National Guard or the U.S. reserves are entitled to 30 days of paid leave and 180 days of unpaid leave per year for training and duty. Cal. Mil. & Vet. Code §§394 through 395.9 |
| Colorado | Public employees who are members of the National Guard or federal reserves are entitled to 15 days of unpaid leave per year for military training. If required to serve more than 15 days, they are entitled to take leave without pay and to be reinstated. Colo. Rev. Stat. §§28-3-601 and 602 |
| | Private, nontemporary employees who are members of the National Guard or federal reserves are entitled to 15 days off without pay per year for training, and are entitled to return to their jobs provided they are still qualified to fill the positions. Colo. Rev. Stat. §28-3-609 |
| Connecticut | Employees who are members of the military reserves or National Guard are entitled to paid leave for up to 30 days for training or active duty. Conn. Gen. Stat. Ann. §27-33 |

| | |
|---|---|
| **Delaware** | State and school employees may take up to a three-year leave of absence for service in the armed forces or National Guard. Del. Code Ann. tit. 14, §1327; tit. 29, §5105 |
| **District of Columbia** | Employees may take up to 15 or 22 days of paid leave per calendar year, depending on the type of military service. This applies to members of the armed forces and the National Guard. District employees serving in the D.C. National Guard may take an unlimited amount of paid leave. D.C. Code Ann. §1-613.3 |
| **Florida** | Employees cannot be fired or penalized for active service in the National Guard. Fla. Stat. §250.482 Public employees get 17 days paid leave per year for reserve and National Guard training and unpaid leave when called to duty. Fla. Stat. §115.07 |
| **Georgia** | Public employees ordered into military duty are entitled to 18 days of paid leave per year. National Guard members called to active duty are entitled to 30 days of paid leave. Public employees attending service school may take up to six months unpaid leave. Ga. Code Ann. §38-2-279 Privately employed employees who are ordered into military service are entitled to reinstatement provided they are still qualified to do the job, present proof of completion of military duty and request reemployment within 90 days of discharge. Employees attending service school for a maximum of six months are entitled to reinstatement if they request reinstatement within ten days. Reinstatement is not required if the employer's circumstances have so changed as to make rehiring impossible or unreasonable. Ga. Code Ann. §38-2-280 |
| **Hawaii** | Private employees are entitled to unpaid leaves of absence for National Guard duty. Hawaii Rev. Stat. §121-43 Public employees with at least six months of service are entitled to 15 days of paid leave per year for National Guard or reserves duty. Hawaii Rev. Stat. §79-20 |

| | |
|---|---|
| **Idaho** | All employees are entitled to 15 days of unpaid leave per year for serving in National Guard or military reserves. Idaho Code §46-224<br>Public employees who leave their employment, voluntarily or not, to perform military duty are entitled to reinstatement or, if reinstatement is not possible, placement in a state job with similar seniority. The employee must have been honorably discharged and have served four or fewer years. The request must be made within 90 days of discharge or within one year of discharge from hospitalization. An employee who is disabled as a result of military service must be placed in an appropriate job. Idaho Code §65-511 |
| **Illinois** | It is a petty offense to deprive a member of the state militia or the United States forces of his or her employment. 20 Ill. Comp. Stat. 1805/100 |
| **Indiana** | An employee who is a member of the U.S. reserves and who is called for training is entitled to 15 days of leave without pay per year. The employee must give notice, as soon as practicable, of the dates of departure and return and, upon presenting proof of his or her satisfactory completion of training, is entitled to reinstatement. Ind. Code Ann. §§10-5-9-2-1 to 2 |
| **Iowa** | Employees may not be fired, discriminated against or penalized for membership in the National Guard or military reserves. Employer must give leaves of absence for training or service and must reinstate the employee if he or she presents evidence of satisfactory completion of service and is still qualified to do the job. Iowa Code §29A.43 |
| **Kansas** | Employees may not be fired or punished for absence for National Guard service. Kan. Stat. Ann. §48-222 |
| **Kentucky** | Employees cannot be fired or discriminated against for service in National Guard or active militia. Ky. Rev. Stat. §38.460<br>An employer must grant a member of the National Guard leave without pay to perform active duty or training. Ky. Rev. Stat. §38.238 |

| | |
|---|---|
| Louisiana | Any employee who gave advance notice and who is absent from employment due to service in the uniformed services is entitled to reemployment. The cumulative leaves must total less than five years. The employee may not be discharged except for cause within one year of reemployment. Employers are excused if their circumstances have changed so that reemployment is unreasonable or impossible, or if an undue hardship would result. La. Rev. Stat. Ann. §29:410<br>Permanent employees cannot be fired or discriminated against for duty in state militia or National Guard and are entitled to unpaid leaves of absence for such service. La. Rev. Stat. Ann. §29:38<br>Public employees are entitled to 15 days of paid leave per year for fulfilling military reserves or National Guard duty. La. Rev. Stat. Ann. §42:394 |
| Maine | Employees cannot be fired or penalized for membership in National Guard or state military reserves. Public employees are entitled to paid leave while on annual training duty. Me. Rev. Stat. Ann. tit. 37-B, §342.5 |
| Maryland | Employees cannot be fired or penalized for taking time off for duty in the state militia. Md. Ann. Code art. 65, §32A<br>Public employees may take up to 15 days paid leave annually for training and unlimited paid leave for active duty under the authority of the Governor. Md. Ann. Code art. 65, §42 |
| Massachusetts | Employees may not be fired or denied employment for membership in National Guard or the reserves. Mass. Gen. Laws Ann. ch. 33, §13<br>Fulltime employees must be given 17 days per year of unpaid leave of absence for military training. Mass. Gen. Laws Ann. ch. 149, §52A |
| Michigan | Employees cannot be fired, hindered or dissuaded from performing duty as a member of the U.S. reserves, the National Guard or state naval militia. Statute applies to enlistments as well as those already enlisted. Mich. Comp. Laws §§32.271-274 |

| | |
|---|---|
| **Minnesota** | Employees cannot be fired for being members of military. Minn. Stat. Ann. §192.34<br>Public employees are entitled to 15 days per year of paid leave for National Guard or reserves active duty or training and are entitled to leave without pay if called to extended duty. Minn. Stat. Ann. §§192.26 and 192.261 |
| **Mississippi** | Any person in the federal reserves or state military reserves who leaves a fulltime position for duty or training is entitled to leave without pay and reinstatement upon receiving a discharge that is anything but dishonorable. Applies only if the employee is still qualified to do the job. Miss. Code Ann. §33-1-19<br>Public employees in state or federal armed forces are entitled to reinstatement and 15 days of leave with pay for training. Miss. Code Ann. §33-1-21 |
| **Missouri** | Employees cannot be fired or threatened for membership in the state militia or U.S. armed forces or hindered or prevented from performing their militia service. Mo. Ann. Stat. §41.730<br>Public employees who are in the reserves or the state militia get 15 days of leave with pay per year for service or training. Mo. Ann. Stat. §105.270<br>Public employees are entitled to extended leaves without pay for federal or state military service or training without loss of position or benefits. Mo. Ann. Stat. §41.942 |
| **Montana** | Members of the state militia may not be deprived of employment, or an employment benefit, due to their membership in the militia. Mont. Code §10-1-603<br>Public employees who have been employed for at least six months get 15 days paid leave of absence for military or state militia duty. Mont. Code Ann. §10-1-604 |
| **Nebraska** | Permanent public employees who are members of the National Guard or reserves are entitled to an unpaid leave of absence for up to four years during active duty. All employees who are members of the National Guard or reserves are entitled to 15 days with pay per year for training or duty. |

|  | If the governor declares a state of emergency, employees called to active service get additional leave and are entitled to be paid the difference between their regular pay and their service pay. Neb. Rev. Stat. §§55-160 to 161 |
|---|---|
| **Nevada** | Employers cannot fire or discriminate against employees because of National Guard duty or membership. Nev. Rev. Stat. §§412.1393 and 412.606 |
| **New Hampshire** | Employers cannot fire employees because of membership in or absence from work due to performance of duty in the National Guard. N.H. Rev. Stat. Ann. §110-B:65 |
| **New Jersey** | Anyone who deprives an employee of employment or otherwise obstructs him or her on the job because of membership in the organized militia or because he or she is performing or about to perform military duty is guilty of a misdemeanor. N.J. Stat. Ann. §38A:14-4 |
| **New Mexico** | Employers cannot fire employees because of membership in the National Guard. N.M. Stat. Ann. §§20-11-6 and 20-4-6<br>Public and private employers must give members of the reserves or National Guard unpaid leaves of absence during active duty. Such employees cannot be fired except for cause within one year of their return to work. N.M. Stat. Ann. §§28-15-1 to 28-15-3 |
| **New York** | It is the policy of the state of New York that employers should not discriminate against nor refuse to employ employees who are subject to military duties, but there are no specific remedies for those discriminated against, nor are there penalties for those employers who discriminate. N.Y. Mil. Law §318<br>Public and private fulltime employees are entitled to unpaid leaves of absence when called for active or inactive duty or training. Employees must apply for reemployment within ten days of completion of service. N.Y. Mil. Law §317 |

| | |
|---|---|
| **North Carolina** | Employers cannot fire employees because of National Guard duty, and must reinstate the employee if he or she is still qualified to do the job (an employee who is not qualified must be placed in another position for which he or she is qualified), unless restoration would be unreasonable due to the employer's changed circumstances. N.C. Gen. Stat. §127A-202<br>Employers cannot fire employees because of emergency state militia or reserves duty. N.C. Gen. Stat. §127B-14 |
| **North Dakota** | Public employees cannot be fired for performance of National Guard, military reserves or federal service duty. Employees who have been employed for at least 90 days must be granted 20 days of paid leave when ordered to active service and 30 days of paid leave per year for full or partial mobilizations. Such employees may not be fired for one year from the date of reinstatement except for cause. N.D. Cent. Code §§37-01-25 and 25.1 |
| **Ohio** | Public employees must be granted leave to be inducted into military service. If they are not accepted, they must be reinstated. No public employer may discriminate against or discharge any person because of membership in the National Guard, state militia or U.S. reserves. Ohio Rev. Code Ann. §5903.02 |
| **Oklahoma** | Employers cannot hinder or prevent employees who are members of the National Guard from performing their military duty. Okla. Stat. Ann. tit. 44, §208<br>Public employers must give a leave of absence when a service member is called to active duty and 20 days of paid leave per year for training. If the leave extends beyond 20 days, the state and its political subdivisions may elect to make up the difference between the employee's regular pay and the National Guard pay. Okla. Stat. Ann. tit. 44, §209<br>Employers who refuse to allow an employee to participate in National Guard duties are guilty of a misdemeanor. Okla. Stat. Ann. tit. 44, §71 |

| | |
|---|---|
| **Oregon** | Public employees cannot be discharged for performing military duty. They are entitled to reinstatement to the same or similar positions. Statute does not cover leaves over four years—five years if the orders are from the federal government. Or. Rev. Stat. §408.240<br><br>Any employee who is a member of the state militia who is called to active service must be granted a leave without pay. Or. Rev. Stat. Ann. §399.230<br><br>Public employees are entitled to 15 days of paid leave for training per year. Or. Rev. Stat. §408.290 |
| **Pennsylvania** | Employers cannot fire or discriminate against employees because of performance of military duty in the National Guard or reserves. Pa. Cons. Stat. Ann. tit. 51, §7309<br><br>In the event of war, armed conflict, a draft or an emergency declared by the president or the governor, employees who enlist or are drafted into active service and reservists called to duty are entitled to unpaid leaves. Pa. Cons. Stat. Ann., tit. 51, §7302(A)<br><br>Public employees who are members of the National Guard are entitled to 15 days of paid leave for training and active duty. Pa. Cons. Stat. Ann. tit. 51, §4102 |
| **Rhode Island** | Employers cannot fire or discriminate against employees for duty in the National Guard or reserves. R.I. Gen. Laws §§30-11-2 and 30-11-6<br><br>Employees who are National Guard members are entitled to unpaid leave for training periods and active military service. R.I. Gen. Laws §30-11-3<br><br>An employee who enters the land, naval or air forces and is honorably discharged must be reinstated to his or her position or one of similar seniority if the employee is still qualified to do the job and makes the request within 40 days of discharge. The statute does not apply if the employer's circumstances have so changed so that it would be unreasonable to force compliance. R.I. Gen. Laws §§30-21-1 through 30-21-7 |

| | |
|---|---|
| **South Carolina** | Private and public employers cannot fire employees for membership or performance of duty in National Guard. S.C. Code Ann. §§25-1-2310 and 2320<br>Public employees who are members of the National Guard or U.S. Reserves are entitled to up to 15 days paid leave for training or active service and an additional 30 days if called to serve in an emergency. S.C. Code Ann. §8-7-90 |
| **South Dakota** | Fulltime employees who are members of the National Guard or reserves are entitled to 15 days per year of unpaid leave of absence for training or when called to active duty. S.D. Codified Laws Ann. §33-17-15 |
| **Tennessee** | It is a felony for an employer to refuse employment or terminate an employee because he or she is a member of the National Guard, or to terminate employment because the employee is absent while attending any prescribed drill or training. Tenn. Code Ann. §58-1-604 |
| **Texas** | Private employers cannot fire a permanent employee who is called to active service in the state militia. Tex. Govt. Code Ann. §431.006<br>Public employees are entitled to 15 days of paid leaves of absence per year for training or duty in the state militia or armed forces reserves. Tex. Govt. Code Ann. §431.005 |
| **Utah** | Employers cannot fire employees who are members of the National Guard or U.S. reserves and must grant them up to five years of leaves of absence for service. Public employees may not be discharged within one year of return except for cause. State employees are entitled to 15 days per year with pay for training and instruction. Utah Code Ann. §§39-1-36, 39-3-1 and 39-3-2 |
| **Vermont** | Employers cannot fire fulltime employees who are members of the U.S. reserves for engaging in military training and must grant them 15 days of unpaid leave per year. Vt. Stat. Ann. tit. 21, §491 |

| | |
|---|---|
| **Virginia** | Employers cannot fire nor refuse to hire members of the National Guard, nor may they dissuade employees from joining the Guard. Va. Code §44-98<br>Public employees who are members of the reserves, National Guard or state naval militia are entitled to 15 days per year of paid leave for the performance of military duties. Va. Code §44-93 |
| **Washington** | Employers cannot fire fulltime employees for military service and must grant an unpaid leave of absence when employees are called to active duty or training in the National Guard, armed forces reserves or U.S. public health service. An employer does not have to reemploy a returning employee if circumstances have changed so much that it is impossible or unreasonable to do so. Wash. Rev. Code Ann. §73.16.033 |
| **West Virginia** | Employees in the National Guard are entitled to the same reemployment rights guaranteed to members of the U.S. Reserves by applicable federal law. W. Va. Code §15-1F-8<br>Public employees are entitled to 30 days paid leave per year for training or active duty. Employees called to active duty by the president are entitled to an additional 30 days of leave. W.Va. Code §15-1F-1 |
| **Wisconsin** | Employers must grant fulltime employees up to four years of unpaid leave for enlistments, inductions and orders to active service in the U.S. reserves or National Guard. Wis. Stat. Ann. §§45.50 and 45.51 |
| **Wyoming** | Employers cannot fire, hinder or penalize employees for performing National Guard duty. Wyo. Stat. §19-11-104<br>Public employees are entitled to 15 days of unpaid leave per year for National Guard or U.S. reserves training or duty. Wyo. Stat. §19-11-108 |

# E. Family and Medical Leave

A federal law, the Family and Medical Leave Act or FMLA (29 U.S.C. §2601 and following) requires that you give an employee up to 12 weeks of unpaid leave during a year's time:

- for the birth or adoption or foster placement of a child, as long as the leave is taken within a year of the child's arrival
- to care for the health needs of a spouse, parent or children, or
- to recuperate from the employee's own physical or psychological health conditions.

You must not only allow an employee to take the time off, but must allow the employee to return to the same or a similar position to the one he or she held before the leave. According to the Department of Labor, which is charged with enforcing the law, this is the provision employers are guilty of violating most often. To be on the safe side, be sure that the position to which any employee returns after a leave is not only similar to the one he or she left, but that it has the same "terms, conditions and privileges," including the same job security.

During the leave, you must continue to make the same benefit contributions, such as paying insurance policy premiums, that you made before the employee went on leave. However, the FMLA does not require that you pay any benefits that are not generally provided to employees—and seniority and pension benefits need not accrue during an employee's leave.

Employers who violate the Act, including its provisions against retaliating against those who take advantage of its protections, may be required to pay backpay, damages, attorneys' and expert witnesses' fees—and importantly, for the cost of up to 12 weeks of caring for a child, spouse or parent.

The FMLA applies to all private and public employers with 50 or more employees—an estimated one-half of the workforce. In addition, to be covered under the law, an employee must have:

- been employed at the same workplace for a year or more, and
- worked at least 1,250 hours—or about 24 hours a week—during the year preceding the leave.

There are a number of exemptions to the FMLA. Companies with fewer than 50 employees within a 75-mile radius are exempt from the FMLA. So are the highest paid 10% of employees. And those who work as schoolteachers or instructors are partially exempt from the FMLA—that is, they may be restricted from taking their unpaid leave until the end of a teaching period.

## CHANGING DIAPERS, CHANGING THEIR MINDS

A common sore point with employers is that some employees officially state they will take a parental leave of only a few months, but when it ends decide to become fulltime parents and quit their jobs outright. This practice is attractive to many employees because it seems to allow the option of going back to a job after experimenting with a few months of stay-at-home parenting.

Many companies now require employees who take paid parental leaves and then decide to leave their jobs permanently to pay back compensation received during the leave. The FMLA does not prohibit such a policy. And the FMLA specifically allows employers to recover the cost of maintaining health insurance coverage from employees who do not return after a leave.

If you wish to adopt this type of policy, it is best to ask employees taking leave to sign an agreement pledging to make such a repayment.

The majority of states now also have leave laws, but their provisions differ wildly—leaving a patchwork of protections, benefits and loopholes that are often confusing to both employers and employees. These laws differ greatly as to the size of workplace covered, the reasons allowed for time off, who is covered, the length of leave allowed and a host of other matters. Check your own state law below, which may give workers more liberal rights to take leaves than the FMLA allows.

## STATE FAMILY AND MEDICAL LEAVE LAWS

**Alabama**
Employees of certain state and local educational agencies may use sick leave to attend to a sick immediate family member or individual with a close personal tie. Statute applies to bus drivers and employees of state or local Board of Ed., Institute for the Deaf & Blind, Youth Services Dept., School of Fine Arts, School of Mathematics & Science, State Senate, State House of Reps, Lt. Governor, organizations participating in the Teacher's Retirement System. Ala. Code §§16-1–18.1

**Alaska**
Public employers with 21 or more employees must grant any employee who has worked fulltime for six months or halftime for one year 18 weeks of unpaid leave per 12-month period for pregnancy, childbirth or adoption, or 24 months for care of a family member during a serious illness. Employees who take such leave must be restored to their same or comparable position. Alaska Stat. §§23.10.500, .550

**Arizona**
No statute

**Arkansas**
Public employees can use sick leave to care for a sick parent or guardian, spouse, child, sibling, grandparent or in-law. Ark. Code Ann. §21-4-206
School district employees may use sick leave to care for a sick spouse, child, parent or other relative in the household. Ark. Code Ann. §6-17-1304

| | |
|---|---|
| **California** | It is an unfair employment practice for an employer to refuse to grant a leave of up to four months for a female employee who is disabled as a result of pregnancy, childbirth or related medical conditions. Cal. Govt. Code §12945 |
| | Employees who have worked for at least one year and have done 1,250 hours of work during the previous year may take up to 12 working weeks in any 12-month period for family care and medical leave, with reemployment guaranteed. Applies only to employers with more than 50 employees. Does not apply to an employer with fewer than 50 employees within 75 miles of the employee's worksite. Cal. Govt. Code §1245.2 |
| | A government employer may not refuse to hire and may not discharge or discriminate against any person who has exercised his or her rights to family and medical leave. Cal. Govt. Code §19702.3 |
| | Employers with 25 or more employees working at the same location must grant parents, guardians or custodial grandparents up to 40 hours per school year—but not more than eight hours per calendar month—to participate in the school activities of a child in grades K through 12, as long as the employee gives reasonable advance notice. Employer may require verification from the school. Cal. Labor Code §230.8 |
| | Employers may not discharge or discriminate against employees who are called to attend their children's schools following suspension. Employees must give reasonable advance notice. Cal. Labor Code §230.7 |
| **Colorado** | Employer policies applying to leaves for biological parents must also be extended to adoptive parents. Colo. Rev. Stat. §19-5-211 |
| **Connecticut** | Employers with at least 75 employees are required to give 16 weeks of unpaid leave within any two-year period. Leave may be for birth or adoption of a child or for care of a child, spouse or parent during serious illness. Employees who take such leave must be allowed to return to either their original or equivalent jobs. Employers may request certification by a health care provider. Conn. Gen. Stat. §§31-51kk-pp |
| | State employers must give 24 weeks of unpaid leave within any two-year period. |

Leave may be for birth or adoption of a child or for care of a child, spouse or parent during serious illness. Employees who take such leave must be allowed to return to either their original or equivalent jobs. Employees must provide written certification from a physician before going on leave. Conn. Gen. Stat. §5-248a

An employee who knows he or she is going to need to take leave for a planned medical treatment or for birth or adoption must give the employer 30 days notice or as much advance notice as possible.

**Delaware**      State employees who have been employed fulltime for at least one year may take six weeks unpaid leave for the adoption of a child. Del. Code Ann., tit. 29, §5116

Public school employees may take five days paid leave for the death of an immediate family member or one day paid leave for the death of a near relative. This leave is in addition to any other sick leave or vacation. School employees can use their sick leave to attend to an immediate family member who is seriously ill. If the absence is more than five days, a doctor's certification is required. Del. Code Ann., tit. 14, §1318

**District of Columbia**      An employee who has worked with a company of at least 20 employees for at least one year, and who has worked at least 1,000 hours during the previous 12-month period, must be granted up to 16 weeks of unpaid leave during any 24-month period in connection with the birth or adoption of a child or serious illness of a family member. Family member includes a child who lives with the employee and for whom the employee assumes parental responsibility. It also includes a person with whom the employee shares and maintains a residence. If the necessity of taking such leave is foreseeable, the employee must give the employer a reasonable amount of advance notice. The employer may request certification by a healthcare provider. Employees who take such leaves must be restored to either their original or equivalent jobs. D.C. Code Ann. §§1301-1305

| | |
|---|---|
| Florida | Career service state employees are entitled to up to six months unpaid time off for parental or family leave if needed to attend to a serious family illness, a condition that poses imminent danger of death or any mental or physical condition that requires constant in-home care. Fla. Stat. §110.221 |
| Georgia | No statute |
| Hawaii | Employers with at least 100 employees must grant employees an unpaid leave of up to four weeks per calendar year for the birth or adoption of a child or for the care of a child, spouse or parent during a serious illness. The employer may require certification by a healthcare provider. Employees who take such leave must be restored to their same or comparable positions. Haw. Rev. Stat. §§398-1 to 11 |
| Idaho | No statute |
| Illinois | Township employees (60 Ill. Comp. Stat. 1/100-5), highway commissioners' employees (605 Ill. Comp. Stat. 5/6-201.20) and town tax assessor employees (35 Ill. Comp. Stat. 200/2-65) are entitled to maternity leaves as developed by their employers. <br><br> All employers must give an employee up to eight hours during each school year to attend their child's classroom activities and conferences that cannot be scheduled during nonworking hours. The employee must first exhaust all vacation and compensatory time and must give the employer seven days of notice except in an emergency. 820 Ill. Comp. Stat. 147/15 |
| Indiana | No statute |
| Iowa | Employers with at least four employees must grant employees who are disabled by pregnancy, childbirth or related medical conditions an unpaid leave for the duration of their disabilities, up to a maximum of eight weeks. Iowa Code Ann. §216.6 |
| Kansas | No statute |
| Kentucky | An employer of any size must grant up to six weeks of unpaid leave to an employee who has adopted a child under seven years old. Ky. Rev. Stat. Ann. §337.015 |

| Louisiana | Employers must give employees up to six weeks of disability leave and must grant additional leaves for a "reasonable period of time" not to exceed four months. La. Rev. Stat. Ann. §§23:341, 342 |
| | An employer may grant up to 16 unpaid hours per year for an employee to attend or participate in school conferences and activities of a child for whom the employee is the legal guardian if those activities cannot be scheduled during nonworking hours. Employees must give reasonable notice and schedule the time off so that it does not unduly disrupt the employer's operations. La. Rev. Stat. Ann. §23:1015 |
| Maine | An employee who has worked at least 12 consecutive months with a company employing at least 15 people at the worksite must be granted up to ten consecutive weeks of unpaid leave in any two-year period for the birth or adoption of a child 16 years old or younger or to care for a family member during illness. Employees who take such leaves must be restored to either their original or equivalent jobs. Me. Rev. Stat. Ann. tit. 26, §§843, 844 |
| Maryland | No statute |
| Massachusetts | Employers of at least six employees must grant those who have completed their probationary periods or have worked fulltime for at least three months up to eight weeks of unpaid leave for the birth or adoption of a child under 18 or the adoption of a child under 23 if the child is mentally or physically disabled. Mass. Gen. Laws Ann. ch. 149, §105D |
| Michigan | No statute |
| Minnesota | An employer employing 21 or more people must grant employees up to six weeks of unpaid leave for the birth or adoption of a child. However, only employees who have worked for the company an average of at least 20 hours per week for at least 12 months before the request for leave is made are covered. During the leave, the employer must offer the employee the option of continuing group healthcare insurance coverage. Employees who take such leave must be returned to either their original or equivalent jobs, unless the employees would have been laid off. Minn. Stat. Ann. §§181.9410 and following |

An employee may use paid sick leave to care for a sick child. Minn. Stat. Ann. §181.9413

An employer must grant up to 40 hours with pay to enable an employee to donate bone marrow. Minn. Stat. Ann. §181.945

An employee is entitled to 16 paid hours of leave per year to attend school conferences or classroom activities that can't be scheduled during nonworking hours. Minn. Stat. Ann. §181.9412

| | |
|---|---|
| **Mississippi** | No statute |
| **Missouri** | Public employees who are adoptive parents have the same rights as biological parents to take time off without pay and vacation time to arrange for the adoption itself or for care, but only if the adoptive parent is the person primarily responsible for the care of the child. A stepparent may use sick leave or vacation or take leave without pay to care for a sick stepchild. Mo. Ann. Stat. §105.271 |
| **Montana** | An employer of any size may not dismiss an employee who becomes pregnant, or refuse to allow a reasonable unpaid leave for pregnancy, or refuse to allow accrued disability or other leave benefits for a pregnancy leave. Employees also cannot be required to take pregnancy leave for an unreasonable period of time. Employees who take pregnancy-related leaves must be returned to their original jobs or equivalents unless, in the case of a private employer, the employer's circumstances have so changed as to make it unreasonable or impossible to do so. Mont. Code Ann. §49-2-310 and §49-2-311 |
| **Nebraska** | No statute |
| **Nevada** | The same leave policies that apply to other medical conditions must be extended to female employees before and after childbirth, or after a miscarriage. Nev. Rev. Stat. §613.335 |

| | |
|---|---|
| **New Hampshire** | Employers must allow female employees to take leave for period of temporary disability resulting from pregnancy, childbirth or related condition. When the employee is able to return to work, she must be restored to the same or a comparable position unless the employer's business necessity makes this impossible or unreasonable. N.H. Rev. Stat. Ann. §354-A:7y |
| **New Jersey** | Employers of at least 50 employees must grant to those who have worked for at least 12 months, and who have worked at least 1,000 hours in the preceding 12 months, up to 12 weeks of unpaid leave in any 24-month period for the birth, adoption or care during the serious illness of a child under 18 years old, or one older than 18 who is incapable of self-care or a parent or a spouse. The employer may require certification by a healthcare provider. Employees who take such leaves must be restored to either their original or equivalent jobs. An employer may deny leave if the employee is among the seven highest paid employees or is in the highest 5%, whichever is greater, and if substantial and grievous economic injury to the business would result. The employer must notify the employee of the intent to deny leave upon determining that denial is necessary. If leave has commenced, the employee must return within ten days. Family Leave Act, N.J. Stat. Ann. §§34:11B-1 to B16 |
| **New Mexico** | No statute |
| **New York** | If an employer permits leave for the birth of a child, then leave must be granted for adoption. N.Y. Labor Law §201-c |
| | An employer with 20 or more employees must grant an employee up to 24 hours leave to donate bone marrow and may not retaliate against an employee who requests a leave for this purpose. N.Y. Labor Law §202-a |

| | |
|---|---|
| **North Carolina** | An employee who is a parent, guardian or who acts in place of a parent may take up to four hours per year without pay to be involved in the child's school— including a public or private school or daycare. The hours taken must be at a mutually agreed-upon time; the employer may require 48 hours notice for the request and may require verification that the employee actually attended or was involved. No retaliatory action may be taken against an employee who exercises rights under this law. N.C. Gen. Stat. §95-28.3 |
| **North Dakota** | State employees, but not employees of subdivisions of the state, may take unpaid leave to care for a newborn child or to care for a child, spouse or parent with a serious health condition. The amount of leave depends on the average number of hours per week the employee works, up to a maximum of four months per year. Employees may also take up to 40 hours per year of sick leave to care for a sick parent, spouse or child.

Employees must give employers reasonable notice before taking leave. Employers may require certification by a healthcare provider. N.D. Cent. Code §§54-52.4-01 and following |
| **Ohio** | Permanent state employees are entitled to up to six weeks paid leave for the birth or adoption of a child— the last four weeks to be paid at 70% of base pay. Ohio Rev. Code Ann. §124.136

Fulltime permanent state employees are entitled to three paid days' bereavement leave for a death within the employee's immediate family. Ohio Rev. Code Ann. §124.387 |
| **Oklahoma** | No statute |
| **Oregon** | Employees who have worked for a company with at least 25 employees for at least 90 days must be granted up to 12 weeks of unpaid leave for childbirth or the adoption of a child less than six years old. The employer may require employees to give 30 days notice of intent to take such a leave, and employees returning from such a leave must be returned to either their original or equivalent jobs. Pregnant employees must also be given the right to transfer to a less strenuous job. Or. Rev. Stat. §659.360

Employees may take up to 40 hours of leave for a bone marrow donation procedure. Or. Rev. Stat. §659.358 |

| | |
|---|---|
| Pennsylvania | No statute |
| Rhode Island | Employers with 50 or more employees must grant those who have worked for them for at least 12 consecutive months up to 13 weeks of unpaid leave in any two calendar years for the birth or adoption of a child or for the care of a family member during illness. Employees who take such leaves must be restored to either their original or equivalent jobs. R.I. Gen. Laws §§28-48-2 and 28-48-3 |
| South Carolina | State employees may use up to six weeks of sick leave to care for an adopted child after placement. S.C. Code Ann. §8-11-155 |
| South Dakota | State employees who have worked at least 12 months may take up to 12 weeks of unpaid leave to care for a newborn, adopted or foster child or to care for a spouse, child or parent who has a serious health condition. S.D. Admin. Code §55:01:22:08:02 |
| Tennessee | Companies with 100 or more employees must grant up to four months of unpaid leave for pregnancy or childbirth to any fulltime female employee who has worked at least 12 consecutive months. If the employee gives the employer at least three months advance notice of her intent to take such a leave or if a medical emergency makes the leave necessary, she must be restored to her original job or its equivalent upon returning to work. The employer must allow an employee who takes such a leave to continue benefits such as healthcare insurance, but the employer is not required to pay for the benefits during the leave period. |
| | If the employee's job is "so unique" that the employer cannot, with reasonable efforts, fill the position temporarily, the employer need not reinstate the employee. Reinstatement rights do not apply if the employee uses the time to actively pursue other employment opportunities or work fulltime or parttime for another employer. Tenn. Code Ann. §4-21-408 |
| Texas | No statute |
| Utah | No statute |

| | |
|---|---|
| **Vermont** | Companies with 15 or more employees must allow employees who have worked with them an average of at least 30 hours per week, for at least one year, to take up to 12 weeks of unpaid leave per year for pregnancy, childbirth, the adoption of a child under the age of 16 or the serious illness of the employee or a family member. The employee must provide the employer with written notice of intent to take such a leave and of its anticipated duration. The employee must be allowed to use accrued vacation or sickness leave for up to six weeks of leave. The employee must also be given the option of continuing benefit programs at his or her own expense. After returning from such a leave, the employee must be restored to his or her original job or its equivalent—unless the employer can demonstrate that the employee performed unique services and hiring a permanent replacement worker, after giving notice to the employee, was the only alternative to preventing substantial and grievous economic injury to the employer's business. An employee who does not return to the job after taking such a leave for reasons other than the serious illness of the employee must refund to the employer any compensation paid during the leave, except payments for accrued vacation or sickness leave. Vt. Stat. Ann. tit. 21, §472 Employees may also take up to four hours of unpaid leave in a 30-day period but not more than 24 hours in 12 months, to participate in a child's school activities, to take a family member to a medical or professional appointment or to respond to a family member's medical emergency. Vt. Stat. Ann., tit. 21, §472a. |
| **Virginia** | No statute |
| **Washington** | Employers with 100 or more employees, including political subdivisions of the state, and the state, must grant up to 12 weeks of unpaid leave during any two-year period in connection with the birth or adoption of a child or to care for a child under the age of 18 who is terminally ill. The employee must provide the employer with at least 30 days of advance notice in most situations. Employees who take such leaves must be |

restored to their original or equivalent jobs. If circumstances have changed to the point that no equivalent job
is available, the employee must be given any vacant job
for which he or she is qualified. An employer may limit
or deny family leave to either the highest paid 10% of the
employees or 10% designated as key personnel. Wash.
Rev. Code §§49.78.010 and following

Employees may use sick leave to care for a sick child.
Wash. Rev. Code §49.12.270

Employers are not required to provide parental leave
but, if they do, leave policies allowing employees to
take leave to care for a newborn child must also apply
to adoptive parents and stepparents. Wash. Rev. Code
§§49.12.350 and .360

**West Virginia**    Fulltime state or county board of education employees
who have worked at least 12 consecutive months are
entitled to 12 weeks of unpaid leave, after using up
available personal leave, for the birth or adoption of a
child; or to care for a child, spouse, parent or dependent who has a serious medical condition. The employer may require verification from the healthcare
provider. The Parental Leave Act, W. Va. Code §§21-
5D-1 to 9

**Wisconsin**    Employers with 50 or more employees must grant
employees who have been with the company one year
and worked 1,000 hours up to six weeks of unpaid
leave for the birth or adoption of a child and up to two
weeks for the care of a parent, child or spouse with a
serious health condition. This leave, when combined
with any other family-related leave, may not exceed a
total of eight weeks within a 12-month period. The
employee must give notice of the leave and the employer may require certification by a healthcare
provider.

Statute specifically prohibits discharge of or retaliation
against anyone who opposes a practice permitted under
the Family and Medical Leave Act, and provides a
complaint procedure in the Department of Industry,
Labor and Human Relations. Wis. Stat. Ann. §103.10

**Wyoming**    No statute ■

## CHAPTER 7

# Complying With the Americans With Disabilities Act

Among the alphabet soup of acronyms that now control workplace rights, there is one unrivaled in causing employers' brows to furrow. The Americans With Disabilities Act, or ADA (42 U.S. Code §12102 and following), aims to prohibit employment discrimination on the basis of workers' disabilities. Although it was debated, haggled over and honed by both employees and employers before it was passed, the law is not a panacea for either group. It is widely criticized as poorly drafted—and since it took effect in 1992, it has churned up a bevy of lawsuits, resulting in still more confused and confusing opinions as to its meaning.

Generally, Title I of the ADA prohibits you from:

- discriminating on the basis of virtually any physical or mental disability (see Chapter 8)
- asking job applicants questions about their past or current medical conditions (see Chapter 1)
- requiring job applicants to take pre-employment medical exams (see Chapter 3), and
- creating or maintaining worksites that include substantial physical barriers to the movement of people with physical handicaps.

The Act requires you to make reasonable accommodations for qualified individuals with disabilities, unless that would cause undue hardship. But those dictates are frustrating. As discussed below, it is often unclear whether an individual worker is protected under the law. And perhaps most irritating for employers, there are no clear guidelines about what you must do to accommodate a worker's disability—and when you can legally claim it is simply too onerous to do so.

## THE LAW MAY APPLY TO YOUR BUILDING, TOO

In addition to laying down rules for employment, the ADA spells out what a business must do to make its services and facilities accessible to customers and other visitors with disabilities. That part of the law, known as Title III, has shown itself to be more straightforward and far less confounding to employers than has Title I of the same law.

Title III applies to a wide range of businesses that serve the public, including:

- places that serve food or drink—such as restaurants and bars
- businesses that sell or rent goods—such as bakeries, grocery stores and hardware stores
- service businesses—such as laundromats, dry cleaners, barber shops, travel agencies, shoe repair services and doctors' and lawyers' offices, and
- recreational facilities—such as gyms, health spas and bowling alleys.

Businesses covered by Title III must take reasonable steps to remove barriers in existing buildings that can limit access by disabled people. More strict rules apply to new buildings and those undergoing major renovation.

Portions of the ADA and the regulations affecting employment practices are available on the Department of Justice website at: http://www.usdoj.gov.

For an explanation of the portions of the Act and the regulations covering the accessibility of services and facilities, see The Americans with Disabilities Act Title III Technical Assistance Manual, available from the Government Printing Office for $25.

## A. Who Is Covered

You must comply with the ADA if you have 15 or more employees for 20 or more weeks during the current or previous calendar year. This count includes parttime employees. And the law's coverage broadly extends to private employers, employment agencies and labor organizations.

The Act protects workers who, although disabled in some way, are still qualified for a particular job—that is, they would be able to perform the essential functions of a job, either with or without some form of accommodation. This is the saving grace for employers, as it means quite simply that you need not hire or retain any worker who is not qualified to perform a job. And whether a disabled worker is deemed qualified for a job seems to depend on whether he or she has appropriate skill, experience, training or education for the position.

To determine whether a particular function is considered an essential one that an applicant or employee must be able to perform, look first at the written description you have composed to define the job. (See Chapter 1, Section A.) If a function is described there, it is likely to be considered an essential part of the job from a legal standpoint.

But your own discretion and the reality of an individual workplace enter in, too. For example, if other employees would be available to take over some tangential part of a job, or if only a small portion of the workday is spent on the function, or if the work product will not suffer if the function is not performed—then that function may not be deemed essential to the job.

## B. Disabled Defined

The ADA does provide disabled workers with some powerful, relatively new protections against discrimination on the job. But it is important for employers not to be overanxious when dealing with disabled individuals; most want only to be treated like other workers on the job. And not every impairment has the status of a legally protected disability.

A disabled individual is defined as a person who:

- has a physical or mental impairment that substantially limits a major life activity
- has a record of impairment, or
- is regarded as having an impairment.

This definition makes clear why this law provides just cause for pause. Several of the terms used in it are broad—and not well-defined. Some of their intended meanings were hinted at during the congressional debates on the legislation and some have been clarified by the EEOC, but many will simply have to be hammered out in the courts over time.

The ability to work is one of the major life activities that is protected. Some cases have attempted to refine the meaning of this term, mostly by focusing on when an individual is considered not to be disabled. According to emerging and sometimes conflicting judicial wisdom, an individual is not disabled if he or she:

- is only prevented from performing a particular type of work
- can work regular hours, but not overtime or rotating shifts, and
- can perform the daily tasks of life.

## 1. Impairments Limiting a Life Activity

Impairment includes both physical disorders, such as cosmetic disfigurement or loss of a limb, and mental and psychological disorders. Physical disabilities which can be easily seen are those most often protected, presumably for the simple reason that they are easiest to prove to others.

The ADA specifically protects workers with Acquired Immunodeficiency Syndrome (AIDS) and Human Immunodeficiency Virus (HIV), alcoholism, cancer, cerebral palsy, diabetes, emotional illness, epilepsy, hearing and speech disorders, heart disorders, learning disabilities such as dyslexia, mental retardation, muscular dystrophy and visual impairments.

A number of other conditions are also protected under the ADA upon proper proof that they are limiting in some way. To be covered, an individual condition must restrict a life activity—broadly defined as the ability to walk, talk, see, hear, speak, breathe, sit, stand, reach, reason, learn, work or provide basic care. However, the ADA does not cover conditions that impose short-term limitations, such as pregnancy or broken bones. And it does not protect people who claim they are disabled because they use illegal drugs or abuse prescription drugs.

Anxiety disorders triggered by specific events such as long workhours and conditions such as colorblindness that are only disabling for certain tasks have been held not to be disabilities protected under the ADA. And the U.S. Supreme Court recently ruled that the ADA does not protect individuals who have disabilities that can be corrected—for example, poor eyesight correctable to 20/20 with glasses or contact lenses.

**Total Disability Is Totally Different.** And in a recent decision that seems contradictory on its face, the U.S. Supreme Court held that workers who are totally disabled so as to qualify for Social Security Disability benefits may simultaneously be protected by the ADA, which requires them to be able to work, with accommodation.

In a tricky twist, whether a particular condition is considered a disability may depend on its genesis. A good example is the delicate matter of an employee who exceeds normal weight. If the extra pounds are caused by the employee's penchant for lifting weights, he or she would not likely be considered to have a disability that is recognized under the ADA. However, if the extra poundage can be traced to a glandular disorder, courts are more apt to consider the condition a disability. Similarly, a worker who is unable to read because he or she dropped out of school would not likely be deemed disabled; the conclusion would be opposite if the condition is caused by dyslexia. A murkier refinement: A worker who is generally stressed by life and work does not likely have a disability protected by law; a worker diagnosed by a psychiatrist as having a stress disorder is likely protected.

### ARE THE EMPLOYEES SICK—OR IS IT THE BUILDING?

The latest wave of controversy in ADA claims based on conditions some workers contend limit them, but are difficult for outsiders to detect. For example, some workers claim that Multiple Chemical Sensitivity, or MCS, caused by carpet, glue or furniture fumes makes them dizzy, tired and headachy. Other workers claim that mold and mildew on the job aggravate or cause respiratory problems. And some claim latex gloves and chemical coatings have given them asthma. Where the symptoms can be traced to chemicals or growths in the building aggravated by poor ventilation, they are commonly dubbed Sick Building Syndrome. But employees who attempt to link the Syndrome to a successful ADA claim still face a tough climb uphill. A few complaints have resulted in money awards from employers—but paradoxically, most workers have had to prove they were unable to work to collect. The greater success stories come from employees and employers who work together to come up with a solution to a complaint before it produces a disabling condition—often as simple as improving ventilation or setting up an office with air filtration and without carpeting.

## 2. Records of Impairment

Because discrimination often continues even after the effects of a disability have abated, the ADA prohibits discrimination against those who have had impairments in the past. This includes many groups of workers such as former cancer patients, rehabilitated drug addicts, recovering alcoholics and even those misclassified as having a condition, such as someone misdiagnosed as being HIV-positive.

## 3. Regarded as Impaired

In recognition of the fact that discrimination often stems from prejudice or irrational fear, the ADA protects workers who have no legal physical or mental impairment, but may be viewed by others as disabled—for example, someone who is badly scarred. You cannot refuse to hire a person because you suspect that others will react negatively to him or her.

So far, this legal requirement has drawn the most questions. Most judges who have decided the issue have blatantly held that a mistakenly perceived limitation is simply not a handicap under the Act.

### ALL IN THEIR MINDS?
### THE ADA AND MENTAL DISABILITY CLAIMS

In the newest wave of ADA complaints, workers claim that post-traumatic stress makes them hyperactive or short-tempered. Others claim that Attentive Deficit Disorder, or ADD, makes it difficult for them to concentrate and be productive on the job. Even where diagnosed and treated with drugs, employers have argued that mental conditions such as these are not true disabilities within the meaning of the law.

The EEOC issued new guidelines on mental illness in March of 1997, mostly reiterating that the ADA protects workers who have mental impairments that limit "a major life activity" such as learning, thinking, concentrating, interacting with others, caring for himself or herself or performing manual tasks. The EEOC opined that protected conditions may include major depression, bipolar disorder, anxiety disorders such as panic and obsessive compulsive disorders. But the agency also emphasized that the impairment must be lasting; while a serious depression lasting a year or more might qualify under the ADA, a down spell of a month probably would not.

Reactions to the EEOC guidelines have varied. Some applaud the increase as a harbinger of the agency's heightened sensitivity to recognizing the truly debilitating effects of mental disabilities. Others say its new guideline will only encourage workplace slackers. And another contingent blames the usual bogeyperson, The Media, for stirring emotions and focusing what they deem is undue attention on the issue.

Despite this gentle nudge from the EEOC to heed mental disability claims, many judges and juries around the country continue to reject them out of hand. The gulf between guideline and practice may be due to the problem of definition. The lack of objective criteria for assessing mental diseases often makes their diagnoses murky—and the most skeptical observers claim that some employees seek a finding of mental disability as an excuse to shirk work.

And workers who claim mental disabilities are often faced with a Catch-22 when proving their cases: The ADA covers only those who are still able to perform their jobs; a worker who makes a convincing case of mental disability may have a tough time persuading others that he or she is still fit to work.

Finally, there may be problems accommodating a worker with a mental disability in a way that realistically meets the needs of worker and workplace. Some accommodations may be effective and easy to provide— for example, moving an employee away from noisy machinery or allowing beverages in the workplace to combat a dry mouth caused by medication. But other accommodations, such as allowing more time to complete a work activity, may look like favoritism to other workers. And in the meanest workplaces, doctors' orders not to startle or ridicule a particular employee may cause co-workers to escalate the bad behavior.

# C. Illegal Discrimination

The ADA prohibits you from discriminating against job applicants and employees who have disabilities in a number of specific situations.

## 1. Screening Tests

You may not use pre-employment tests or ask interview questions that are designed to expose or focus on an applicant's disabilities rather than skills related to the job. For example, although these questions used to be routine, employers can no longer ask: Have you ever been hospitalized? Have you ever been treated for any of the following listed conditions or diseases? Have you ever been treated for a mental disorder? (See Chapter 1, Section C.)

However, in screening applicants to find the best match to fill a job opening, you are free to ask questions about an individual's ability to perform job-related tasks, such as: Can you lift a 40-pound box? Do you have a driver's license? Can you stand for long periods of time?

## 2. Insurance Benefits

Before the ADA was passed, many employers railed that their insurance costs would skyrocket if they were forced to provide coverage for the special medical needs of disabled workers. But the ADA does not require that all medical conditions be covered; your workplace policy can still limit coverage for various treatments or design exclusions for preexisting conditions. However, you must provide the same coverage for workers with disabilities as you do for workers without disabilities.

## 3. Disabled Relatives and Friends

Employers are banned from discriminating against people who are not disabled, but who are related to or associated with someone who is disabled.

For example, an otherwise qualified worker cannot be denied employment because a family member, roommate or close friend has AIDS.

## 4. Segregation

On the job, you cannot segregate or classify disabled workers in a way that limits their opportunities or status—for example, by placing them in jobs with different pay, benefits or promotion opportunities from workers who are not disabled.

# D. Making Accommodations

The core of the ADA requires employers to make accommodations—changes to the work setting or the way jobs are done—so that disabled people can work. It is this requirement that initially got many employers up in arms over its passage; some felt the law imposed difficult, nebulous decisions on them.

In reality, since the law does not require an employer to propose reasonable accommodations—only to provide them—the onus of suggesting workable and affordable changes falls at least initially on the employee who wants the accommodation. Courts early on took issue with this practice, holding that because an employer is better situated to know whether other positions within a company may be suitable and available, the employer ought to tell disabled employees about other positions for which they may qualify.

The emerging bottom line is this: Once an employee requests a reasonable accommodation, you must consider it. But the buck no longer stops there. Employers must also propose their own solutions—a reserved handicapped parking space, a modified work schedule, a telephone voice amplifier—that might make it possible for a disabled worker to do a job. You may still refuse to make accommodations that are too expensive or implausible.

**YOU DON'T HAVE THAT EXCUSE TO KICK AROUND ANYMORE**

Recent tallies of the cost to employers of making reasonable accommodations for disabled workers show that the workplace investments are surprisingly inexpensive.

| | |
|---|---|
| Percent of accommodations that cost nothing | 31 |
| Percent that cost less than $50 | 19 |
| Percent that cost $50 to $500 | 19 |
| Percent that cost $500 to $1,000 | 19 |
| Percent that cost $1,000 to $5,000 | 11 |
| Percent that cost more than $5,000 | 1 |

Source: Job Accommodation Network, 1993

## 1. What Is a Reasonable Accommodation

The ADA points to several specific accommodations that are likely to be deemed reasonable—some of them changes to the physical set-up of the workplace, some of them changes to how, when or where work is done. They include:

- making existing facilities usable by disabled employees—for example, by modifying the height of desks and equipment, installing computer screen magnifiers or installing telecommunications for the deaf

- restructuring jobs—for example, allowing a ten-hour/four-day workweek so that a worker can receive weekly medical treatments

- modifying exams and training material—for example, allowing more time for taking an exam, or allowing it to be taken orally instead of in writing

- providing a reasonable amount of additional unpaid leave for medical treatment

- hiring readers or interpreters to assist an employee

- providing temporary workplace specialists to assist in training, and

- transferring an employee to the same job in another location to obtain better medical care.

These are just a few possible accommodations that you might make. The possibilities are limited only by your imagination.

## 2.  What Is an Undue Hardship

The ADA does not require you to make accommodations that would cause an undue hardship—a weighty concept poorly defined in the ADA as "an action requiring significant difficulty or expense." To show that a particular accommodation would present an undue hardship, you would have to demonstrate that it was too costly, extensive or disruptive to be adopted in that workplace.

The Equal Employment Opportunity Commission (EEOC), the federal agency responsible for enforcing the ADA, has set out some of the factors that will determine whether a particular accommodation presents an undue hardship on a particular employer:

- the nature and cost of the accommodation

- the financial resources of the employer—a large employer, obviously, may reasonably be asked to foot a larger bill for accommodations than a mom and pop business

- the nature of the business, including size, composition and structure, and

- accommodation costs already incurred in a workplace.

It is not easy to prove that an accommodation is an undue hardship. Financial difficulty alone is not usually sufficient. Courts will look at issues other than direct costs—including tax credits and deductions available for making some accommodations, as well as the disabled employee's willingness to pay for all or part of the costs.

 For additional information on the ADA, contact:

Job Accommodation Network (JAN)
918 Chestnut Ridge Road; Suite 1
West Virginia University
P.O. Box 6080
Morgantown, WV 26506-6080
800-232-9675 or 800-526-7234
Computer bulletin board: 800-342-5526
Provides free consulting services to employers seeking to accommodate employees with disabilities. Maintains a database of companies nationwide that have accommodated workers and organizations, support groups, government agencies and placement agencies that assist the disabled.

National Organization on Disability
910 16th Street, NW; #600
Washington, DC 20006-2988
202-293-5960
800-248-2253
TDD: 202-293-5968
FAX: 202-293-7999
Internet: http://www.nod.org
Administers the Community Partnership program, a network that works to address educational, employment, social and transportation needs of people with disabilities. Provides members with information and technical assistance, makes referrals, monitors legislation.

President's Committee on Employment of People With Disabilities
1331 F Street, NW; Suite 300
Washington, DC 20004-1107
202-376-6200
TDD: 202-376-6205

FAX: 202-376-6219
Internet: http://www.pcepd.gov
Independent federal agency facilitates employment of people with
disabilities and enforces Americans With Disabilities Act (ADA). Provides education, information, training and technical assistance.

# E. Tips on Avoiding Problems

You can go a long way toward avoiding potential legal pitfalls in dealing
with workers you know or suspect of having a disability if you follow a
few guidelines.

➡ Make sure the person is qualified to do the job. In making this
determination, it is essential to pay attention to the sometimes
subtle differences between a disability and an inability to take on the
required work tasks.

➡ Make all work-related decisions based on a particular
individual's abilities. When deciding to hire, promote or fire a
particular employee, do not give yourself over to stereotyped prejudices.
If you have doubts about whether a person can do a job or specific task,
allow him or her to prove you wrong.

➡ Consider changing the job or conditions. The crux of the legal
requirement to make reasonable accommodations is that you are
accommodating. If you can alter the tasks of the job or workspace
without exorbitant cost or untenable inconvenience so that a disabled
person can be a good fit, then make those changes.

➡ Remember what many employers forget: Temporary disabilities
are not covered by the ADA. And covered employees must be
excluded from a large class of jobs, not just a few. ■

# Guarding Against Discrimination

The most powerful law prohibiting discrimination in the workplace is a portion of the federal Civil Rights Act, Title VII (42 U.S.C. §2000 and following). Today, a number of additional federal laws—several of them amendments to Title VII—are used to clamp down on illegal workplace discrimination. And state statutes mirror these protections, many of them giving employees broader protections and applying to greater numbers of employers. (See Section B.)

This chapter discusses Title VII and a cornucopia of other major laws prohibiting various forms of discrimination on the job.

- The Equal Pay Act of 1963 specifically outlaws discrimination in wages on the basis of gender. (See Section C below.)

- The Age Discrimination in Employment Act (ADEA) outlaws workplace discrimination on the basis of age. The law has been amended several times since it was passed in 1967, and now applies only to employees who are at least 40 years old. (See Section D1 below.)

- The Older Workers Benefit Protection Act is an amendment to the ADEA, passed in 1990, that specifically outlaws discrimination in employment benefit programs on the basis of employees' age, and it too applies only to employees age 40 and older. It also deters employers' use of waivers in which employees sign away their rights to take legal action against age-based discrimination. (See Section D2 below.)

- The Pregnancy Discrimination Act (PDA), which makes it illegal for an employer to refuse to hire a pregnant woman, to terminate her employment or to compel her to take maternity leave, was passed in 1978 as an additional amendment to Title VII. (See Section E below.)

- In 1986, in *Meritor Savings Bank v. Vinson* (477 U.S. 57), the U.S. Supreme Court held that Title VII also protects against sexual harassment, another form of illegal workplace discrimination. (See Chapter 9, Guarding Against Sexual Harassment.)

- The Americans With Disabilities Act (ADA), enacted in 1990, makes it illegal to discriminate against people because of their physical or mental disability. (See Chapter 7, Complying With the ADA.)

# A. Title VII

Title VII originally outlawed discrimination based on race, skin color, religious beliefs or national origin, and it created the Equal Employment Opportunity Commission (EEOC) to administer and enforce the legal standards it set.

## 1. Who Is Covered

Title VII applies to all companies and labor unions with 15 or more employees. It also governs employment agencies, state and local governments and apprenticeship programs.

Title VII does not cover:

- federal government employees; special procedures have been established to enforce anti-discrimination laws for them, and
- those who work as independent contractors rather than employees.

### COUNTING EMPLOYEES: NOT AS EASY AS IT SOUNDS

The Civil Rights Act is clearly written to apply to employers with 15 or more employees. But courts across the nation have been of differing minds when it comes to deciding which employees you should include in your final tally.

Some courts, in determining whether an employer has 15 employees and so is controlled by the dictates of Title VII, used a counting system in which hourly and parttime employees were considered in the total, but only on the days they were at work or on paid leave.

The U.S. Supreme Court recently ruled that this is a disingenuous shell game. The Court held that employees should be defined and tallied for purposes of Title VII according to the payroll method. Under the payroll method, employers are covered if they have 15 or more employees on the payroll for each working day in 20 or more weeks, regardless of the actual work the workers perform or whether they are compensated (*Walters v. Metropolitan Educational Enterprises, Inc.*, 117 S.Ct. 660 (1997)).

## 2. Prohibited Discrimination

Under Title VII, you may not intentionally use race, skin color, age—if at least 40—gender, religious beliefs or national origin as the basis for decisions on hirings, promotions, dismissals, pay raises, benefits, work assignments, leaves of absence or just about any other aspect of employment. Title VII covers everything about the employment relationship—from pre-hiring ads to working conditions, to performance reviews, to giving post-employment references.

## RETALIATION: A SNEAKY LIABILITY

While prohibiting discrimination on the job, Title VII also prohibits you from retaliating against those who file a discrimination complaint, or who cooperate in the investigation of one. To make out such a claim, the employee must be able to prove that the retaliation occurred because he or she filed a complaint. As evidence, the offended employee will more often than not point to some workplace reprimand or correction, such as performance reviews that suddenly became critical after the discrimination complaint was raised.

These days, retaliation claims—or even the threat of them—have become powerful weapons in the employee arsenal. Most employers are unaware that such a claim exists—and become aware of it only after a disgruntled employee's lawyer makes use of the possibility.

In truth, once an employee is feeling angry, hurt or disgusted enough to bring a claim of discrimination, the bathwater is already sullied. And you, as an employer, must proceed cautiously while on this terrain. For example, be sure that your employee evaluations and other decisions are based on quantifiable, objective assessments of how well the employee gets the job done.

Some of the most common claims brought under Title VII—those alleging discrimination based on race, religion and ethnicity—are discussed here.

### a. Race

Race discrimination cases are complex to prove—and frequently laden with charged feelings. Employees who want to prove cases of race discrimination must show that they were intentionally treated differently than other employees because of their race. In an agency investigation or a court case, you have the right and opportunity to counter this with evidence that there was a legitimate, nondiscriminatory reason for the action you took. The employee can counterclaim your evidence with still more evidence that your excuses were not valid, merely a pretext for discriminating.

At first, these burdens and evidence sound daunting—impossible for both sides. But courts are increasingly liberal as to what they will accept as evidence. And keep in mind that evidence shows up in many places in the workplace: memos, email messages, voicemail messages, performance reviews, watercooler conversations, documented patterns of promotions or firings.

These days, even the line between free and prohibited speech is less blurry when the speech itself is full of hatred and bigotry. Judges seem less willing to tolerate racist hectoring on the job—and juries are generally loath to do so. The conventional wisdom for employers is to do all you can to settle race claims out of court.

## DISCRIMINATION AGAINST GAY AND LESBIAN WORKERS

Gay men and lesbians have historically been subjected to painful measures that would legalize discrimination: initiatives barring them from teaching in public schools, public resolutions urging opposition to legislation combatting sexual orientation discrimination, local ordinances allowing private clubs to bar them from their doors, loud and heavy lobbying against same-sex marriage laws. On the job, the discrimination often continues—with homophobic comments and jokes, lectures about upholding The Company Image, promotions denied and jobs lost.

There is no federal law that specifically outlaws workplace discrimination on the basis of sexual orientation. However, depending upon your corporate culture or the part of the country in which you live, there may be some bans against discrimination based on sexual orientation. Laws that do outlaw discrimination on that basis have been enacted by nearly a quarter of the states—including California, Colorado (state employees only), Connecticut, the District of Columbia, Hawaii, Massachusetts, Minnesota, New Jersey, Rhode Island, Vermont and Wisconsin. (See the chart in Section B.) In addition, over 100 cities prohibit discrimination based on sexual orientation.

In states and cities that do not have laws forbidding workplace discrimination on the basis of sexual orientation, workers have sued employers who fire or otherwise discriminate against them because they are gay or lesbian by filing a lawsuit claiming invasion of privacy.

## b. Religion

In the last few years, there has been a significant increase in the number of religious discrimination lawsuits filed. Theologians hail this burst in litigation as a sign that Americans are returning to the fold. Pessimists say that workers are looking for just another excuse to work less. Whether the litigants are heaven-sent or slothful, the law is often on their side.

Title VII of the Civil Rights Act and most state laws prohibit employers from discriminating on the basis of religious beliefs. Where workers articulate a need to express their religious beliefs and practice in the workplace, employers are generally required to accommodate them— unless doing so would cause the employer undue hardship. As in all other contexts where the term comes up, the meaning of undue hardship in this context gives employers and courts cause for confusion.

The U.S. Supreme Court has pronounced twice on the issue.

In *Trans World Airlines Inc. v. Hardison* (432 U.S. 135 (1977)), an airline employee claimed that his religion, the Worldwide Church of God, forbade him from working on Saturdays. In subsequent meetings, TWA union officials argued that allowing the employee to change shifts would violate a collective bargaining agreement that banned the arrangement for workers without sufficient seniority. The Court agreed, holding that the union agreement was more sacrosanct than the religious practices.

Nearly a decade later, the Court again heard the pleas of a member of the Worldwide Church of God—this time arguing that he needed six days off per school year for religious observance. The sticking point again was a collective bargaining agreement providing only three days of paid leave for religious observation. The Court waffled some in its opinion, holding that the court below could decide whether providing unpaid leave to make up the balance was a reasonable accommodation (*Ansonia Board of Education v. Philbrook,* 479 U.S. 60 (1979)).

Since the Supreme Court's pronouncements in the '70s, the lower courts that have faced the issue have reached differing conclusions about what is an undue burden for employers. A Florida police officer's request for Saturdays off was denied "for public safety reasons." But a New Mexico court ruled that a truck driver was illegally denied a job because of his practice of smoking peyote during a Native American ritual. And a California court shot down an employer's order that banned religious artifacts in all workers' cubicles and prevented them from any type of "religious advocacy" on the job.

For now, employers and employees grappling with the issue would be best served to work together to reach an accommodation—and keep the issue out of the uncharted territory of court decisions.

## c. Ethnicity

Traditionally, unkind and nasty words—slurs and bigoted speech—were the usual weapons of ethnic discrimination in workplace. The emerging hotbed of workplace claims in this area involves rules requiring that workers speak only English while on the job. The controversy is not likely to end soon. The U.S. Census Bureau predicts that by the year 2050, 20% of the population of the United States will be Hispanic—and Asians and Pacific Islanders will make up an additional 10% of it. Faced with this future, American workplaces need better direction on the legality of rules that limit or prohibit employees from speaking languages other than English on the job.

Supporters of English-only rules claim they are essential, enabling employers to determine whether workers are obeying company rules and being polite and respectful to co-workers and clients. Opponents denounce the rules as punishing and demeaning to workers who are not fluent in English, and claim they are a thinly veiled method to target and discriminate against immigrant workers. Some also point up that in parts of the country such as southern California, where the workforce is rich in immigrants, it is a boon to businesses to have a multi-lingual workforce, making it possible to communicate with customers in their native languages.

In most situations, you must allow employees to use the language of their choice when speaking among themselves while working or during breaks. In fact, English-only rules are presumed to be illegal unless there is a clear business necessity for requiring them—such as for air traffic controllers or for those who must deal with company customers who speak English.

Whenever there is some stricture requiring that employees speak only English on the job, employers must first:

- notify all employees of the rule

- inform all employees of the circumstances under which English is required, and

- explain the consequences of breaking the rule.

So much for theory. In reality, drawing the line between permissible English-only policies and impermissible ones is difficult indeed. In recent legal challenges, courts have upheld some form of English-only rules:

- when they were passed so that supervisors could better manage employees' work, or because customers might object to hearing conversations in a language they could not understand (*Garcia v. Gloor,* 618 F.2d 264 (5th Cir. 1980))

- to improve the rating of a radio program, where speaking "street" Spanish on-air allegedly did not boost ratings among Hispanic listeners (*Jurado v. Eleven-Fifty Corp.,* 813 F.2d 1406 (9th Cir. 1987)), and

- to promote racial harmony after non-Spanish-speaking employees claimed that hearing Spanish spoken distracted them while operating machinery (*Garcia v. Spun Steak,* 998 F.2d 1480 (9th Cir. 1993)).

Courts in many of the cases have intimated, however, that employers must exempt employees who are not bilingual from the requirements of English-only rules—or provide training in English so that they may learn to speak it.

## 3. Enforcement

The Equal Employment Opportunity Commission (EEOC) is the federal agency responsible for evaluating and pursuing nearly all cases of workplace discrimination. Compared to most other government agencies, the EEOC has very well-defined procedures for handling complaints.

The agency's burden of business is burgeoning—the caseload increased nearly 40% from 1990 to 1998. But the budget is not; there has been no increase in several years. Despite its beleaguered condition, the EEOC has consistently vowed to rout out all reported discrimination on the job. But that resolve might be changing. The EEOC recently quietly issued a new policy setting its sights a little lower: It will deal with the worst cases; the rest are anyone's call. The new dictate will likely make EEOC staff lawyers more prone to cut deals in cases that are not clear winners.

If the courts or the EEOC find that an employee has suffered illegal discrimination on the job, there are a number of remedies you might be required to provide, including paying penalties, reinstating or promoting the employee, paying lost salary, benefits, damages and attorneys' fees and changing your policies to prevent similar incidents in the future.

## HOW COMPLAINTS ARE HANDLED—OR NOT HANDLED

When an individual files a complaint charging discrimination, typically an EEOC staff lawyer or investigator will initially evaluate whether or not your actions appear to violate Title VII. Theoretically, the EEOC has 180 days to act on a complaint. If the interviewer does not feel that the incident warrants charging you, he or she will notify the complaining employee within this time.

If the EEOC interviewer feels the complaint warrants additional attention, he or she will fill out an EEOC Charge of Discrimination form describing the incident and send it to the employee who initially complained to review and sign. After receiving a complaint, the EEOC is supposed to interview you and then try to mediate a settlement of the complaint between you and the employee who felt wronged.

That is what the EEOC's operating regulations provide. And for the most part, the EEOC does what it is supposed to do. But do not expect every claim to proceed as described. EEOC offices differ in caseloads, local procedures and the quality of their personnel. Investigations are usually slow, sometimes taking three years or more. The EEOC takes only a small portion of its cases to court—as few as 1% of those that are filed with it. These and other factors can have an impact on how a case is actually handled.

## 4. Tips for Avoiding Claims

There are several proven practices and policies that will go a long way to lessening the chances that your business will be hit with a claim of discrimination.

Your best defense against a charge of discrimination is that there was a legitimate business reason—not a discriminatory one—for a decision or a policy. These days, there is also an unspoken necessity to have written evidence to support your decision—for example, spreadsheets supporting your claim that lost profits made it necessary for you to cut the workforce as you did.

➡ Treat all employees as nearly the same as possible. Most discrimination cases start as festering resentment. If it is your consistent policy, for example, to deny medical leave to employees who have a track record of less than a year with your company, an employee with only four months on the job will be hard-pressed to claim you singled him or her out because of age or pregnancy or gender or some other discriminatory status.

➡ Leave a trail, but choose your crumbs carefully. With discrimination claims, perhaps more than any other type of claim, it is the documentation that can keep you from the losing end of a claim. Keep written records of slouchy performance, excessive absences and tardiness and also document all attempts to help the employee improve. It is hard for any panel of jurors—most of them likely to be workers themselves—to empathize with an employee who decries discrimination when he or she is only sporadically on the job, or only occasionally good at it.

➡ Allocate hiring and firing responsibilities wisely. If an employee who is fired later files a claim of discrimination, it may make a difference who wielded the hatchet. A number of courts have held, for example, that it is presumed not to be a discriminatory firing where the same person makes the decision to hire and fire a particular employee.

**WHAT THE COURTS WILL PONDER**

In investigating discrimination claims, courts and investigating agencies will be most swayed by evidence of:
- history—especially companywide statistics showing evenhanded promotions
- similar treatment of employees in similar positions, and
- statistics of those of the same age, race or gender that hold higher positions.

# B. State and Local Anti-Discrimination Laws

Nearly all state and local laws prohibiting various types of discrimination in employment echo federal anti-discrimination law in that they outlaw discrimination based on race, color, gender, age, national origin and religion. But the state and local laws typically tend to go into more detail, creating categories of protection for employees that are not covered by federal law. And they may impose remedies or offer penalties not provided in their federal counterpart.

In Louisiana, for example, it is illegal to discriminate in employment matters on the basis of a worker's sickle cell trait. In Minnesota, it is illegal to discriminate against people who are collecting public assistance. And in Michigan, employees cannot be discriminated against because of their heights or weights.

Many state anti-discrimination laws also provide faster and more effective procedures for pursuing complaints about illegal workplace discrimination than the EEOC process. An employee in New Jersey, for example, may go directly into superior court with a lawsuit based on age discrimination without first complaining to the EEOC.

As an employer, it behooves you to beware of the twists and turns in state laws prohibiting discrimination in employment. A summary of the state laws, along with agencies responsible for enforcing them, is in the chart below. There are several states that have discrimination laws, but no state agency to enforce them. In these states, discrimination actions must be based on the federal law or enforced in a private lawsuit.

You can research municipal anti-discrimination laws at the headquarters of your community's government, such as your local city hall or county courthouse. Also, many local ordinances are available on the Internet. Start with the site maintained by the Seattle Public Library: http://www.spl.org/govpubs/municode.html. It includes links to many cities.

## 1. Time Limits

Ordinarily, a charge with the EEOC must be filed within 180 days of the date of the action about which the employee is complaining. State laws have their own separate time limits. There is a special wrinkle for age discrimination claims: If a state has an agency that enforces its own age discrimination law and an employee has filed a complaint there first, an EEOC complaint must be filed within 30 days of notice that the state is no longer pursuing the case, even if the normal 180-day period is not up. All of these time limits are counted from the date of the alleged discriminatory action—a cut in pay, demotion, layoff, forced retirement.

## 2. State Laws and Enforcing Agencies

This section offers a synopsis of factors that may not be used as the basis for employment decisions under state laws. Keep in mind that it is only a synopsis, and that each state has its own way of defining important terms, such as what conditions qualify as a physical disability.

## STATE LAWS PROHIBITING DISCRIMINATION IN EMPLOYMENT

| | |
|---|---|
| **Alabama** | Age discrimination (40 years or older) for employers with 20 or more employees. Ala. Code § 25-1-20<br>No other anti-discrimination law, but employers are encouraged to employ people who are blind or otherwise physically disabled. Ala. Code §21-7-1<br>If an employer has an affirmative action program, the term minority, in addition to an ethnic group or other classification, shall also include American Indians or Alaskan Natives, as identified by birth certificates or tribal records. Ala. Code §25-1-10<br>Enforcing agency: None |
| **Alaska** | Race, religion, color, national origin, age, physical disability, gender, marital status, changes in marital status. Alaska Human Rights Law (Alaska Stat. §18.80.220)<br>Pregnancy or parenthood. Alaska Stat. §18.80.220<br>Mental illness. Alaska Stat. §§47.30.865, 18.80.220<br>Enforcing agency:<br>Human Rights Commission<br>800 A Street, Suite 204<br>Anchorage, AL 99501<br>907-274-4692 |
| **Arizona** | Race, color, religion, gender, age, physical disability (excluding current alcohol or drug use), national origin. Arizona Civil Rights Act (Ariz. Rev. Stat. Ann. §41-1461 and following)<br>Enforcing agency:<br>Civil Rights Division<br>1275 West Washington Street<br>Phoenix, AZ 85007<br>602-542-5263 |
| **Arkansas** | No discrimination on basis of race, religion, national origin, gender or physical or mental disability. Ark. Code Ann. §§16-123-107, -108<br>Prohibits discrimination in wages on the basis of gender. Ark. Code Ann. §11-4-601<br>For state employees only: age if 40 years old or older. Ark. Code Ann. §§21-3-201 to 203<br>Enforcing agency: None |

| **California** | Race, religious creed, religion, color, national origin, ancestry, physical disability, mental disability, medical condition, marital status, gender, age if 40 or older, pregnancy, childbirth or related medical conditions. Cal. Govt. Code §§12940, 12941, 12945 |
| --- | --- |
| | AIDS or HIV: If an employee's participation in a research study regarding AIDS or HIV is disclosed, the information shall not be used to determine the employability or insurability of that person. Cal. Health & Safety Code §121115 |
| | Political activities or affiliations, including sexual orientation. Cal. Lab. Code §§1101, 1102 and 1102.1 |
| | Enforcing agency: |
| | Department of Fair Employment and Housing |
| | 2014 T Street, Suite 210 |
| | Sacramento, CA 95814 |
| | 916-445-9918 |
| **Colorado** | Race, religion, color, age, gender, national origin, ancestry. Fair Employment Practices Act (Colo. Rev. Stat. §24-34-401 and following) |
| | Physical or mental disability. Colo. Rev. Stat. §27-10-115 |
| | Sexual orientation, state employees only. Executive Order No. D0035; December 10, 1990 |
| | Enforcing agency: |
| | Civil Rights Commission |
| | 1560 Broadway, Suite 1050 |
| | Denver, CO 80202-5143 |
| | 303-894-2997 |
| **Connecticut** | Race, color, religion, age, gender, pregnancy, marital status, sexual orientation, national origin, ancestry, present or previous mental or physical disability. Fair Employment Practices Act (Conn. Gen. Stat. Ann. §§46a-60, 81c; Conn. Public Act 98-180) |
| | Enforcing agency: |
| | Commission on Human Rights and Opportunities |
| | 1229 Albany Avenue |
| | Hartford, CT 06112 |
| | 203-566-7710 |

| | |
|---|---|
| **Delaware** | Race, color, religion, gender, national origin, marital status, age if between ages 40 and 70 or physical disability as long as the cost to the employer of accommodating the employee's physical disability does not exceed 5% of that employee's annual compensation. Fair Employment Practices Act (Del. Code Ann. tit. 19, §710 and following)<br>Enforcing agency:<br>Department of Labor<br>Labor Law Enforcement Section<br>State Office Building, 6th Floor<br>820 North French Street<br>Wilmington, DE 19801<br>302-761-8200 |
| **District of Columbia** | Race, color, religion, national origin, age if between ages 18 and 65, gender, personal appearance, marital status or family responsibilities, sexual orientation, political affiliation, matriculation or physical disability. Human Rights Act (D.C. Code Ann. §1-2512)<br>Enforcing agency:<br>Human Rights Commission<br>441 4th Street, NW<br>Washington, DC 20001<br>202-724-1385 |
| **Florida** | Race, color, religion, gender, national origin, age, marital status, physical disability. Human Rights Act (Fla. Stat. Ann. §760.01)<br>AIDS or HIV condition. Fla. Stat. Ann. §760.50<br>Enforcing agency:<br>Commission on Human Relations<br>325 John Knox Road, Bldg. F, Suite 240<br>Tallahassee, FL 32303-4149<br>850-488-7082 |
| **Georgia** | In public employment:<br>Race, color, national origin, religion, sex, age, disability—excluding alcohol or drug use. Fair Employment Practices Act (Ga. Code Ann. §45-19-20)<br>In private employment: |

|  | Mental or physical disability—excluding the use of alcohol or any illegal or federally controlled drug and excluding disabilities based on communicable diseases and disabilities that interfere with the person's ability to do the job. Ga. Code Ann. §34-6A-4<br>Age if between 40 and 70 years old. Ga. Code Ann. §34-1-2<br>Enforcing agency: None |
| **Hawaii** | Race, religion, color, ancestry, gender, sexual orientation, age, marital status, mental or physical disability, pregnancy, childbirth or related medical conditions. Fair Employment Practices Law (Haw. Rev. Stat. §378-1 and following)<br>Enforcing agency:<br>Hawaii Civil Rights Commission<br>888 Mililani Street, 2nd Floor<br>Honolulu, HI 96813<br>808-586-8640 |
| **Idaho** | Race, color, religion, national origin, gender, age or physical or mental disability. Fair Employment Practices Act (Idaho Code §67-5909)<br>Enforcing agency:<br>Commission on Human Rights<br>450 West State Street<br>Boise, ID 83720<br>208-334-2873 |
| **Illinois** | Race, color, gender, national origin, ancestry, religion, age if over 40, marital status, physical or mental disability (excluding substance abuse). Human Rights Act (775 Ill. Comp. Stat. 5/1-101 and following)<br>Enforcing agency:<br>Department of Human Rights<br>James R. Thompson Center<br>100 West Randolph Street, 10th Floor<br>Chicago, IL 60601<br>312-814-6245 |

| Indiana | Race, color, gender, national origin, ancestry, religion, age if between 40 and 70 years old or physical or mental disability. Civil Rights Law (Ind. Code Ann. §§22-9-1-1 and following)<br>Enforcing agency:<br>Civil Rights Commission<br>100 N. Senate Avenue, Room N-103<br>Indianapolis, IN 46204<br>317-232-2600 |
|---|---|
| Iowa | Race, color, religion, age, gender, national origin, pregnancy, AIDS or physical disability. Does not apply to workplaces with fewer than four employees or to workers under age 18. Civil Rights Act (Iowa Code Ann. §216.1 and following)<br>Enforcing agency:<br>Civil Rights Commission<br>211 East Maple Street, 2nd Floor<br>Des Moines, IA 50319<br>515-281-4121 |
| Kansas | Race, color, religion, gender, age if over age 18, national origin or ancestry or physical disability. Act Against Discrimination (Kan. Stat. Ann. §§44-1001 and following)<br>Enforcing agency:<br>Human Rights Commission<br>Landon State Office Building<br>900 SW Jackson, Suite 851 South<br>Topeka, KS 66612-1258<br>785-296-3206 |
| Kentucky | Race, color, religion, national origin, gender, age if between ages 40 and 70, physical or mental disability. Civil Rights Act (Ky. Rev. Stat. §344.040)<br>Physical disability. Ky. Rev. Stat. §207.130<br>In addition, no employee can be fired, refused employment or discriminated against because of being diagnosed with level 1/0, 1/1 or 1/2 pneumoconiosis (black lung disease) with no respiratory impairment. Ky. Rev. Stat. §342.197 |

Enforcing agency:
Human Rights Commission
332 West Broadway, 7th Floor
Louisville, KY 40202
502-595-4024

**Louisiana**     Race, color, religion, gender, national origin, pregnancy, sickle cell traits. Discrimination in Employment Act (La. Rev. Stat. Ann. §§23:332, 342, 352)
Physical or mental disability. La. Rev. Stat. Ann. §§46:2251, 23:323
Age (40 to 70 years old). La. Rev. Stat. Ann. §23:312
Participation in investigations relating to state's employment laws. La. Rev. Stat. Ann. §23:964
Enforcing agency: none

**Maine**     Race, color, gender, religion, national origin, ancestry, age or physical or mental disability. Human Rights Act (Me. Rev. Stat. Ann. tit. 5 §4572)
Enforcing agency:
Human Rights Commission
Statehouse, Station 51
Augusta, ME 04333
207-624-6050

**Maryland**     Race, color, religion, gender, national origin, age, marital status, past or current physical or mental illness or disability as long as the disability does not prevent the worker from performing the job. Human Relations Commission Act (Md. Code Ann. art. 49B, §16)
Enforcing agency:
Commission on Human Relations
20 East Franklin Street
Baltimore, MD 21202
301-333-1700

**Massachusetts**     Race, color, religion, gender, sexual orientation, national origin, ancestry, age or physical or mental disability. Fair Employment Practices Act (Mass. Gen. Laws Ann. ch. 151B, §4)
Enforcing agency:
Commission Against Discrimination
One Ashburton Place
Boston, MA 02108
617-727-3990

| | |
|---|---|
| **Michigan** | Race, color, religion, gender, national origin, height, weight, marital status or age. Elliot Larsen Civil Rights Act (Mich. Comp. Laws §37.2202)<br>Physical disability and mental disability. Mich. Comp. Laws §37.1202<br>Enforcing agency:<br>Department of Civil Rights<br>1200 6th Street, 7th Floor<br>Detroit, MI 48226<br>313-256-2615 |
| **Minnesota** | Race, color, religion, creed, gender, marital status, pregnancy, sexual orientation, national origin, age, physical disability or receipt of public assistance. Minn. Stat. Ann. §363.03<br>Enforcing agency:<br>Department of Human Rights<br>Bremer Tower<br>7th Place and Minnesota Streets<br>St. Paul, MN 55101<br>612-296-5663 |
| **Mississippi** | State employer cannot discriminate based on race, color, religion, sex, national origin, age or physical disability. Miss. Code Ann. §25-9-149<br>Small businesses may not receive assistance from the state unless they certify that they do not discriminate based on race, color, religion, sex, national origin, age or physical disability. Miss. Code Ann. §57-10-519<br>Enforcing agency: None |
| **Missouri** | Race, color, religion, gender, national origin, ancestry, age between ages 40 and 70 or physical or mental disability. Human Rights Act (Mo. Ann. Stat. §§213.010 to 055)<br>AIDS condition, except individuals currently contagious and who pose a direct threat to the health and safety of others or who, because of current contagious disease, are unable to perform the duties of their employment. Mo. Ann. Stat. §191.665<br>Enforcing agency:<br>Commission on Human Rights<br>3315 West Truman Boulevard<br>Jefferson City, MO 65102-1129<br>573-751-3325 |

| | |
|---|---|
| **Montana** | Race, color, religion, creed, gender, age, national origin, marital status or physical or mental disability. Human Rights Statute (Mont. Code Ann. §49-2-303)<br>Enforcing agency:<br>Human Rights Commission<br>1236 Sixth Avenue<br>Helena, MT 59624<br>406-444-2884 |
| **Nebraska** | Race, color, religion, gender, national origin, age between ages 40 and 70, marital status or disability—excluding addiction to alcohol, other drugs or gambling. Fair Employment Act (Neb. Rev. Stat. Ann. §48-1104)<br>Enforcing agency:<br>Equal Opportunity Commission<br>301 Centennial Mall South<br>Lincoln, NE 68509-4934<br>402-471-2024 |
| **Nevada** | Race, color, religion, gender, age if over 40 years old, national origin, physical disability. Fair Employment Practices Act (Nev. Rev. Stat. Ann. §613.330)<br>Enforcing agency:<br>Equal Rights Commission<br>2450 Wrondel Way, Suite C<br>Reno, NV 89502<br>702-688-1288 |
| **New Hampshire** | Race, color, religion, gender, age, national origin, marital status, sexual orientation or physical or mental disability. Law Against Discrimination (N.H. Rev. Stat. Ann. §354-A:6)<br>Enforcing agency:<br>Human Rights Commission<br>163 Loudon Road<br>Concord, NH 03301<br>603-271-2767 |
| **New Jersey** | Race, color, religion, gender, national origin, ancestry, age between ages 18 and 70, marital status, sexual or affectional orientation, genetic information, atypical hereditary cellular or blood trait, past or present physical or mental disability or draft liability for the armed forces. Law Against Discrimination (N.J. Stat. Ann. §10:5-12) |

Enforcing agency:
Division of Civil Rights
31 Clinton Street, 3rd Floor
Newark, NJ 07102
201-648-2700

**New Mexico** Race, color, religion, gender, age, national origin,
ancestry, medical condition or physical or mental
disability. Human Rights Act (N.M. Stat. Ann. §28-1-7)
Enforcing agency:
Human Rights Commission
1596 Pacheco Street
Aspen Plaza
Santa Fe, NM 87505
505-827-6838

**New York** Race, color, religion, creed, gender, age if age 18 or
older, national origin, marital status, physical or mental
disability, genetic predisposition, pregnancy, political
activities. Human Rights Law (N.Y. Exec. Law §§292,
296; Labor Law §201-d)
Enforcing agency:
Division of Human Rights
55 West 125th Street
New York, NY 10027
212-961-8400

**North Carolina** Race, color, religion, gender, age, national origin.
Applies only to employers who regularly employ more
than 15 employees. Equal Employment Practices Act
(N.C. Gen. Stat. §143-422.2)
Sickle cell or hemoglobin C traits. N.C. Gen. Stat. §95-28.1
Physical or mental disability. N.C. Gen. Stat. §§168A-1
to A-5
AIDS or HIV condition. Statute specifically allows
employers to request applicants to take an AIDS test
and to deny employment based solely on a positive test
result, but protects existing employees from AIDS/HIV-
related discrimination. N.C. Gen. Stat. §130A-148
Enforcing agency:
Human Relations Commission
121 West Jones Street
Raleigh, NC 27603
919-733-7996

| North Dakota | Race, color, religion, gender, national origin, age if 40 or older, marital status, status with regard to public assistance or physical or mental disability and participation in lawful activity off the employer's premises during nonworking hours. N.D. Cent. Code §14.02.4-03 Enforcing agency: None |
|---|---|
| Ohio | Race, color, religion, gender, national origin, ancestry, age or physical or mental disability. Civil Rights Act (Ohio Rev. Code Ann. §4112.02) Age, if 40 years old or over. Ohio Rev. Code Ann. §4107.14 Enforcing agency: Civil Rights Commission 220 Parsons Avenue Columbus, OH 43266-0543 614-466-5928 |
| Oklahoma | Race, color, religion, gender, national origin, age if age 40 or older or physical disability. Applies to public employers and private employees with more than 20 employees. Civil Rights Act (Okla. Stat. Ann. tit. 25, §1302) Enforcing agency: Human Rights Commission 2101 North Lincoln Boulevard, Room 480 Oklahoma City, OK 73105 405-521-2360 |
| Oregon | Race, color, religion, gender, national origin, marital status, age if age 18 or older or because of a juvenile record that has been expunged. Protection is also extended to persons who associate with members of the protected groups. Fair Employment Act (Or. Rev. Stat. §659.030) Physical or mental disability. Or. Rev. Stat. §659.400 Enforcing agency: Civil Rights Division Bureau of Labor & Industry 800 NE Oregon Street, Box #32 Portland, OR 97232 503-731-4075 |

| Pennsylvania | Race, color, religion, gender, national origin, ancestry, age if between ages 40 and 70, familial status, physical or mental non-job-related handicap or disability or the use of a guide or support animal because of blindness, deafness or physical handicap. Human Relations Act (43 Pa. Cons. Stat. Ann §§953, 954)<br>Enforcing agency:<br>Human Relations Commission<br>Uptown Shopping Plaza<br>2971-E North 7th Street<br>Harrisburg, PA 17110-2123<br>717-787-4410 |
|---|---|
| Rhode Island | Race, color, religion, gender, pregnancy, ancestry, age if between ages 40 and 70, sexual orientation or physical or mental disability. Fair Employment Practices Act (R.I. Gen. Laws §§28-5-6 and 7)<br>AIDS condition or the perception of it. R.I. Gen. Laws §23-6-22<br>Enforcing agency:<br>Commission for Human Rights<br>10 Abbott Park Place<br>Providence, RI 02903-3768<br>401-277-2661 |
| South Carolina | Race, color, religion, gender, age if age 40 or older, national origin. Human Affairs Law (S.C. Code §§1-13-30 and -80)<br>Physical or mental disability. S.C. Code §43-33-530<br>Enforcing agency:<br>Human Affairs Commission<br>2611 Forest Drive, Suite 200<br>Columbia, SC 29204<br>803-253-6336 |
| South Dakota | Race, color, religion, creed, gender, national origin, ancestry or physical and mental disability. Human Relations Act (S.D. Codified Laws Ann. §20-13-10)<br>Enforcing agency:<br>Commission on Human Relations<br>224 West 9th Street<br>Sioux Falls, SD 57102<br>605-339-7039 |

| | |
|---|---|
| **Tennessee** | Race, creed, color, religion, gender, age, national origin. Fair Employment Practices Act (Tenn. Code Ann. §4-21-401)<br>Physical or mental disability. Tenn. Code Ann. §8-50-103<br>Enforcing agency:<br>Human Rights Commission<br>531 Henley Street, Suite 701<br>Knoxville, TN 37902<br>615-594-6500 |
| **Texas** | Race, color, religion, gender, pregnancy, age, national origin or physical or mental disability. Commission on Human Rights Act (Texas Code Ann. Lab. §§21.051, 21.105, 21.106, 21.108, 21.110, 21.119)<br>Enforcing agency:<br>Commission on Human Rights<br>8100 Cameron Road, #525<br>Austin, TX 78754<br>512-837-8534 |
| **Utah** | Race, color, religion, gender, age if over age 40, national origin, pregnancy, childbirth or related medical conditions or physical or mental disability. Anti-Discrimination Act (Utah Code Ann. §§34A-5-106)<br>Enforcing agency:<br>Anti-Discrimination Division of the Industrial Commission<br>160 East Third, South, 3rd floor<br>Salt Lake City, UT 84111<br>801-530-6801 |
| **Vermont** | Race, color, religion, gender, national origin, ancestry, age if age 18 or older, place of birth, sexual orientation, HIV-positive condition or requiring a blood test for the presence of HIV or physical or mental disability. Fair Employment Practices Act (Vt. Stat. Ann. tit. 21, §§495 and 495a and tit. 3, §961)<br>Enforcing agency:<br>Attorney General's Office<br>Civil Rights Division<br>109 State Street<br>Montpelier, VT 05609<br>802-828-3657 |

| | |
|---|---|
| **Virginia** | Race, color, religion, gender, national origin, age, marital status, pregnancy or physical or mental disability. Human Rights Act (Va. Code Ann. §2.1-714 and following)<br>Enforcing agency:<br>Council on Human Rights<br>1100 Bank Street<br>Richmond, VA 23219<br>804-225-2292 |
| **Washington** | Race, color, creed, gender, age if between age 40 and 70, national origin, marital status or the presence of any sensory, physical or mental disability, or the use of any trained guide or service dog by a disabled person. Wash. Rev. Code Ann. §49.60.180<br>Enforcing agency:<br>Human Rights Commission<br>1511 Third Avenue, Suite 921<br>Seattle, WA 98101<br>206-464-6500 |
| **West Virginia** | Race, religion, color, national origin, gender, familial status, age if 40 or older, physical or mental disability. Human Rights Act (W.V. Code §5-11-9)<br>Enforcing agency:<br>Human Rights Commission<br>1321 Plaza East, Room 106<br>Charleston, WV 25301<br>304-348-6880 |
| **Wisconsin** | Race, color, religion, gender, age if age 40 or older, national origin, sexual orientation, marital status, arrest or conviction record or physical disability. Fair Employment Practices Act (Wis. Stat. Ann. §111.321)<br>Enforcing agency:<br>Department of Industry, Labor and Human Relations Equal Rights Division<br>201 East Washington Avenue, Room 402<br>Madison, WI 53708<br>608-266-6860 |

| Wyoming | Race, color, creed, gender, national origin, ancestry, age if between ages 40 and 69 or physical or mental disability. Fair Employment Practices Act (Wyo. Stat. §27-9-105)<br>Enforcing agency:<br>Fair Employment Commission<br>6101 Yellowstone, Room 259C<br>Cheyenne, WY 82002<br>307-777-7262 |
|---|---|

# C. Equal Pay

A federal law, the Equal Pay Act (29 U.S.C. §206), requires you to pay all employees equally for equal work, regardless of their gender. It was passed in 1963 as an amendment to the Fair Labor Standards Act.

An employee who wishes to raise a claim under the Equal Pay Act must show that two employees, one male and one female, are:

- working in the same place
- doing equal work, and
- receiving unequal pay.

He—but more likely she—must also show that the employees in those jobs received unequal pay because of their genders.

**GOOD INTENTIONS, SMALL GAINS**

While the Equal Pay Act technically protects both women and men from gender discrimination in pay rates, it was passed to help rectify the problems faced by female workers because of sex discrimination in employment. And in practice, this law almost always has been applied to situations where women are being paid less than men for doing similar jobs.

The wage gap has narrowed slowly since 1980, when women's earnings were only 60% of men's; the 1998 figure has women earning about 76% as much as working men. But the Equal Pay Act likely has little to do with it. The law's biggest weakness, from an employee's perspective, is that it is strictly applied only when men and women are doing the same work. Since women have historically been banned from many types of work and had only limited entree to managerial positions, the Equal Pay Act in reality affects very few women.

## 1. Who Is Covered

The Equal Pay Act applies to all employers covered by the Fair Labor Standards Act, which means virtually all employers are covered. (See Chapter 5.) But the Equal Pay Act covers a number of additional categories of workers, including professional employees, executives, managers and administrators and teachers in elementary and secondary schools.

## 2. Equal Work

In equal pay cases, the issue often turns on whether the jobs are legally equal, rather than the number of dollars that go into a man's or woman's wallet for getting the job done. Jobs do not have to be mirror images for the courts to consider them equal. Minor differences in skill, effort and responsibility are not usually relevant. But significant differences—such as working in a department that produces significantly more revenue for the company than another—may be enough to differentiate the two jobs for equal pay purposes.

The focus is on the duties actually performed. Job titles, classifications and descriptions may weigh in to the determination, but are not the be all and end all.

## 3. Equal Pay

In general, pay systems that result in employees of one gender being paid less than the other gender for doing equal work are allowed under the Equal Pay Act if the pay system is actually based on a factor other than gender, such as a merit or seniority system.

## 4. Tips for Avoiding Claims

While it is a tough juggle, there are a number of steps you can take to help ward off discrimination claims in your workplace.

➡ Make sure that job descriptions are current and job titles accurate. Although these are not dispositive in proving or disproving a charge of illegal disparities in pay, they can be essential to you if they clearly show that two different employees perform two different jobs.

➡ Take an honest look at who gets the bigger bucks. The biggest problems arise where two jobs are basically the same, but one includes a few extra duties. It is perfectly legal to award higher pay for the extra duties, but some courts have looked askance at workplaces in which the higher-paying jobs with extra duties are consistently reserved for workers of one gender.

➡ If you need to cure a pay disparity between a male employee and female employee, the wiser approach is probably to pay the female more. Lowering the male employee's earnings will not cure an equal pay violation—and realistically, will leave you with two disgruntled employees rather than one who feels underpaid.

➡ Claims of unfairness in gender-based pay most often arise when a workforce is reorganized or reduced, leaving gender differences in pay. If business changes result in glaring disparities in pay based on gender, waste no time in righting the situation.

# D. Age Discrimination

A number of laws have been passed to protect the growing ranks of older employees. With the workforce aging rapidly and many workers staying on the job longer, employers can expect age discrimination claims to be the cause célèbre of the new millennium.

## 1. The Age Discrimination in Employment Act

The federal Age Discrimination in Employment Act, or ADEA (29 U.S.C. §§621 to 634), provides that workers over the age of 40 cannot be arbitrarily discriminated against because of age in any employment decision. Perhaps the single most important rule under the ADEA is that no worker can be forced to retire.

The Act also prohibits age discrimination in hiring, lay-offs, promotions, wages, healthcare coverage, pension accrual, firing, other terms and conditions of employment, referrals by employment agencies and union membership. It requires that you must have a valid reason not related to age—for example, economic reasons or poor job performance—for all employment decisions, but especially firing.

The ADEA applies to employees age 40 and older—and to workplaces with 20 or more employees. But some types of workers are exempt from the Act's coverage. They include:

- executives or people "in high policy-making positions" can be forced to retire at age 65 if they would receive annual retirement pension benefits worth $44,000 or more, and

- police and fire personnel, tenured university faculty and certain federal employees having to do with law enforcement and air traffic control are exempt from the ADEA.

**State Laws May Add Twists.** Most states have laws against age discrimination in employment. In many cases, the state law provides employees with broader protection than the federal law. For example, several states provide age discrimination protection to workers before they reach age 40, and other states protect against the actions of employers with fewer than 20 employees. (See Section B.)

## WHO'S ON SECOND MAY OR MAY NOT MATTER

Courts uniformly used to require proof that an employee who was discharged or demoted was replaced by someone younger than 40 years old. However, the U.S. Supreme Court recently held that a worker need not be replaced by a whippersnapper to make a case.

In one of the briefest opinions on record, the Court held that what is important is that a worker is discriminated against because of age; who takes over the job is irrelevant. The Court held that: "there can be no greater inference of age discrimination when a 40-year-old is replaced by a 39-year-old than when a 56-year-old is replaced by a 40-year-old" (*O'Connor v. Consolidated Coin Caterers Corp.,* 116 S.Ct. 1307 (1996)).

But in spite of the Supreme Court's directive to ignore the age of the replacing worker, many courts continue to do so. A number of courts have ruled that it is not enough for an employee to prove that he or she was displaced by a younger worker—that worker must be significantly younger. While the definition of the laden phrase significantly younger is still evolving, the meaning so far seems to be that there must be a gap of at least ten years before the law will mind it. For example, a court recently dismissed the age discrimination claim of a 51-year-old manager who was reorganized out of a workplace while other managers, ages 44 and 45, were allowed to remain on staff.

While decisions such as this may help make employers somewhat less skittish when dealing with the rapidly aging workforce, keep in mind that the best prevention for age discrimination lawsuits is to base all hiring, promoting and firing decisions on legitimate business reasons. Be sure you back them up with paperwork.

## 2. The Older Workers Benefit Protection Act

The Older Workers Benefit Protection Act (29 U.S.C. §§623, 626 and 630) was passed in 1990 to clarify how and when the ADEA applies to employee benefit programs. Its main purpose is to make it illegal to:

- use an employee's age as the basis for discrimination in benefits, and

- target older workers for cuts in staff.

This law is far-reaching; it covers all nonunion employees in private industry who are at least 40 years old. Unfortunately, most of the effects of this law are very difficult for anyone but a benefits administrator who is immersed in the lingo to understand. You might be wise to consult with one if you plan to cut benefits to older workers now on staff.

However, one provision of the law that you are most likely to use—regulating the legal waivers you may ask employees to sign in connection with early retirement programs—is relatively clear and specific. By signing a waiver—often called a release or covenant not to sue—an employee agrees not to take any legal action, such as an age discrimination lawsuit, against you. In return for signing the waiver, you give the employee an incentive to leave voluntarily, such as a severance pay package that exceeds the company's standard policy.

Under the Older Workers Benefit Protection Act, you must give an individual employee at least 21 days to decide whether or not to sign such a waiver. If the waiver is presented to a group of employees, you must give each of them at least 45 days to decide whether or not to sign. In either case, they have seven days after agreeing to such a waiver to change their minds.

There are a number of other key restrictions the Older Workers Benefit Protection Act places on agreements not to sue.

- You must make the waiver understandable to the average individual eligible for the program in which the waiver is being used.

- The waiver may not cover any rights or claims that arise after an employee signs it, and it must specify that it covers an employee's rights under the ADEA.

- You must offer something of value—over and above what is already owed to the employee—in exchange for his or her signature on the waiver.

- You must advise the employee in writing that he or she has the right to consult an attorney before signing the waiver.

- If you are making the offer to a class of employees, you must inform them all in writing how the class of employees is defined; the job titles and ages of all the individuals to whom the offer is being made; and the ages of all the employees in the same job classification or unit of the company to whom the offer is not being made. Because the law does not specify how many employees are required for a class, it is best to include this information whenever you make the offer to two or more people.

**This Is One Serious Piece of Paper.** Employers are allowed no room to hedge on any one of these requirements—and a waiver that does not comply with all the absolute requirements is the same as no waiver at all. The U.S. Supreme Court reaffirmed this in a recent decision—and pointedly held that an employee who signed a deficient waiver could not only sue for age discrimination, but did not need to return severance pay she received from her former employer (*Oubre v. Entergy Operations, Inc.,* 118 S.Ct. 838 (1998)).

## STICKS AND STONES MAY BREAK YOUR BONES,

But Words Can Land You in Court

Jokes, jibes and teasing can be healthy signs of camaraderie and pleasant tensionbreakers on the job. But age—always a touchy issue for many people—has recently become one of the prime ingredients in a growing number of discrimination lawsuits.

Given that reality, it may be better to ban the banter that might be subtle—or not so subtle—evidence of age discrimination. This is particularly true when supervisors use potentially loaded epithets to describe workers they mange.

Examples of phrases bandied about in workplaces that later were used as fodder in age discrimination claims include: "not keeping up with the times," "over the hill," "set in his ways," and those of the common canine variety: "you can't teach an old dog new tricks" and "old dogs won't hunt." The juries who heard these utterances—panels traditionally composed of older people—heard them in the vacuum of a courtroom. Apparently, all attempts to explain them away or prove their innocent intentions fell on deaf ears.

## 3. Tips for Avoiding Claims

There is some commonsense guidance you can follow to cut back on the possibility of age discrimination claims in your workplace.

Sharpen your ears for comments around the workplace that may reveal a bias against older workers. Terms such as Old Dog, Pops and Oldtimer may feel less than endearing to those on the receiving end. Do not use them yourself. And emphasize to all workers that your business will not tolerate these dangerous and rude epithets.

➡️ Give benefits and enforce performance standards evenhandedly, without regard to age. Those investigating claims of age discrimination will be especially attuned to patterns of treating older employees differently from younger ones.

➡️ Offer equal training opportunities to employees of all ages and stages. Avoid even the appearance that you are willing to invest more in younger workers on the theory that they will be on the job for a longer time.

➡️ Think both long and hard before imposing age limits on job requirements. You must be able to prove the limit is necessary because a worker's ability to adequately perform that job does in fact diminish after the age limit is reached.

# E. The Pregnancy Discrimination Act

The Pregnancy Discrimination Act, or PDA (92 Stat. §2076), passed in 1978 as an amendment to Title VII, gives some specialized workplace protections to new parents. The law clearly outlaws discrimination based on pregnancy, childbirth or any related medical condition.

## 1. Who Is Covered

Like other provisions of Title VII, the federal law that widely prohibits many types of discrimination, the PDA applies to your workplace if you:

- engage in some type of interstate commerce—today, broadly construed to include all employers that use the mails or telephones, and
- have 15 or more employees for any 20 weeks of a calendar year.

## 2. Prohibited Discrimination

The PDA specifies that pregnant employees—and those recovering from childbirth or an abortion—who need time off from work, must be treated the same as other temporarily disabled employees. For example, if you allow employees to return to work with full seniority and benefit rights after taking time off for a surgical operation and recovery, you must similarly reinstate women who take time off because of a pregnancy.

On the flip side, this law does not require you to provide more benefits for a pregnant worker than you provide for other temporarily disabled workers. If it is company policy, for example, to suspend seniority rights and benefits for employees who require extended medical leave, you can deny those work benefits to pregnant workers on leave.

Also, while the PDA bars discrimination based on pregnancy, it does not require you to provide a pregnant employee with leave—and does not guarantee job security while a worker is out on leave.

The PDA does include a few restrictions, however, of which employers are frequently unaware.

• The PDA bars mandatory maternity leaves—and those that are prescribed for a set time and duration. The focus instead is on whether an individual pregnant worker remains able to perform her job. And you cannot require a pregnant worker to take a leave from work during her pregnancy as long as she remains able to do her job.

• In addition, you cannot refuse to hire or promote a woman solely because she is pregnant—or because of stereotyped notions of what work is proper for a pregnant woman to do or not to do.

• The PDA also states that an employer cannot refuse to provide healthcare insurance benefits that cover pregnancy if it provides such benefits to cover other medical conditions. The sole exception here is you need not pay for health insurance benefits for an abortion—except where the life of the pregnant woman would be endangered if the fetus is carried to term or where there are medical complications following the abortion.

- And finally, you must grant men the same options for taking leave from their jobs to care for a child as you grant to women. To do otherwise would constitute illegal discrimination based on gender.

## 3. Tips on Complying

Given the growing number of confusing laws bestowing rights in the workplace, employers often crave one piece of advice above all others: They want to know what the law does not require them to do. This is particularly true in the case of laws passed to protect the ubiquitous goal of fostering Family Values. For example, an employer who needs to discipline or fire an employee who may be protected by the PDA may feel especially hamstrung; it seems somehow impolitic or callous to tread on those who are balancing work and home. Fortunately, however, there are some guidelines.

If a job applicant would miss out on critical training because of pregnancy, you may justifiably deny the job without risking a claim of pregnancy discrimination.

You may fire employees who miss an excessive amount of work because of pregnancy-related morning sickness if you also fire other employees with excessive absences.

Apart from leave mandated by the PDA, family and medical leave is not available to those who have a temporary disability— the non-familial-sounding category into which pregnancy is placed. (See Chapter 6.) Courts have held, for example, that it is not pregnancy discrimination to fire employees who needed leaves of absence— including medical leaves—during their first year of employment. ■

**CHAPTER 9**

# Guarding Against Sexual Harassment

**A**sk employers what potential workplace problem haunts their dreams these days, and most will offer the same unequivocal response: sexual harassment. There is good cause for unrest. The number of claims filed with the EEOC has soared since 1991, when the Thomas-Hill hearings made sexual harassment a workplace buzzword and the Civil Rights Act was amended to allow damage awards to those who make out a case. The bigger number of claims filed do not mean more harassment is occurring—just more awareness of the issue and a greater willingness to take action against it. This reality should act as a wake-up call to employers: Be Prepared.

This chapter sets out the policies and procedures an employer can adopt to monitor, detect and deal with sexual harassment on the job. Unlike other chapters in this book, this one is heavy on forms—offering a sample sexual harassment policy, complaint form and workplace monitoring survey. The reason is that employers can do much to avoid the volatile problems of workplace sexual harassment. A solid policy against harassment and scrupulous enforcement of it are musts.

Courts occasionally require a company to write up a comprehensive policy as part of the legal relief ordered in a sexual harassment case. But more often these days, the impetus to rid the workplace of sexual harassment comes from within. Fear of lawsuits is not the only reason. The link between decreased productivity and workplace harassment is now well-documented. As a result, more employers are taking an active role, adopting formal policies to prevent sexual harassment where possible and to deal with it when it occurs. Those who choose to ignore the problem in the hope it will go away find that it only gets worse.

For comprehensive information about sexual harassment, see *Sexual Harassment on the Job: What It Is and How to Stop It*, by William Petrocelli and Barbara Kate Repa (Nolo).

# A. Sexual Harassment Defined

In legal terms, sexual harassment is any unwelcome sexual advance or conduct on the job that creates an intimidating, hostile or offensive working environment. Simply put, sexual harassment is any offensive conduct related to an employee's gender that a reasonable woman or man should not have to endure.

The forms that sexual harassment can take are as varied as a perverse imagination can create. An employee who has been led to believe she must sleep with her boss to keep her job has been sexually harassed, as has one whose co-workers regularly tell offensive, sex-related jokes and plaster their walls with pictures of nude women. An employee who is pinched or fondled against her will by a co-worker has been sexually harassed, as has one whose colleagues leer at her, block her path or act like they're going to grab her.

An employee who is constantly belittled and referred to by sexist or demeaning names has been sexually harassed, as has one who is subjected to repeated lewd or pornographic remarks. Sexual harassment occurs when a supervisor acts as if the women working under him owe him sexual favors, and it also occurs when a co-worker attacks or intimidates a woman because he doesn't think she should be doing what he considers Man's Work.

Although it is usually men who sexually harass women on the job, such harassment can be inflicted by women against men, by women against women, and by men against men. Hostility based on gender is the test, rather than the gender of those involved.

# B. The Employer's Duty

In two of its most recent pronouncements on sexual harassment, the U.S. Supreme Court began to define what steps employers must take to help stamp out this unwanted behavior in their workplaces.

In one case, the Court held that an employer may be liable for sexual harassment even when an employee did not succumb to sexual advances or suffer adverse job consequences. But the employer could defend itself against liability and damages by showing that it used reasonable care in stopping harassment—a strong written anti-harassment policy or an investigation procedure. An employee who does not take advantage of the workplace policy by reporting the harassment has a considerably weaker case (*Burlington Industries, Inc. v. Ellerth*, 524 U.S. 742 (1998)).

In another case, the Court held again that an employer could defend itself against a sexual harassment charge by showing it acted reasonably to prevent it. But it found that an employer acted unreasonably by failing to distribute its anti-harassment policy or establishing a complaint procedure—and as a result, was liable for the harassment (*Faragher v. City of Boca Raton, Florida*, 524 U.S. 775 (1998)).

Yet another recent case—this one decided by a California appellate court—commended an employer for its "textbook example of how to respond appropriately to an employee's harassment complaint." The court was impressed that, immediately after receiving a letter from an employee alleging she was sexually harassed, the employer:

- requested a meeting with her to discuss the allegations
- questioned the accused harasser

- interviewed employees and former employees the accused harasser supervised, and

- promptly gave the accusing employee a letter summarizing its investigation and the action it took.

While the company found no evidence of sexual harassment, it did find the accused had "exhibited extremely poor judgment" in a number of words and deeds. It added a written reprimand and warning to his personnel file—specifying the errors he made and warning him from "initiating any contact whatsoever" with the accuser, on pain of immediate termination (*Casenas v. Fujisawa USA, Inc.*, 58 C.A. 4th 101 (1997)).

# C. Sexual Harassment Policies

A well-crafted sexual harassment policy can offer both employees and employers guidance and certainty in dealing with harassment in the workplace.

## 1. Benefits to Employees

If an employer has a clear written policy prohibiting harassment, all who work there will have a firmer idea of what behavior will not be tolerated in the workplace. If a worker is harassed, a strong policy can guide him or her as to how to take action against it.

Despite some paranoid perceptions, very few workers who bring complaints about sexual harassment on the job are seeking big bucks or vengeance. Their goal, at least initially, is to make the harassment stop—and to take all practical steps to see that it stays stopped. It is typically only where an employer offers no fair way to resolve the problem that sexual harassment complaints evolve into lawsuits.

And when an employer does not take heed of complaints, an employee armed with a sexual harassment policy that has been ignored will often be best armed to pursue more formal legal options to end the harassment.

## 2. Benefits to Employers

Employees who are sexually harassed on the job often become distressed, depressed, frightened or angry. It is not easy to hold a job while also working fulltime to keep a harasser at bay. And the challenge often takes its toll: Sexually harassed workers often become demoralized and miss work—and even while on the job, are much less able to concentrate and to work efficiently.

All of this runs counter to every employer's prime goal: workplace productivity. A number of recent workplace studies show the high cost of tolerating sexual harassment:

- over 25% of women who are sexually harassed on the job use leave time to avoid the uncomfortable work situation.
- at least 15% of women who are harassed at work quit their jobs because of it, and
- nearly 50% of those harassed try to ignore it—and they suffer about a 10% drop in productivity; the harassed worker's peers who know of the situation also suffer a 2% drop in productivity.

But perhaps money talks most loudly: Ignoring sexual harassment can cost the average company up to $6.7 million a year in absenteeism, employee turnover, low morale and low productivity.

In addition to these indirect costs, an employer who tolerates sexual harassment risks the high administrative costs involved in EEOC and other agency complaint investigations, as well as the pricey possibility of a successful lawsuit against it. Since many employers hire expensive corporate lawyers at the first scent of legal trouble, the costs of defending a sexual harassment lawsuit are extremely high.

And of course, if the harassed employee wins, costs to the employer will be even higher—sometimes a lot higher. Several employers have been hard hit with jury verdicts ranging into several million dollars for emotional distress, lost wages and wrongful discharge.

## 3. Tips for Good Policies

An effective sexual harassment policy discourages harassment. And it should also encourage employees to report all serious incidents of harassment promptly—with an eye to eliminating them. Employees cannot be required to report sexual harassment; that would be coercive and illegal. But if there is a sensible and sensitively written policy against harassment, backed by good policies to deal with it as confidentially as possible and to prevent retaliation against the person making the complaint, most employees will gratefully comply.

A model policy is offered here, but keep in mind that a sexual harassment policy will be effective only if it is appropriate and realistic for your workplace. A conservative, multi-tiered accounting conglomerate based in New York City, for example, may find it reasonable to have more buttoned-down strictures on permissible workplace behavior than a small computer graphics company based in San Francisco or a tractor dealership in Pocatello, Idaho.

Also, to be effective, a sexual harassment policy must be clear and comprehensible. A growing number of employers pridefully point to the fact that they have written sexual harassment policies. However, a quick look at most policies reveals that they are so replete with legalese and cross-references to other workplace documents that they are more confusing than curing. Be sure your company adopts a policy that is meaningful and written so that it can be easily understood by everyone.

Finally, a sexual harassment policy should be seen by all as a work in progress. It will surely need to be changed with the times and perhaps even altered to reflect the changing roles and numbers of employees. To make sure that this happens, the policy should be reviewed and amended regularly. One good way to do this is to pass it around to all employees each year for comments and suggestions.

The most effective sexual harassment policies have a number of common elements.

➡️ The policy should include a statement that sexual harassment will not be tolerated. A short, direct statement that sexual harassment will not be endured is most effective. In addition, let employees know that sexual harassment is against the law.

➡️ Define what behavior is prohibited. This used to be no small task. Fortunately, after struggling for years to come up with meaningful definitions of prohibited harassing behavior, the EEOC, legislatures and courts have made considerable progress. Today, it is possible to provide a number of clear definitions and rules. For example, it is clearly sexual harassment to suggest that future promotions will be bestowed in exchange for sexual favors.

While even the best policy cannot set out every kind of prohibited behavior, a good one should go beyond declarative language to list some specific examples. For example, a sexual harassment policy may ban:

- Verbal harassment, including making sexual comments about a person's body, telling sexual jokes or stories, spreading rumors about a co-worker's sex life, asking or telling about sexual fantasies, preferences or history
- Nonverbal harassment, such as giving unwanted personal gifts, following a person, staring at a person's body, displaying sexually suggestive material such as pornographic photos
- Physical harassment, including touching yourself in a sexual manner in front of another person, brushing up against another person suggestively.

➡️ Spell out what action will be taken for first-time offenses and repeated unacceptable conduct. Punishments should be appropriate, certain and reasonably strict. Appropriate action can range from a written warning in the employee's personnel file to counseling, suspension from work, transfer to a different position or dismissal.

➡️ Give guidelines on how to report harassment. Detail how, when and where employees can complain about harassment. For example, if the first step is to contact a particular person within the company, make clear exactly how to do that. The complaint process should be as confidential as possible. If a form is required to initiate a complaint, include a copy in every employee handbook—or at least be sure that the form is easily accessible. (See Section D for a sample.)

Provide an alternative to employees who do not wish to file the complaint with their own supervisors, some of whom may either be responsible for the harassment or guilty of ignoring it. Make it possible to report the harassment to any other supervisor—or to anyone on a panel of employees designated to handle company grievances.

➡️ Provide for prompt and confidential investigations. Despite all best intentions to keep the matter hushed, news of a harassment investigation tends to circulate fast. And people often take sides quickly. Proceeding speedily and appropriately with the investigation helps take the strain from the workplace, stems the tides of worry and gossip and, above all, is the best way to get at the truth of the matter. During the investigation, as during the initial complaint filing, make every effort to respect the confidentiality of all involved.

➡️ Make the results known. A report of the findings of a harassment investigation and a notation about whether any action is to be taken should be given to both the harassed employee and the accused harasser.

➡️ Take a strong stand against retaliation. The fear of retaliation is what keeps many employees from reporting even the most egregious workplace harassment. The retaliation may come from the harasser who, as a manager or supervisor, transfers an employee to an undesirable position, changes his or her work duties to be either mundane or overwhelming or fires the worker.

Co-workers, especially friends and supporters of the harasser, sometimes retaliate against an employer who has rocked the boat by reporting harassment. They may refuse to cooperate with the employee—so it becomes evermore difficult for her to work—or they may shun him or her.

A good harassment policy should also assure employees that there will not be any retaliation for filing a complaint against workplace harassment or for cooperating in the investigation of another's complaint. The policy should also spell out the kinds of discipline—reprimand, suspension, transfer, dismissal—that will be imposed against those who retaliate.

➡️ Provide training sessions and monitoring. A sexual harassment policy should also provide for regular education and training—and for periodic monitoring of the workplace.

## 4. Sample Policy

Here is a good start for a sexual harassment policy that can be modified to fit the needs of most workplaces.

## SEXUAL HARASSMENT POLICY

[Employer name] is committed to providing a work environment where women and men can work together comfortably and productively, free from sexual harassment. Such behavior is illegal under both state and federal law—and will not be tolerated here.

This policy applies to all phases of employment—including recruiting, testing, hiring, upgrading, promotion or demotion, transfer, layoff, termination, rates of pay, benefits and selection for training, travel or company social events.

### Prohibited Behavior

Prohibited sexual harassment includes unsolicited and unwelcome contact that has sexual overtones. This includes:

- written contact, such as sexually suggestive or obscene letters, notes, invitations
- verbal contact, such as sexually suggestive or obscene comments, threats, slurs, epithets, jokes about gender-specific traits, sexual propositions
- physical contact, such as intentional touching, pinching, brushing against another's body, impeding or blocking movement, assault, coercing sexual intercourse, and
- visual contact, such as leering or staring at another's body, gesturing, displaying sexually suggestive objects or pictures, cartoons, posters or magazines.

Sexual harassment also includes continuing to express sexual or social interest after being informed directly that the interest is unwelcome—and using sexual behavior to control, influence or affect the career, salary or work environment of another employee.

It is impermissible to suggest, threaten or imply that failure to accept a request for a date or sexual intimacy will affect an employee's job prospects. For example, it is forbidden either to imply or actually withhold support for an appointment, promotion, or change of assignment, or to suggest that a poor performance report will be given because an employee has declined a personal proposition.

Also, offering benefits, such as promotions, favorable performance evaluations, favorable assigned duties or shifts, recommendations or reclassifications in exchange for sexual favors is forbidden.

### Harassment by Non-Employees

In addition, [Employer name] will take all reasonable steps to prevent or eliminate sexual harassment by non-employees including customers, clients and suppliers, who are likely to have workplace contact with our employees.

### Monitoring

[Employer name] shall take all reasonable steps to see that this policy prohibiting sexual harassment is followed by all employees, supervisors and others who have contact with our employees. This prevention plan will include training sessions, ongoing monitoring of the worksite and a confidential employee survey to be conducted and evaluated every six months.

### Discipline

Any employee found to have violated this policy shall be subject to appropriate disciplinary action, including warnings, reprimand, suspension or discharge, according to the findings of the complaint investigation.

If an investigation reveals that sexual harassment has occurred, the harasser may also be held legally liable for his or her actions under state or federal anti-discrimination laws or in separate legal actions.

### Retaliation

Any employee bringing a sexual harassment complaint or assisting in investigating such a complaint will not be adversely affected in terms and conditions of employment, or discriminated against or discharged because of the complaint. Complaints of such retaliation will be promptly investigated and punished.

### Complaint Procedure and Investigation

[Title of person appointed] is designated as the Sexual Harassment Counselor. All complaints of sexual harassment and retaliation for reporting or participating in an investigation shall be directed to the Sexual Harassment Counselor or to a supervisor of your choice, either in writing, by filling out the attached Complaint Form, or by requesting an individual interview. All complaints shall be handled as confidentially as possible. The Sexual Harassment Counselor will promptly investigate and resolve complaints involving violations of this policy and recommend to management the appropriate sanctions to be imposed against violators.

### Training

[Employer name] will establish yearly training sessions for all employees concerning their rights to be free from sexual harassment and the legal options available if they are harassed. In addition, training sessions will be held for supervisors and managers, educating them in how to keep the workplace as free from harassment as possible and in how to handle sexual harassment complaints.

A copy of the policy will be distributed to all employees and posted in areas where all employees will have the opportunity to freely review it. [Employer name] welcomes your suggestions for improvements to this policy.

# D. Complaint Procedures

A good harassment policy is a crucial first step in ridding a workplace of offensive, unwanted behavior. But it won't count for much unless an employer also adopts a trustworthy and energetic procedure for handling and investigating complaints. (See Chapter 11 for a discussion of effective investigations.)

A helpful attachment to a sexual harassment policy is a complaint form to record important dates, facts, names and flag important follow-up procedures.

---

**SAMPLE SEXUAL HARASSMENT COMPLAINT FORM**

Name: _____

Department: _____

Job Title: _____

Immediate Supervisor: _____

1. Who was responsible for the harassment? _____

_____

2. Describe the sexual harassment. _____

First incident: _____

_____

_____

Approximate date, time and place: _____

What was your reaction? _____

_____

_____

Second incident: _____

_____

_____

---

Approximate date, time and place: _____

What was your reaction? _____

_____

_____

Subsequent incidents: _____

_____

_____

Approximate date, time and place: _____

What was your reaction? _____

_____

_____

3. List any witnesses to the harassment: _____

_____

_____

_____

I understand that these incidents will be investigated, but this form will be kept confidential to the highest degree possible.

Employee: _____

Date: _____

**FOR EMPLOYER'S USE**

Dates of investigation of complaint: _____

_____

_____

Date of final report: _____

_____

_____

Copy sent to employee: _____

Action taken: _____

_____

_____

_____

_____

Date of follow-up conference with employee: _____

Results: _____

_____

_____

_____

Date of follow-up conference with employee: _____

Results: _____

_____

_____

_____

Date of follow-up conference with employee: _____

Results: _____

_____

_____

_____

_____

## THE IMPORTANCE OF PROPER TRAINING

Sexual harassment in the workplace can be curbed or even eliminated by training supervisors and employees to recognize its signals and head it off. Doing this will end the need for harassment-related lawsuits, increase productivity and make the workplace more comfortable for everyone. Often, such training requires guidance from experts.

Sexual harassment training can take many different forms, depending on the size and budget of a company. The best training programs involve all levels of employees so that the entire workplace gets a better understanding of sexual harassment—why it happens, who it affects, typical reactions of both the harasser and harassed and effective ways to make the harassment stop.

An increasing number of employers now offer anti-harassment training on the job, according to the American Management Association; 40% of the companies it surveyed provided training in 1991, 65% in 1996.

Typically, a trainer will visit a workplace and diagnose what is needed there. Most trainers offer:

- help with writing a sexual harassment policy and a procedure for enforcing it—both tailored to the individual workplace
- seminars to increase staff awareness of sexual harassment, including strategies for preventing and addressing workplace harassment
- programs specifically geared to teach managers how to investigate and deal with sexual harassment complaints, so that everyone in the workplace will have some confidence in the process, and
- additional training for managers and supervisors in how to lead periodic sexual harassment prevention workshops in their own workplaces.

Large employers often require a full range of training services. Smaller employers without the resources for full-blown training and follow-up programs can still get expert, cost-effective help in designing a good sexual harassment policy. Also, for a reasonable cost, a few employees can attend one of the growing number of seminars offered by outside workplace consultants. Many trainers offer discount rates if a number of employees, such as three or more, attend their training.

# E. Monitoring the Workplace

In addition to adopting a sexual harassment policy and complaint procedure and providing employees with training, employers who are truly committed to eradicating sexual harassment should actively monitor their workplaces. The best way to do this is to regularly remind employees that sexual harassment is illegal and will not be tolerated—and to urge them to assess whether it is a problem in the workplace. You may also consider conducting a survey of the workplace every year or so—encouraging employees to give confidential assessments of whether sexual harassment affects their worklives. ■

## CHAPTER 10

# Guarding Against Violence

**W**orkplaces are places of human intrigue, where mixes of personality in proximity breed the best and worst in emotions. In the best of times and places, workers reach new levels of understanding and harmony. In the worst, resentments fester into violence.

## A. Violence in the Workplace

The numbers and pronouncements about our chances of being attacked or killed while at work are scary.

The number of violent acts committed in the workplace has increased 300% in the last decade. An increasing amount of the violence is lethal. Homicide reigns as the leading cause of workplace death among women. In fact, the National Institute for Occupational Safety and Health lists homicide as a leading cause of all work-related deaths in the United States, second only to motor vehicle crashes. An average of 20 people are murdered each week in American workplaces.

In addition to this, an estimated one million workers suffer assaults that are not fatal on the job each year—with 85% of these assaults occurring to those who work in the retail trade and service industries. The U.S. Postal Service alone reported 500 cases of employees being violent toward supervisors in a recent period of 18 months—and an additional 200 cases of supervisors acting violently toward employees. Frightening results of a recent study claim that an employee in California is more likely to be murdered at work than to die in a car accident commuting to or from work. And the state boasts many, many commuters.

## B. Recognizing Potentially Violent Workers

In the past, employers contending with the threat of violence in the workplace had little more constructive to do than advise workers to duck and take cover. But a closer look reveals the helpful information that there were a number of common warning signals. The individuals who have erupted have usually been displeased with how a co-worker, supervisor or the impersonal entity The Company have treated them on the job—and most have been vocal about this angst or have dropped some hint that they intend to act.

That said, it is also true that part of what makes violent behavior difficult to control is that it often comes unannounced and uncontrolled. Still, there is a common pattern. Most workplace killers are disgruntled former employees who have been laid off or fired or they are the obsessed spouse or lover of an employee.

And those who kill at work, experts say, usually give off red flags that typically include:

- following or stalking an employee to or from work
- entering the workplace
- following an employee at work, and
- telephoning or sending correspondence to the employee.

Co-workers describe many individuals who have committed violence in the workplace as: loners, not team players, having a history of interpersonal conflict and displays of anger, having made threats of violence in the past, being withdrawn, showing symptoms of current drug or alcohol abuse, being argumentative and quick to blame others for their own problems and frustrations.

Both employers and employees may be able to help ward off violence by heeding these signs of trouble and taking immediate action. Encourage employees to report threatening co-workers. As an employer, be prepared to act quickly to both refer problem workers to a ready source of help and tell them, in no uncertain terms, that they will be fired if their bad behavior continues.

Your duties to clamp down on potential assailants may extend beyond those people on the payroll. Some workplace experts posit that nearly 20% of all violent episodes on the job are committed not by one employee against another, but by a worker's spouse, partner or family member who tracks them down at work. If you learn that an angry relative or former lover is on an employee's trail, take the warning seriously. And take action to protect all those on the job.

## WHO'S AT RISK?

Workplace violence is clustered in particular occupations, with well over half of all recent workplace homicides occurring in retail trade and service occupations. In these types of jobs—as well as in finance, insurance and real estate—homicide is the leading cause of workplace death.

Several researchers have isolated facts that they believe increase a worker's risk for workplace assault. They include:
- having contact with the public
- exchanging money
- delivering passengers, goods or services
- having a mobile workplace, such as a taxicab
- working with unstable or volatile people such as healthcare, social or criminal justice clients
- working alone or in small numbers
- working late at night or in the early morning hours
- working in areas with high crime rates
- guarding valuable property or possessions, and
- working in community-based settings.

Source: National Institute for Occupational Safety and Health, Public Health Summary, "Violence in the Workplace"

## C. Taking Action

Employers who try to ward off violence often get caught in the conundrum of balancing employees' safety against the rights of the potential perpetrator. On one hand, employers are charged with keeping the workplace safe. Several have been successfully sued for negligent hiring, negligent supervision and wrongful death because they kept suspicious employees on staff who ultimately maimed or killed others on the job. But employers have also been sued by employees who claimed that overzealous investigations have violated laws protecting them from discrimination or invasions of their privacy.

Of late, scales are tipping in favor of keeping workplaces safe. In 1994, for example, a Massachusetts court held that an employer, the U.S. Postal Service, was well within its rights when it fired a worker who screamed obscenities, swept the contents off a supervisor's desk, threw a typewriter and chair and knocked down several office partitions. The employee defended that he had an explosive personality disorder that entitled him to protection as a disabled employee rather than a pink slip. But the court concluded that a fundamental requirement of any job is that an employee must not be violent and destructive (*Mazzarella v. U.S. Postal Service*, 849 F.Supp. 89 (D. Mass. 1994)).

And a Florida court held shortly after that an employee—even one diagnosed with a chemical imbalance—could be fired on the spot for bringing a loaded gun to work (*Hindman v. GTE Data Services*, 4 A.D. Cas. (BNA) 182 (M.D. Fla. 1995)).

Increasingly, the pressure to act comes from victims of workplace violence and their survivors. And an increasing number of courts find employers directly liable for violence when they turn a deaf ear to workers' complaints about inadequate security—or a blind eye to knowledge that a worker's past actions might make him or her likely to attack co-workers and others on the job.

It is essential that you encourage employees to report co-workers' threatening behavior and promptly investigate any such reports. (See Chapter 11.) It is particularly important to give the angry or disgruntled employee a chance to vent his or her dissatisfaction, preferably in a private place in a confidential conversation. In many cases, this can defuse the anger enough to avert a volatile situation.

You must also stand at the ready to act quickly. It may be frightening to confront someone you suspect might be irrational and volatile. But here's a reality that will help you overcome your fear and loathing of taking action: Unchecked violent behavior usually becomes more severe and more frequent over time.

### STOP—IN THE NAME OF THE LAW

In a response to the perception that workplace violence is careening out of control, California recently enacted the Workplace Violence Act (Cal. Civ. Code §527.8).

The most powerful provision in the law's arsenal allows employers to get a court order called a permanent injunction against an employee or others who threaten or actually commit violence against employees in the workplace. The injunctions, which typically forbid a person from continuing threats or coming to a worksite, will only be issued if there has actually been violence in the past or there is a current serious threat of death or injury.

A number of employers have obtained injunctions against threatening employees since the law took effect in January 1995. But all report that what is most important is the not the injunction itself, but obtaining cooperation from police, district attorney's offices and city attorney's offices—the agencies ultimately responsible for enforcing the law and removing the threat of harm from the workplace.

# D. Tips for Preventing Violence

It is important not to overreact to a report of erratic behavior in a way that creates an atmosphere of panic in the workplace. But it is essential to take appropriate action once you are privy to such intelligence.

If a particular employee has been singled out as a target, there are a number of definitive things you can do to protect him or her.

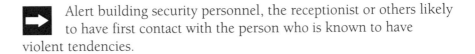 Alert building security personnel, the receptionist or others likely to have first contact with the person who is known to have violent tendencies.

➡️ Move the targeted employee's office or workstation— preferably to a spot that is busy.

➡️ Offer the employee a work schedule with varied hours or arrange to have him or her work at home for a time.

➡️ Install a silent alarm or other security device at the employee's desk.

If you have a greater fear about potential violence coming from outsiders such as clients, customers or other members of the public, you might consider a few other or additional changes to your workplace.

➡️ Adjust the way you handle cash—for example, by using locked drop safes, retaining only small amounts of cash on the site, posting notices stating that only limited amounts of cash are available.

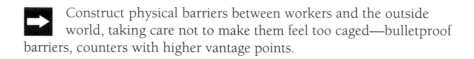

Construct physical barriers between workers and the outside world, taking care not to make them feel too caged—bulletproof barriers, counters with higher vantage points.

Install good internal and external lighting.

Be sure that employees have easy access to and from work areas—and that the work building has no obvious hiding spots, such as overgrown vegetation, where attackers might lurk and hide. This change might involve spending some money on reconfiguring the building, but the investment may be worth the pace of mind it provides.

Consider installing any of the burgeoning types of security devices now on the market—including closed circuit cameras, alarms, two-way mirrors, cardkey access and specialized door locks.

Look into personnel policies that may bolster safety on the job— adding escorts to cars after hours, varying times of money drops, increasing staff during opening and closing, providing training to employees in how to deal with workplace violence. ■

**CHAPTER 11**

# Conducting Investigations

In dealing with complaints—from sexual harassment to discrimination to surly behavior on the job—you must investigate to diagnose what went asunder. Indeed, if legal wrongdoing is reported, you have no choice but to investigate. And if you have someone on staff with the sense and sensitivity to conduct a skillful investigation, that will usually help nip a problem early in its budding—or at least help define it. Employers with the ability to conduct a fair and thorough investigation will often avoid the need to call in outsiders such as lawyers or government agency staffers to perform their own investigations.

And there's more: If a particular complaint cannot be resolved behind your own closed doors and it escalates into a legal claim with an agency or court, the fact that you conducted a reasonable investigation of the alleged wrong will help in your defense.

Begin your investigation with both eyes open, realizing that investigations can be risky business. But the risks will only arise if you are sloppy or incomplete—basing an employment decision on an inadequate or biased investigation, or stirring up rather than stilling the gossip mill after the investigation is concluded. In evaluating investigations, courts look most closely at whether they are timely, fair and effective. These are good watchwords for you to digest, even if you ultimately manage to avoid a more formal claim or complaint.

## THE IMPORTANCE OF QUICK REFLEXES

Employers may get their best protection from legal liability by conducting a prompt and effective investigation of a workplace wrong. But there are other, less tangible benefits to proceeding quickly—generally, within one day of receiving a complaint of wrongdoing.

Investigating sends the message that you are a business committed to doing what is right and to righting perceived wrongs—or at least taking all possible reasonable steps to do so. Again, it is reasonableness and an effort to be fair that carry the day for employers when workplace problems get aired before a judge, jury or investigating agency.

Also, prompt investigations, no matter their result, usually help quash disturbances within the workforce—which may range from mild disquiet among the staff to fractionated camps fed by the office gossip mill to outright revolt. Productivity and morale are salvaged, too.

In addition, prompt investigations may give employees who feel they were wronged the one thing they want most: a forum in which to vent and be heard. That alone saves many employees from turning too quickly to the courts for a resolution.

And finally, an effective and speedy investigation will often help prevent the same type of bad behavior from occurring in the future.

# A. Investigation Basics

Assure employees that not only are they welcome to complain about perceived wrongdoings on the job, but that bringing them to your attention is part and parcel of keeping the workplace safe and sane for all. Emphasize that a true and well-motivated complaint will not get them shunned, demoted or fired. It may help overcome employees' initial reticence if you emphasize that all reports and investigations will be confidential. (See Section B.)

The tone and tenor of the investigation of a workplace complaint often means the difference between achieving a prompt and satisfactory resolution of the problem or having it explode into an expensive legal battle. A shoddy, lip service investigation not only fails to end the workplace problem, but in a later lawsuit, risks becoming key evidence of your failure to take the wrongdoing seriously.

A thorough investigation will have the earmarks discussed in this chapter.

## 1. Getting Started

The key to resolving complaints is promptness. Not only is it extremely demoralizing to all concerned to have an unresolved complaint hanging in the workplace air, but a delayed investigation will likely result in hazy recollections. A good rule is that the investigation should begin no later than a day after a complaint is received.

Prepare for the investigation in advance by sketching out its specific purpose and setting out a timeframe for the steps that will likely follow. Draw up some questions that will help keep you on track and help ensure that you do not tread on any employee's privacy. Secure a safe place for all notes and documents involved in the investigation—preferably a locked file to which few people have access.

## 2. Who Should Investigate

The person who investigates the complaint must be perceived within the workplace as fair and objective.

Sometimes, a knowledgeable Human Resources staffer is the best fit for the job. For larger employers that can bring in an impartial person from another part of the company, it may be best to do so. Depending on your workplace, it may be preferable to bring in an outside investigator. Your state Fair Employment Practices agency make be able to refer one to you.

The nature of the incident being investigated may influence your choice of who does the job. For example, some women feel uncomfortable discussing a sexual harassment incident with a male investigator. A woman who feels this discomfort should have the option of being assigned a female investigator—or at least having a female personnel employee with her during investigation interviews.

For all claims, be sure there are at least two people to whom employees can go to register a complaint and that at least one of them is not an immediate supervisor—a person who may hold the keys to their promotions, raises, even staying on the job itself. Having two people designated as recipients for complaints allows an employee to bypass one who may be perceived as hostile, or in cahoots with the person who is the target of the complaint.

### STOP—IN THE NAME OF THE LAW

When interviewing the employee who has the complaint, the accused employee and any potential witnesses to the wrong, it is best to hold those conversations separately and in a soundproof room—away from the watchful eyes and pricked up ears of other workers. However, make clear to all individuals that they are free to leave at any time, that they are not being arrested or confined against their wills. If anyone utters the magic words "I'd like to talk with my attorney," stop at once and allow the person to make the call.

## 3. Making a Paper Trail

Documentation is a critical part of your investigation. Keep a log of the names and addresses of all the people you interview. You may wish to have the person being questioned summarize the main points in his or her own words and handwriting. At a minimum, summarize the larger points orally—and ask for a confirmation that you heard and understood correctly.

Whether or not you ask the person being interviewed to write out his or her comments, be sure to take your own notes—detailed, objective notes—during all interviews. While you might be tempted to tape record your talks on the theory that the tape would never lie, it is generally a risky idea. Taping tends to rob the interview of candor and spontaneity. And most states have laws about when and whether it is legal to tape record conversations—with most such regulations strictly outlawing secret taping.

## B. Interviewing the Complaining Employee

Ask the worker who has the complaint to recount details of the behavior he or she found offensive—including names, dates, places and specific behavior. This process can be painful, so encourage him or her to bring prepared notes. In addition, a preprinted Complaint Form can help the interview be more organized and focused and less intimidating. (See Section B1, below.)

Be prepared for an outpouring of strong emotion. Workers reporting a wrong often do so only as a last resort. Many have been wrestling with their feelings of embarrassment, sadness, or anger. They may even feel that they are doing something wrong—being snitches. Their conversations may be fraught with tears or rage. Your best response is to listen. Refrain from offering advice or a solution until you have all the facts.

**THE WORD IS MUM**

Stress confidentiality. Do all you can to stem the tide of watercooler chatter that may flow from the knowledge that a complaint has been lodged against a worker.

Do not discuss the investigation with anyone who does not need to know. Contrary to your instincts, an open discussion with other employees will more likely stoke the fires of gossip rather than squelch its flames.

Assure the employee who brings the complaint that the matter will be kept private and discussed with no more people than is necessary. And while the employee must be free to discuss the harassment incidents with outside confidantes and friends, once a complaint has been filed, counsel him or her not to discuss specifics of the investigation too freely with co-workers.

Beware that some complaints are unjustified. Maintaining confidentiality is an important safeguard for you as an employer, as it will likely help stave off claims of libel or slander from the person being investigated.

Also, keep a tight fist on pieces of paper generated by the investigations—reports, interview summaries, witness lists. Show them only to people heading up the investigation who absolutely must see them. Make few copies—and keep tabs on them.

## 1. Sample Complaint Form

As mentioned, employees who complain to you about a workplace slight will often be tearful, fearful, hesitant, reticent, or just plain nervous. It might help begin the investigation process if you give them a few moments alone to compose their thoughts—and to jot them down on the form below. You will then be forewarned and informed—and in a better position to discuss their complaints with them.

Use your fingertips here. Be mindful that staving off the initial interview with this bit of paperwork may not be a good way to deal with workers who have difficulties reading or writing. Others, however, will likely feel assured that you have taken their problem seriously and will relish the opportunity to get the conversation started in a nonthreatening way.

---

**COMPLAINT FORM**

Name: _____

Department: _____

Job Title: _____

Immediate Supervisor: _____

1. Who was involved in the incident? _____

_____

2. Describe what happened. _____

First incident: _____

_____

_____

Approximate date, time and place: _____

What was your reaction? _____

_____

_____

Second incident: _____

_____

_____

Approximate date, time and place: _____

What was your reaction? _____

_____

_____

Subsequent incidents: _____

_____

_____

Approximate date, time and place: _____

What was your reaction? _____

_____

_____

3. List any witnesses: _____

_____

_____

_____

I understand that these incidents will be investigated, but this form will be kept confidential to the highest degree possible.

Employee: _____

Date: _____

**FOR EMPLOYER'S USE**

Dates of investigation of complaint: _____

_____

_____

Date of final report: _____

_____

_____

Copy sent to employee: _____

Action taken: _____

_____

_____

_____

_____

Date of follow-up conference with employee: _____

Results: _____

_____

_____

_____

Date of follow-up conference with employee: _____

Results: _____

_____

_____

_____

Date of follow-up conference with employee: _____

Results: _____

_____

_____

_____

_____

## 2. Tips on Questions to Ask

Even if you do not begin the initial interview by asking the employee to complete a formalized complaint form, you are wise to go into the interview prepared with a list of at least a few points you wish to clarify. This sounds base and basic—and it is. But since your own agitation over the situation may wreak havoc with your presence of mind, it will help to have at least some jottings to jar your memory. You goal is to be as complete as possible from the start, so that the investigation can progress as quickly and painlessly as possible.

Here are some suggestions for initial questions you might ask.

• Who is involved?

Note that if management and other higher ranking employees are involved, there is a greater likelihood that a formal legal claim or lawsuit will be filed over the alleged misconduct.

• What did the person say or do?

It is essential that you get as many specific details as possible. Push for clear details about who said and did what to whom—including dates, times, responses and the names of potential witnesses.

- Can you suggest any possible reasons for the offending words or actions, any event from the past that might be related?
- Were there repeated offenses?
- Were there any witnesses?
- Did you tell anyone else about this?
- Do you know of anyone else who has had a similar problem?
- Do you know of any evidence—either written or oral—that may be related to this claim?
- What do you think would be an appropriate response and solution?
- Does the person with the harassing or threatening behavior know your home telephone and address, or likely social schedule?

If the behavior is potentially violent, suggest additional precautionary measures such as securing a restraining order from the police or courts or purchasing a home security system.

It is likely that the employee will not be able to remember all details or incidents of harassment during the initial interview. Urge him or her to come forward and supply more information if it dawns later.

# C. Interviewing the Alleged Wrongdoer

Be forthright about the purpose of your interview with the employee who has been accused of wrongdoing. Explain the substance of the complaint, then make clear that the purpose of your meeting is to make sure you get a full version of his or her side of the events. Then conduct a thorough interview—and obtain a signed, written statement detailing his or her recollection of the events. If the employee refuses to sign—or acknowledge the behavior—note that on the statement, which will later be put in his or her personnel file.

Be aware that if the accused is a union member, you may have to take additional steps and safeguards during an investigation—such as emphasizing that his or her cooperation is voluntary or offering to have a union representative present if a collective bargaining agreement requires it.

**⚠ You'll Never Talk Alone.** If you harbor the suspicion that the person being investigated has the potential of becoming violent or volatile, ask security personnel to attend the conversation. And do your utmost to isolate or remove the threatening individual from the workplace at once.

If there is no imminent danger, it is still a good idea to have another person or two attend—a human resource person,  an employee assistance counselor, the employee's supervisor, as examples.

## D. Interviewing Witnesses

It is obvious that you need to interview the employee who lodged the complaint and the person alleged to have committed the wrong. But it is often less clearcut which additional individuals you should talk with while investigating a workplace complaint.

Witnesses to be interviewed may include employees, former employees and anyone else who may know about the workplace behavior being investigated. It is particularly helpful if a witness has seen or heard the wrong on which the complaint is based. You should also interview anyone—a client, customer, present or former employee—who claims to have been subjected to similar behavior by the same person.

But be circumspect when interviewing witnesses. Unlike questions put to the alleged wronged and wrongdoing employees aimed at teasing out the broader picture of potential wrongdoing, your queries to potential witnesses should be limited to facts they know and incidents they have seen. If possible, help maintain some confidentiality by couching your initial questions in more general terms rather than naming names. For example, you might say: "We are investigating a complaint from an employee" rather than "Jim Jones says that Coretta Smith passed him over for a promotion because of his age." Concentrate on the specific information you seek from a particular witness—and focus your questions on that. If you are interviewing more than one witness, resist the temptation to influence the conversation by divulging what others have told you during previous interviews. Talk with each potential witness separately to cut down on the possible influences of suggestion peer pressure.

Finally, make neither threats nor promises when questioning witnesses. It is essential for you to stay uncompromised and neutral so that the answers you secure are not suspect. As mentioned, it may also be a good idea to ask witnesses to write their own brief summaries of their views—an act that not only may help impress upon them that the investigation is a serious event, but may also help make their answers more bulletproof should anyone later claim the answers were coerced.

You will likely find it appropriate to ask witnesses some of the same questions you asked the accusing employee. (See Section B2.) In addition, there are a few specific questions you might want to pose to witnesses. They include:

- How did you learn the information you are telling me now?
- Were you present when the alleged wrongdoing occurred?
- Did you hear this information discussed by anyone else?

# E. Evaluating the Evidence

If you hear different versions of what happened—as is often the case—you may have to redouble your efforts to search for relevant information. Objective proof of the charges, such as an eyewitness or incriminating memo, would likely be persuasive evidence. Keep in mind that such evidence is often impossible to gather, since many workplace wrongs take place in private, out of the earshot and view of others. And the alleged bad behavior is usually undocumented.

You may need to delve into whether there is any possible motivation behind the inconsistent stories—such as a bad performance review or a broken romance. You should also carefully evaluate similar complaints against the same employee that might be evidence of a pattern of behavior.

It is particularly tricky to assess statements from current employees, who may feel pressured to cover up for co-workers or compelled to tell an employer what he or she wants to hear rather than the cold, hard truth.

Weigh the dependability of all the statements you have gathered. You can assess the value of your evidence by considering each witness's:

- reputation for honesty
- possible motive for lying or distorting the truth, and
- opportunity to see or hear the important matter firsthand.

### WHERE TO LOOK FOR EVIDENCE

Written evidence is very helpful in rooting out the truth of a situation. But many an employer has been undone by his own smoking guns that have fallen into the hands of employees or former employees looking to bolster their claims. Be mindful of this double-edged paper trail whenever you put pen or cursor to work to record workplace happenings.

**Email messages.** Often overlooked, these bits of paper or stored computer files often contain candid, revealing information. And do not assume that deleted material is lost and gone forever. Most data recovery systems can easily resurrect old files.

**Company memos.** These written statements can often be used to nail an employer to a specific policy or course. For example, a memo that referred to the need to get rid of dead wood was used to substantiate a former employee's claim of age discrimination—even though it was written nearly a year after the employee was asked to leave the company and was not written by anyone involved in the decision to relieve him or his job.

**Employee handbooks.** Formerly used primarily as puff pieces to welcome a new employee, handbooks are increasingly treated as contracts—and employers are learning to be guarded and truthful about promises they make in them.

## F. Taking Action

Train a keen eye on what you uncovered. Commonsense and reasonableness should be your guides in deciding how to act in either closing the investigation or acting further on your findings. Issue a decision as to whether wrongdoing occurred as quickly as possible to avoid prolonging the angst and damaging speculation that often accompanies an investigation in even in the most gossip-free workplaces.

## 1. If You Find No Wrongdoing

If you have thoroughly investigated the situation and uncover no wrong-doing, notify the accused employee at once. Allegations are likely to be personally stressful and damaging to his or her work productivity, too.

Consider also the needs of the person bringing the complaint. Your finding that no wrongdoing occurred may leave the employee feeling angry, frustrated or scared—or just plain ignored. Encourage the complaining employee to discuss his or her feelings with a willing ear—a sympathetic co-worker or supervisor, company counselor, workplace specialist, psychologist or psychiatrist. In some situations, it may be sensible to make workplace changes that separate the complaining employee from the person he or she accused, or at least to change the chain of reporting command.

Finally, inform the employee bringing the complaint that your decision may not be the last legal word on the matter. Whatever the decision reached during your investigation, he or she is free to go forward with federal or state complaints or file other legal action against the workplace behavior.

## 2. If the Results Are Inconclusive

Unfortunately, not every workplace investigation can be tied up neatly with a bow. In some cases, despite your most thorough attempts, the results of your investigation will be inconclusive.

It is important to be frank about the status of your findings, for both the sakes of the complaining and the accused employees. To hedge your bets, remind the accused employee of the rule or policy he or she was alleged to have violated. Be sure to write up a report or memo summarizing the results and commenting on why no additional action was taken. Keep in mind that if the complaining employee takes his or her beef to a court or government agency, your report will likely be seen by lawyers and possibly a judge.

And know that an inconclusive investigation can still be a powerful thing. It can act as a reminder to all involved to maintain straight and narrow workplace behavior. And if the same employee is later accused to the same or similar wrongdoing, you will have an established track record.

## 3. If You Find Wrongdoing

If you conclude that there has been a serious wrong in the workplace, promptly issue a written apology to the person bringing the complaint. For many workers, this is extremely welcome, as it signals your understanding and acknowledgment of the problem.

You should also take quick disciplinary action against the wrongdoer. What is appropriate will depend on the type and severity of the offense and on whether it is a first time or repeated offense. Appropriate action may include: a verbal or written warning accompanied by the request to attend training sessions, probation—or, in the more serious cases, transfer to a different position, suspension or dismissal.

If you decide on a course of action short of firing, be sure to monitor the accused employee's behavior after a given time—and tell him or her you will do so. But do not be threatening or pedantic about this. Frame your monitoring proposal in terms and tone that shows you care about providing a safe and sane workplace, not that you are Big Brother Watching.

### SEPARATING THE PROTAGONISTS

Where emotions are running high, it may be best to try to separate the accused and the accuser, giving either or both the option of transferring to a different position within the company. If it is the accusing employee who will be transferred, provide total assurance that the transfer is not in retaliation for making the complaint. This means that the transfer must be acceptable to the employee, and must not be to a lower paying, geographically isolated or otherwise less desirable position.

## 4. Preparing a Report

Prepare a draft report of the investigation and your conclusion—and give a copy to any others who help head up the investigation for a thorough critique.

If a person was harmed, get his or her reaction—and record whether and why you could not act to reach a different result. Air out objections. This might go the longest in helping to ward off later claims that you acted unreasonably or unfairly.

Give a copy of your report to the target of the investigation and allow a response. This may open another round of interviews and probes, but it is better to correct things at this stage—or at least doublecheck your conclusions—than to stubbornly adhere to your initial conclusions. Closed-minded employers do not play well before judges and juries.

# G. Monitoring the Workplace

Old habits may die hard. Even prompt and strict action against the wrongdoer may not end his or her bad behavior. And there may also be delayed retaliation against the person filing the complaint, coming from the accused worker or from his or her friends or co-workers.

To guard against these possibilities, make clear that the situation will be monitored for an extended period. Schedule follow-up meetings with the employee who originally complained at regular intervals—two weeks, one month, three months, six months and one year. You will want to be sure both that the wrong has been eliminated and that there has been no retaliation for taking action against it. ■

**CHAPTER 12**

# Firing Workers

**S**urprisingly, there are but a few legal sandtraps in the firing process. Still, doing the deed ranks among the most dreaded you may ever undertake. Even the most callous employers describe firing scenarios with the same refrain: "It was the hardest thing I ever had to do."

Take some heart in knowing that just as it is often a relief to be rid of an employee who performed poorly, it can often be a relief for him or her to be removed from a job that was not a good fit. And certainly, it is better for co-workers to have a subpar performer removed from their midst.

But bright gloss aside, firing is usually at least momentarily tough on all involved. There are countless tomes written for human resource personnel that offer varying views on the mechanics and psychology of firing; you might search for one that meets your needs and philosophies.

Just a few words to the wiser here: If It Were Done, It Were Well It Were Done Quickly. Friday afternoons are usually the best time to fire. Make sure the room in which you deliver the news is as soundproof as possible so that your conversation is confidential. And in most cases, you should make that day the fired employee's last day on the job. You might allow some time for goodbyes, but it benefits no one to let the fired and retained workers mix uneasily for very long. Allow some time at the end of the day after workhours or over the weekend for the employee to remove personal effects; best to have someone on staff present during this final cleanup to ensure that the only effects that leave are personal, not company property. And finally, resist the strongarm tactic of having the employee escorted from the building with a guard—unless you have good reason to believe the employee will become violent or pose some other danger.

This chapter offers help beyond the mechanics—possible alternatives to firing, a reassuring explanation of when terminating is your best course of action and practical tips on what to do and what not to do when you can do no other.

# A. Disciplining Workers

Except in the most egregious cases—such as where a worker has suddenly become violent or has stolen company property—a firing normally should not come as a surprise to you or the employee. Ideally, you will have spotted an employee who is having trouble or has caused trouble on the job and will have set out a plan for what needs to be cured and a timeline by which to do so.

Attempting to smooth a slightly rocky situation this way allows you to keep an employee who is willing to change for the better—and allows the employee the invaluable opportunity of righting a wrong or improving performance. And on the chance that things cannot be salvaged and the employee goes away disgruntled and sues, your corrective attempts will count in your favor to a tallying judge, jury or investigating agency.

Be sure that all negative comments and evaluations relate to work performance. For example, an individual's private life—such as his or her dating and mating behavior—is irrelevant; what matters is whether she or he is performing up to snuff and toeing the line on company policies. If the employee falls short on either of these counts, it is time to take some corrective action.

There are neither hard nor fast rules on what your first corrective step should be. The wisest but least helpful-sounding advice is that you must evaluate each situation on its own before proceeding. If possible, aim for a solution that allows the employee to correct the wrongdoing; 60 to 90 days should be sufficient. And if you have a written workplace policy that promises progressive discipline for poor performance or wrongdoing, it should also make clear that you have the ultimate discretion to skip steps if necessary, to dole out a punishment that fits the crime. As a guide, consider:

- the type of offense
- the effect it has on your business, including co-workers

- the employee's response to calling him or her on the behavior—
along with your sense of the likelihood that the behavior will
repeat or continue, the employee's attitude and willingness to
change, and

- what disciplinary action you have taken in the past against other
employees for similar offenses.

These diagnostic steps will not necessarily result in the best action
for you to take. But they should help you gauge the relative seriousness
of the conduct, whether a quick fix or longer reform will be needed and
whether the employee should go or stay on the job. Actions to take short
of firing, in roughly escalating order, include:

- training in a particular area of weak performance either by
someone on staff or through outside schooling or seminars

- counseling, particular apt if the problem involves interpersonal or
communication difficulties

- warnings, either oral or in the weightier written form

- probation, usually from one to several months, after which the
employee is again evaluated

- suspension, either unpaid or paid, which is often accompanied
by the requirement that the employee use the time off to formu-
late a revised workplan or set specific new goals

- money repercussions, such as denying a raise or temporarily or
permanently reducing pay, and

- agreements to perform, commonly setting out an employer's
expectations and the employee's vow to meet them—frequently
used when the employee has shown some aberrant outside
behavior such as drug or alcohol abuse.

Whatever course you choose, be sure to write a memo summarizing
the terms of the discipline. Keep the summary in the employee's personnel file and give the employee a copy, both to eliminate any suspicion of

duplicitous dealing and to emphasize that the corrective action is serious business. By taking this interim step of disciplining the employee rather than firing him or her outright, you will accomplish the lofty goal of fostering a behavior change for the better. And by documenting it, you are also accomplishing the more pragmatic step of creating a paper trail that can substantiate your actions should you and the employee later disagree over what took place or what was expected.

### THE HIGH COST OF GIVING THEM UP AND LETTING THEM GO

A recent poll offers some enlightenment for employers wondering whether the ebb and flow of their workforce is normal. Businesses in the survey reported an average annual turnover rate of around 15%— and more than a third weighed in with a rate higher than 20%.

Most blamed the same culprits: a relatively booming economy, tight job market and low unemployment rate—all leading to a shortage of skilled employees.

In the survey, 30% of businesses tallied the costs of replacing an employee who leaves at an average of more than $10,000—and 34% reported it costs between $5,000 and $10,000.

Source: 1998 Retention and Staffing Survey by Manchester Partners International, an employment consulting firm based in Bala Cynwyd, Pa.

# B. Firing Workers

Despite the fact that firing is hard on both you and the unfortunate employee, you are generally perfectly within your legal rights to do so.

## 1. Employment at Will

Despite the worrisome specter of wrongful termination lawsuits, employers can rest assured that, most of the time, people employed in private industry have no automatic legal right to keep their jobs. That is because of the long-established legal doctrine of employment at will—a term that stems from a 1894 case (*Payne v. Western & Atlantic RR,* 81 Tenn. 507), in which the court ruled that employers do not need a reason to fire employees; they may fire any or all of their workers at will. Even if the reason for dismissal is morally wrong, the court held, no legal wrong has occurred and the government has no basis to intervene.

The at will doctrine has been reinforced over and over again by subsequent court rulings. But it has been weakened a bit since the 1970s by some laws and court rulings in which former employees have questioned the legality of their firings. For example, employees in Montana who have completed probation are protected from being fired, unless there is good cause (Mont. Code Ann. §§39-2-901 to 905).

There are a few important exceptions to the employment at will doctrine that may make it possible for employees to hang unto their jobs. And as anxieties deepen over job security, more employees are taking the time and effort to contradict their employers' assertions that it is time for them to go.

For example, if you have been foolhardy enough to issue a written statement signifying that an employee is excepted from the employment at will doctrine, you may be held to your word—and virtually stuck with the employee.

Also, many collective bargaining agreements state that union members can be fired only "for good cause." So while union members are still technically employees at will, the work agreements negotiated by their unions often make them exceptions to the general rule, requiring that employers point to a specific, legally valid reason before firing them.

Some employers negotiate and sign detailed contracts with their employees—contracts which set out the specific terms of their employment, including salary and relocation rights. Employment contracts are rare—usually reserved for only the uppermost company executives and other notables such as professional athletes. Those holding employment contracts are usually not subject to the employment at will doctrine; their contracts spell out the length of their employment and specifically note when and how the employment relationship can end.

Finally, some former employees have successfully contested their dismissals by pointing to the promising words uttered or handed to them when they were hired. Promises made while hiring are frequent culprits. (See Chapter 1.) But the newest fertile ground for lawsuits is employee manuals. A few courts held, for example, that where company manuals have stated that employees became permanent after a certain time, or that they must be given a hearing before being fired, employers must deliver on those promises. However, most savvy businesses these days are well-acquainted with this legal loophole, so few of them now include such vague promises in their employee manuals.

## WHEN GOOD CAUSE IS GOOD ENOUGH

Airing a wrongful discharge case before a jury can be a good or bad gamble, depending on your stance and circumstance. At the outset, the jury was traditionally asked to determine three questions:

- Was there an actual or implied contract under which the employer needed good cause to fire?
- If so, did the employee commit the offense with which he or she was charged?
- If so, was it an offense that warranted being fired?

This traditional approach is being challenged by courts that are not so concerned with whether the employee committed the alleged wrong. In a recent case, the California Supreme Court injected a good deal of commonsense into the judicial reasoning process and trained the spotlight on the employer's integrity rather than the actual conduct of the fired employee. It held that it is enough if the employer conducted an adequate investigation and had a reasonable belief that the offense was committed before handing out the pink slip. The court summarized that an employer has good cause to fire an employee if he or she believes in good faith that there is a fair and honest reason to do so—not a trivial, arbitrary, capricious, unrelated to business needs or pretextual reason (*Cotran v. Rollins Hudig Hall Int'l, Inc.,* 17 Cal. 4th 93 (1998)). Courts in Oregon, Washington and New Mexico have also imposed objective, good faith standards for employers evaluating workplace misconduct. It is still too soon to tell whether this reasoning will catch on back east.

Some posit that one upshot of this trend of legal reasoning is that in the future, more former employees will attack their firings based on inadequate workplace investigations. (See Chapter 11.)

## 2. Valid Reasons for Firing

In spite all that has been said and written about your right to fire at will, it is still best—from both legal and practical points of view—for you to be able to point to a concrete, valid reason for firing an employee. In most situations, finding a valid reason will not be that difficult. Few employers, having spent time and money hiring and training an employee, will fire at whim.

The gallery of firable offenses includes:

- performing poorly on the job
- refusing to follow instructions
- abusing sick leave
- being absent excessively
- being tardy habitually
- possessing a weapon at work
- violating company rules
- being dishonest
- endangering health and safety
- engaging in criminal activity
- using alcohol or drugs at work
- behaving violently at work
- gambling at work, and
- disclosing company trade secrets to outsiders.

Realistically speaking, it is also essential that you have written documentation of your reason for firing—poor performance reviews, a determination of severe sexual harassment, memos of failed disciplinary measures in a personnel file.

## 3. Tips on Firing Workers

Remain calm and in control. Most problems arise when an employer tries to sugarcoat the bad news with half-truths or metaphors. It is always best to focus on your decision to fire and avoid apologizing or backstepping. There are a number of common mistakes that can rear up to haunt you.

➡ Do not blame a layoff or a cutback on the company—unless it is absolutely true. It may appear to be more humane, less judgmental, less accusatory to tell an employee that a position has been eliminated rather than point to his or her poor performance or your own poor management for allowing him or her to overstay a welcome. But if it is not true—or if there is a possibility that someone will be hired to fill the position or even a similar one in the future—do not use it to excuse away the firing. Former employees often have the time, motivation and the contacts to monitor your workplace to see whether their former positions have been filled. If you get caught in this type of fib, you could find yourself on the losing end of a charge that the firing was based on discrimination or some other bad motive.

➡ Do not refer to the composition or culture of the workplace. Avoid talking of your plans to recast the workforce, or implying that the employee somehow does not fit your image. Common words and phrases fraught with potential harm include:
• "We're after a more dynamic, aggressive workforce."
• "We need someone who fits in better with the team."
• "We must have employees with fewer family commitments who are available to court clients after hours."

Any of these pronouncements could leave the impression that the employee is truly being fired for any number of reasons of questionable legality: being too old, too foreign, too married.

➡️ Do not threaten an employee for challenging a firing. It is a natural human yearning to want the unpleasant business of firing to be over and done with in one fell swoop. But it can be a mistake to threaten to take action or to withhold a benefit if an employee later claims the firing was wrongful. For example, where an employee has been fired for stealing or some other criminal activity, you may be tempted to make a deal: You will not report the wrongdoer to the law if he or she does not contest the firing. Or you might agree to tender the employee's final paycheck only if he or she agrees not to challenge the urging to move on. Resist these temptations. This form of persuasion may be deemed illegal coercion. You must decide whether or not to bring criminal charges against a former employee independently of any employment decision you make. And it is also illegal to deny benefits to which a former employee is entitled—pay or vacation earned and owing, for example—in exchange for forbearing on a claim or lawsuit.

➡️ Do not mention an employee's injury or physical condition. This can be a particularly poignant form of poison if the employee you are firing is perceived to have a disability—and so is strongly protected by the Americans With Disabilities Act. It also holds potential danger if the worker has been injured on the job and has filed a workers' comp claim—and so is also strongly protected under the law. While you can fire an employee for excessive absences or for violating clearcut safety rules, you cannot do so because he or she files injury claims—even if they cause your insurance costs to skyrocket.

➡️ Do not attempt to use humor or glibness; the fired employee may have the last laugh. For example, a chuckling manager at a large hotel chain handed one former employee a tome cutely titled *Parting Company* just seconds after announcing that the day was his last on the job. The employee took the book home—and burned it. And the tacky tactics later became persuasive evidence in a wrongful termination lawsuit.

➡️ If you suspect the employee may become violent when you break the news, arrange to have a mental health professional or security personnel stationed near your meeting place. It may be counterproductive to have these outsiders attend the conversation unless needed, however, since their presence may tend to further anger or disrupt a potentially volatile employee.

### EASING THE TRANSITION—WHILE STAYING OUT OF COURT

Given the rapid changes in today's workforces, it should not be surprising to learn that outplacement—services geared to help employees out of their old jobs and into new ones—is the one of the fastest growing industries. Employers typically hire outplacement counselors to provide services for a former employee: an assessment of his or her skills, advice on writing resumes and targeting job prospects and often a temporary office space in which the former employee can conduct the business of job hunting.

It is common to continue to pay salary and benefits for a worker for at least part of the time while he or she gets outplacement help.

Most employers claim the cost is well worth it. One priceless benefit of outplacement is that everyone can move on. Former employees whose time and minds are taken up by a new job are far less likely to sue you for wrongful termination or file claims for unemployment or workers' compensation insurance. Offering some outplacement services can also make you look more sympathetic in the eyes of a judge or jury later evaluating a wrongful discharge against you.

Outplacement is sometimes informal. You might simply offer your worksite for its business paraphernalia that will aid in a job search: access to computers, copiers, phones and voicemail. But if the employee left disgruntled, angry or embarrassed, it may not be good for anyone's morale to invite him or her back on the premises.

# C. Offering Severance

While many employers assume that they must offer fired employees a package of money and benefits known as severance on their way out the door, no law requires it. You are required to provide former employees with severance in only a limited number of circumstances—those in which a worker had good reason to believe he or she was entitled to it, as evidenced by:

- a written contract stating that severance will be paid

- a promise that employees would receive severance pay as documented in an employee handbook
- a history of the company paying severance to other employees in the same position, or
- an oral promise that you would pay severance.

Still, severance packages have become an accepted nicety for employees who are laid off or let go for some reason other than misconduct. Severance helps ease the blow for the fired employee and also helps sweeten the sour grapes he or she may harbor after being given walking papers.

The key is to be as consistent as possible. While it is sensible to make a more generous offer to employees who have been on the job for a longer time, it is essential that you offer similar severance to similarly situated former workers to avoid claims of discrimination. Otherwise, what you offer and how much it is worth is limited by your own resources and creativity. In the last few years, the length of time an employee has worked with a company has taken a backseat, tempered by the economic reality of what you can comfortably afford to pay. Severance rates have become less generous—averaging 30 weeks of pay for nonexempt employees to 39 weeks for those classified as executives.

In addition to severance pay—some amount of pay, generally based on the pay an employee received for a specific period while on the job—the benefits you may wish to consider including in a severance package are:

- continuation of employee benefits, such as payment of health insurance premiums for a limited time
- a favorable letter of reference if your normal policy is to divulge only the former employee's position and term of employment
- releasing the employee from special obligations such as a covenant not to compete
- allowing the employee to keep any advances
- allowing the employee to keep equipment

- agreeing not to contest the employee's right to unemployment compensation

- paying for outplacement services (see Section B), and

- promising to pay an employee's moving expenses, up to a stated limit.

# D. Agreements Not to Sue

Some employers require departing employees to sign a waiver—often called a release or covenant not to sue—in which he or she agrees not to take any legal action against the employer, such as an age discrimination lawsuit. In return for signing the waiver, the employer gives the employee an incentive to leave voluntarily, such as a severance pay package that exceeds the company's standard policy. (See Section C.)

This type of transaction was very popular in the early 1990s among large corporations that wanted to reduce their payroll costs. Because the conventional wisdom was that older workers who have been with a company a long time typically cost more in salary and benefits than younger workers, most staff-cutting programs were directed at older workers. But cutting only older workers was repeatedly held to constitute illegal age discrimination, so companies commonly induced the older workers to sign away their rights to sue.

This practice of ridding the workforce of primarily older workers is now somewhat limited and more often the subject of negotiation, according to the dictates of the Older Workers Benefit Protection Act. (See Chapter 8.) That law requires that you give an older worker— someone who is 40 or over—at least 21 days to decide whether or not to sign such a waiver. If you present the waiver to a group of employees, each of them must be given at least 45 days to decide whether or not to sign. In either case, the former employees have seven days after agreeing to such a waiver to revoke their decisions.

If the discharged worker is under 40, you need not allow any specific think period in which to review the agreement not to sue, but at least one court has held 24 hours is not enough time to give a former employee to review such an agreement.

The ruse of rushing the employee to judgment will not work; neither will the idea of purposefully making the terms murky or unclear. Short and simple is best. If an attorney has written an agreement not to sue that you intend to tender to workers, make sure it passes the reality test. To avoid the claims that the corporate Goliath is striking out at the cowering and sympathetic David, it is probably best to leave the attorney way in the background during negotiations.

If recent court cases point the trend, the most important safeguard employers can have is to enter a negotiation, a give and take over the terms of the agreement. Whatever you do, do not present the agreement as a threat or a take it or leave it proposition. Urge the employee to discuss the terms of the agreement. Even small concessions—another week or two of salary, use of an office for a limited time while the employee hunts for a new job—can make a big difference in his or her willingness to forgo a lawsuit against you.

# E. Giving References

Giving references for former employees—once a pro forma part of many employers' jobs—now carries with it risks and the potential for liability.

You may feel particularly uncomfortable if contacted as a reference for a former employee who was fired for some egregious act, such as stealing from the company coffers, drug or alcohol abuse or a violent act on the job.

## 1. Possible Liability

No matter how civilized the atmosphere when you asked the employee to leave, when contacted for references, you will likely feel caught between the desire to be truthful and your fear that, if you say anything unflattering, you will be sued. The number of costly defamation lawsuits recently filed over negative references makes this fear a real one. And the U.S. Supreme Court added fuel to the fire when it ruled recently that former employees who sue their employers for retaliatory negative job references are protected by the Civil Rights Act (*Robinson v. Shell Oil Co.,* 519 U.S. 337 (1997)).

These days, conventional legal wisdom cautions all employers to stick to the barest bones. Many companies—an estimated 65% of them in 1995—have steel-clad policies to supply only the dates of employment, job title and final salary to prospective employers.

Some cautious companies even require that employees who leave must sign releases allowing them to give reference information in the future. And some employers ask even prospective employees to sign the same sort of release. Courts have upheld these releases of late, holding that employees who sign away rights to this information have also signed away their rights to bring a lawsuit for defamation based on what beans get spilled. In some states, employers are protected by law from defamation lawsuits if they answer questions about former employees truthfully.

The broad warning for employers giving references is that you should give out only easily documented facts—an employee's attendance record or production record, for example.

But this closed lip approach seems to unfairly penalize prize employees, who may depend on good references to snag their next jobs. And many employers who think that an employee has done a poor job or has blatantly violated company rules feel that they have a responsibility to let prospective employers know about the problem. There is nothing inherently illegal about this, unless a former employee can accomplish the difficult task of proving that you told a bald-faced lie about him or her—for example, that he or she raided the company till when that is not true. A seemingly noncommittal "no comment" in response to a prospective employer's probe about strengths and weaknesses may be the most damaging of all—yet its evasiveness makes it poor evidence upon which to base a defamation lawsuit.

## IF YOU WEREN'T WORRYING BEFORE, YOU MIGHT START NOW

A growing practice may give you additional cause for pause when giving references for former employees. A number of agencies have sprung up recently that collect information about the references you give, then report back to the former employee. If the reference you gave is less than glowing, you may find yourself on the defending end of a defamation lawsuit.

These services pose as companies or recruiters verifying references. Confidentiality is assured: the customers seeking dirt on themselves will not be identified to their former employers. Most reference checkers offer a basic service beginning at around $40 summarizing the views of a single person, such as a former supervisor, as to the employee's job duties. For meatier information, such as someone's take on decisionmaking skills—or to learn the views of a number of people in a former organization—the price is several hundred dollars. Many disgruntled employees, encouraged by a plethora of free time to feed their vendettas and news stories trumpeting big verdicts for defamation, feel that the money is well spent. One satisfied customer noted: "I was vindicated when I received your report showing damaging, malicious, and false remarks. I sued for defamation."

Not surprisingly, the services are armed and ready to enter the legal battlefield—offering, for additional charges, a letter ordering the former employer to quit the badmouthing—and even serving as expert witnesses should the customer decide to file a lawsuit for defamation.

Some cagey former employees engineer this type of monitoring on their own—or enlist friends or relatives to do it.

There are detractors and supporters of this brand of covert reference checking. Some argue it is disingenuous entrapment; others say it merely reinforces The Golden Rule that if you don't have anything nice to say about someone, it's best to remain mum.

No matter where your sentiments sit, you should know that this practice is happening—and gaining in popularity.

## 2. Tips on Giving References

Given the newfound aura of uncertainty surrounding your duties and liabilities when responding to prospective employers about former employees, it is wise to proceed cautiously, perhaps even fueled by a touch of paranoia.

➡️ Verify that the request comes from a genuine source—a prospective employer of a former employee. Do so by requesting the address of company headquarters and at least one other phone number within the organization.

➡️ Maintain a central source. Try to have one trusted person—or a few sophisticated souls—responsible for giving references. Make sure they are familiar with the pitfalls of being overly negative or falsely positive.

➡️ Be consistent. Give the same type and level of information to every prospective employer who asks about a particular employee.

➡️ Avoid surprises. A crafty interviewer can get you to volunteer information you did not intend to offer—and some of that might present a legal danger. If you are wary about answering, rein in your responses to factual information.

➡️ Be minimalist. If your initial sleuthwork does not satisfy you that the request is authentic—or you remain uneasy about giving a reference for any reason—restrict your responses to the barest minimum of information: dates of employment, title and final salary.

➡️ Keep a paper trail. Make sure you have a record of all requests for references. ■

# Index

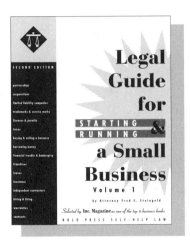
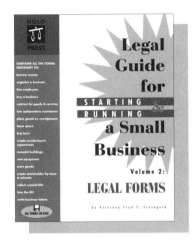

# Take 2 minutes & Give us your 2 cents

**Y**our comments make a big difference in the development and revision of Nolo books and software. Please take a few minutes and register your Nolo product—and your comments—with us. Not only will your input make a difference, you'll receive special offers available only to registered owners of Nolo products on our newest books and software. Register now by:

| **PHONE** | **FAX** | **EMAIL** | or **MAIL** us |
|---|---|---|---|
| 1-800-992-6656 | 1-800-645-0895 | cs@nolo.com | this registration card |

**REMEMBER:**
Little publishers have big ears. We really listen to you.

- - - - - - - - - - - - - - - - - - - - fold here - - - - - - - - - - - - - - - - - - - -

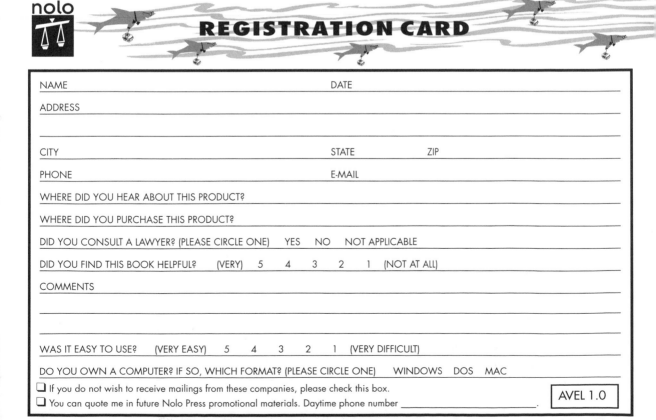

### nolo

# REGISTRATION CARD

NAME _____ DATE _____

ADDRESS _____

_____

CITY _____ STATE _____ ZIP _____

PHONE _____ E-MAIL _____

WHERE DID YOU HEAR ABOUT THIS PRODUCT? _____

WHERE DID YOU PURCHASE THIS PRODUCT? _____

DID YOU CONSULT A LAWYER? (PLEASE CIRCLE ONE)    YES    NO    NOT APPLICABLE

DID YOU FIND THIS BOOK HELPFUL?    (VERY)    5    4    3    2    1    (NOT AT ALL)

COMMENTS _____

_____

_____

WAS IT EASY TO USE?    (VERY EASY)    5    4    3    2    1    (VERY DIFFICULT)

DO YOU OWN A COMPUTER? IF SO, WHICH FORMAT? (PLEASE CIRCLE ONE)    WINDOWS    DOS    MAC

❑ If you do not wish to receive mailings from these companies, please check this box.

❑ You can quote me in future Nolo Press promotional materials. Daytime phone number _____.

AVEL 1.0